CHILDREN'S ENCYCLOPEDIA OF

BRITISH HISTORY

KING*f*ISHER

CHILDREN'S
ENCYCLOPEDIA
OF
BRITISH
HISTORY

KINGFISHER
Kingfisher Publications Plc
New Penderel House
283–288 High Holborn
London WC1V 7HZ
www.kingfisherpub.com

Material in this edition previously published by Kingfisher Publications Plc in
Children's Illustrated Encyclopedia of British History in 1992

A revised, reformatted and updated edition published as
Children's Encyclopedia of British History by Kingfisher Publications Plc
in hardback in 1996, and in paperback in 1998

This revised and updated edition published by
Kingfisher Publications Plc in 2001

BCA/PREMIER/0701/UD.RNB(RNB)140MA

This revised edition produced by PAGE*One* Ltd, Cairn House,
Elgiva Lane, Chesham, HP5 2JD

4 6 8 10 9 7 5

A CIP catalogue for this book is available from the British Library.

ISBN 1 85696 026 9

Printed in China

Consultants: Dr Paul Bahn, David Haycock,
Susan Morris and Valerie St Johnston
Editor: James Harrison
Designer: Edward Kinsey
Picture researchers: Alex Goldberg, Elaine Willis
Indexer: Sylvia Potter
Cover design: Mike Davis

CONTENTS

EARLY BRITAIN

(c. 500,000 BC – AD 440)

THE EARLY STORY OF BRITAIN starts some half a million years ago in prehistory (the vast period of time before written records). The earliest people hunted animals and gathered food from what was around them. These hunters and gatherers began to build camps some of which have been discovered. From the stone tools and other remains found at these sites we can learn what life was like before recorded history. Later hunters discovered how to make and use metals such as bronze and copper, and also started to keep sheep and cattle – the first farmers. They built primitive villages and dug huge ditches to make hill forts. At about the time the Egyptians were building the Great Pyramid of Giza, the earliest Britons started to build Stonehenge (*below*) – one of the most remarkable prehistoric stone structures in the world. Britain was still a fairly primitive land compared with Egypt and other major civilizations. By about 500 BC, however, Celtic tribes had settled in Britain and were making iron weapons and utensils, using wheeled carts and chariots and building impressive hill-forts such as Maiden Castle in Dorset.

Stonehenge may have been laid out to mark the position of the midsummer sunrise.

Early Britain

THE EARLIEST HISTORY OF BRITAIN starts in the period known as prehistory, before writing was invented. In Britain, the first written records were introduced by the Romans, so anything that happened in Britain before the Roman Conquest in 55 BC is prehistory.

THE OLD STONE AGE

Archaeologists, people who dig up and examine the remains of prehistory and later periods of history, have discovered two open-air camps near Clacton-on-Sea in Essex and Boxgrove in Sussex. Both sites contain human and animal bones and masses of stone tools. The earliest people lived on this land as long ago as 500,000 years in what is called the Old Stone Age.

In these prehistoric times, there were four great Ice Ages when much of the land was covered by thick ice sheets. In the warmer spells the ice retreated and Old Stone Age people roamed over tundra. Britain was joined to France by open grasslands over what is now the English Channel. People sheltered in caves, and in tents made from animal skin, and they could make fires – which helped them to survive the harsh conditions.

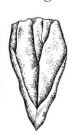

Above **A flint axe from the Old Stone Age, about a quarter of its real size. Early inhabitants also made flint-tipped spears.**

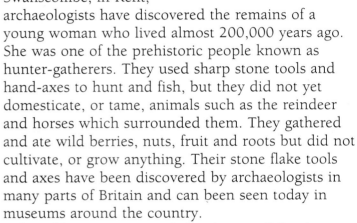

Right: **In the Ice Age Britain was covered by ice north of the Thames estuary (*see dotted line on map*). The land was also joined to Europe across the Channel (*see area shaded in green*).**

HUNTER-GATHERERS

At a place called Swanscombe, in Kent, archaeologists have discovered the remains of a young woman who lived almost 200,000 years ago. She was one of the prehistoric people known as hunter-gatherers. They used sharp stone tools and hand-axes to hunt and fish, but they did not yet domesticate, or tame, animals such as the reindeer and horses which surrounded them. They gathered and ate wild berries, nuts, fruit and roots but did not cultivate, or grow anything. Their stone flake tools and axes have been discovered by archaeologists in many parts of Britain and can been seen today in museums around the country.

The Old Stone Age people lived in small family groups of a dozen or so, and used flint tools to scrape reindeer, mammoth and other animal skins and to bore holes into them. They sewed these hides into clothes using animal tissue threaded on bone needles.

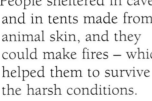

TIME CHART
Note: Dates are approximate

● **500,000 to 4500 BC** Old Stone Age (also called Palaeolithic) period

● **500,000 to 300,000 BC** Early people using flint tools near Clacton-on-Sea

● **500,000 BC** Boxgrove open-air camp in Sussex

● **125,000 BC** Last period of glaciation (ice cover) begins

● **40,000 BC** Early people in caves at Creswell Crags, Derbyshire

---

A NOTE ABOUT DATES
The letters BC indicate the years **B**efore **C**hrist was born; these are placed after the year, and are numbered backwards, so 55 BC (the first Roman invasion), then 54 BC (the second Roman invasion). The letters AD indicate the years after Christ was born (**A**nno **D**omini is Latin for Year of Our Lord.) The letters are placed before the year and are numbered forwards, so AD 410 (when the Romans left Britain) is followed by AD 411.

Left: **Well over 200,000 years ago, Britain's first settlers could make hand-axes using blocks of stones, usually flint.**

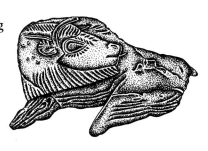

Left: **Making fires and sewing animal hides were key activities for early Britons.**

Right: **The first cave paintings and carvings, such as this bison carved in bone, were made in prehistoric times.**

It was the switch to keeping animals and sowing crops, as well as still hunting and fishing for food, that marks the New Stone Age period in Britain.

With farming and settlement came other skills, such as using deer antlers to break the soil for sowing, and making pottery bowls. Some people became flint-miners, using sharp and polished stone axes. The flint mines at Grimes Graves in Norfolk show they could sink shafts over ten metres deep. People also now buried their dead in long burial mounds called barrows which were like chambers. A New Stone Age camp at Windmill Hill in Wiltshire has a group of round barrows. Another site, at Skara Brae in the Orkneys, is claimed to be the oldest village. In the 1920s a storm washed away the sand-hills that had kept it hidden and protected for 5,000 years.

THE NEW STONE AGE

As the ice melted it released more water into the sea until, around 6000 BC, the last land bridge disappeared and Britain was cut off from Europe by the English Channel. But traders and settlers still came to Britain, on boats and rafts. From about 4500 BC the New Stone Age began as people started farming rather more than hunting and gathering for food. Settlers and traders brought seed corn, sheep and cattle with them and, using sharp axeheads fitted onto wooden handles, they cleared the woods around them so their animals could graze and so they could sow crops of wheat and barley. They were the first farmers.

Below: **At Skara Brae in the Orkneys, north of Scotland, you can visit New Stone Age houses built around 3100 BC. They are well preserved, with cupboards and beds** made from slabs of local Orkney stone. The people here wore beads of teeth and bone, made peat fires and kept sheep. The soil was too windswept to grow crops.

- 3200 BC Stonehenge, Wiltshire, begun

- 3100 BC Stone Age village at Skara Brae, Orkney

- 2600 BC Silbury Hill, a huge barrow in Wiltshire, built

- 2500 BC First known British pottery at Windmill Hill, Wiltshire

- 2000 BC First known weaving

- 1900 BC Beaker Folk arrive in Britain, with bronze tools

- 1800 BC Bronze Age begins in Britain

- 800 BC First Celts invade

- 700 BC Iron Age begins in Britain

- 350 BC Celts settle in Ireland

- 200 BC Celts settle in Taymouth and Moray Firth

Above: **Stonehenge was built in three stages, beginning about 3200 BC and ending about 1300 BC. Huge standing stones such as these are called megaliths (from the Greek *mega-*, large, and *lith*, stone), and are scattered throughout northern Europe. They may have been used to observe the sun, moon and stars, as well as to record the seasons.**

Below: **Around 4,000 years ago the first farming villages appeared made of wood and thatched straw. The people grew barley and wheat and learned to spin and weave wool. They also made simple pots from clay.**

THE BRONZE AGE

From around 1800 BC, people began to make metal tools and knife-daggers of bronze, by mixing copper with tin over very hot fires. Britain had plenty of tin, copper and even gold. Britain first became known to the classical world of Greece and Rome as the Cassiterides, the Islands of Tin. The island inhabitants continued the New Stone Age way of life, clearing woods to make open land for growing crops and erecting more dwellings.

STONEHENGE AND AVEBURY

These early settlers also built the most spectacular Bronze Age site in Europe, at Stonehenge, on Salisbury Plain in Wiltshire. It includes a ring of 80 massive rocks that were brought from the Prescelly Mountains in southern Wales, a journey of about 390 kilometres. The huge sandstone blocks in the centre were dragged from Avebury, 30 kilometres away. Avebury itself has an even larger henge, or stone circle. Though less well preserved, it is even older than Stonehenge. Passing through Avebury is the Ridgeway, an ancient road just over 150 kilometres long, that can still be travelled.

THE CELTS AND THE IRON AGE

Around 700 BC, the first iron-using tribes, the Celts, arrived from Europe. They knew how to make much stronger iron weapons, nails and tools such as axes and saws. They used sturdy war chariots and armour, and made bronze, rather than flint, sickles for reaping corn. They also made the first bronze musical horns, and gold cups and jewellery. By about 500 BC the first wheeled carts were in use on Britain's ancient routes.

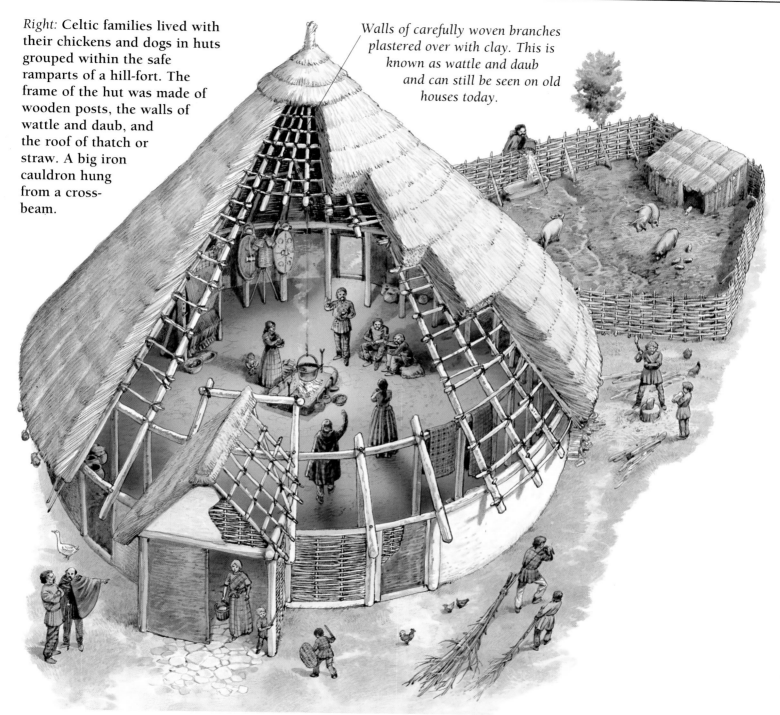

Right: **Celtic families lived with their chickens and dogs in huts grouped within the safe ramparts of a hill-fort. The frame of the hut was made of wooden posts, the walls of wattle and daub, and the roof of thatch or straw. A big iron cauldron hung from a cross-beam.**

Walls of carefully woven branches plastered over with clay. This is known as wattle and daub and can still be seen on old houses today.

The Celtic tribes who settled in Britain, and their descendants, are called Britons. Their language is still spoken today, because Welsh, Gaelic, Irish and Cornish are directly related to Celtic. For example, the Celtic word for river is *avon*. The Celts left no written records themselves, but the Romans wrote about them, and their first accounts of these islands tell of Celtic life in Britain.

These Iron Age Britons built great hill-forts, the best known of which is Maiden Castle in Dorset. They were built on high ground with commanding views of the surrounding countryside, and were made of rock and earth dug out of the ground with very deep and steep-sided slopes. Inside were enough circular thatched dwellings to make up a small town. Tribal life was dominated by the chieftains, their warriors, and by priests called druids.

Although the Celts conquered much of Europe, their power was eventually threatened by the well-organized armies of the Roman empire.

The Romans

BY 100 BC THE ROMANS had an empire that bordered all of the Mediterranean Sea, and stretched across most of Europe, North Africa and the Middle East up to the Red Sea. The Roman army's legions had conquered France, which was called Gaul, and were poised to cross the English Channel. Their knowledge of Britain came from the reports of traders. At first, invasion was not considered worthwhile because the goods the island had to offer – tin, cloth, corn, gold and slaves – could be taken from other tribes on the Continent. But army commanders, including Julius Caesar, the governor of Gaul, wanted more victories. He was troubled by Celtic revolts which had support from tribes in the south of Britain.

ROMAN INVASIONS

Julius Caesar landed on the English coast, probably at Deal, near Dover, Kent, in 55 BC. Although he had 10,000 troops and cavalry, storms damaged his ships and after fierce fighting with the Britons he had to retreat. In 54 BC, the Romans made a second invasion, moving inland and taking the hill-fort of Bigbury, near Canterbury. The British tribes were now under one chief, Cassivellaunus of the Catuvellauni tribe, whose base was north of the River Thames near modern-day St Albans. Caesar's well-organized Roman troops crossed the River Medway, then the Thames, and forced the Britons to submit to him.

But revolt in Gaul and civil war in Rome took Caesar and his army away, never to return. The Catuvellauni grew strong again under their chief Cunobelinus. For the next 100 years they controlled the southeast with their capital at Camulodunum, now Colchester, in Essex.

- **75 BC** Catuvellauni tribe (from present-day Belgium) settle at Colchester

- **55 BC** Julius Caesar invades Britain near Dover, but has to retreat

- **54 BC** Caesar raids again with five legions and reaches Essex

- **c. 5 BC** Birth of Jesus Christ

- **c. AD 30** Crucifixion of Jesus

- **AD 43** Four Roman legions under Aulus Plautius invade Britain

- **AD 44** Emperor Claudius arrives in Britain and captures Camulodunum (Colchester)

- **AD 45** Vespasian (later emperor) captures Vectis (the Isle of Wight)

- **AD 47** Ostorius Scapula defeats the Iceni in East Anglia

- **AD 48** Romans begin conquest of Wales

- **AD 51** Caractacus (Caradog), King of the Silures, is captured and taken to Rome

Above: **A Roman soldier with shield, spear, short stabbing sword and light armour. In total he carried about 30 kg of equipment.**

Below: **Roman soldiers fought in groups called legions, fighting in formation with swords and spears and protecting themselves with shields.**

ROMAN RULE

In AD 43, the Emperor Claudius sent 40,000 troops under the command of Aulus Plautius, to conquer Britain. Claudius came the next year and entered Camulodunum (Colchester) in triumph. Caractacus led the British resistance for the next seven years. He was eventually handed over to the Romans by Queen Cartimandua of the Brigantes, a northern tribe, who had signed a treaty with the Romans when he fled to her for refuge. Caractacus was led through the streets of Rome bound in chains.

BOUDICCA'S REVOLT

In AD 60 Prasutagus, King of the Iceni, a Norfolk tribe, died and left his fortune jointly to his two daughters and the Roman emperor. The Romans proceeded to take over the kingdom, and Catus, the Roman treasurer, seized all of the king's dominions, ill-treated the daughters and had their mother, Queen Boudicca, publicly bound and scourged. Outraged, Boudicca led a fierce revolt. Under her leadership the Iceni burned Camulodunum (Colchester), Verulamium (St Albans) and Londinium (London) and slaughtered many Romans. The Romans rallied under their governor and defeated Boudicca, who killed herself. Organized resistance by British tribes to Rome was over.

Britain was now the furthest northwest province of the Roman empire. The Romans needed to protect the valuable British minerals such as tin, iron ore, gold and lead. Roman troops went as far as Exeter in Devon, and to the coast and valleys of Wales. In 1996 archaeologists reported that they had discovered a Roman fort on the coast of Ireland which shows the Romans might have established a foothold even further west than was previously believed. But the troops could not control what is now Scotland, where they encountered the fierce Pictish, or painted, tribes.

HADRIAN'S WALL

In AD 122 the Emperor Hadrian visited Britain – the first to do so since Claudius – and decided to establish a secure northern frontier for the Roman province. So he ordered a wall to be built across the narrowest part of the country, from the river Tyne to the Solway Firth. Hadrian's Wall, a great work of military engineering, stretched across the country for 117 kilometres.

Above: **Boudicca, Queen of the Iceni (in modern Norfolk) in her war chariot. She headed a great revolt against the Romans but was defeated in AD 62. She took her own life.**

Below: **The Romans left over 9,000 km of straight roads in Britain, including the Fosse Way from Lincoln down into Devon. They also built the famous** Hadrian's Wall, and the not so well known Antonine Wall, made of turf and stretching 60 km from present-day Glasgow to Edinburgh.

Above: Roman roads were paved with thick slabs of stone and raised in the centre so rainwater ran into ditches at the sides. Many stretches of these roads still exist.

Hadrian's Wall took seven years to complete, and long stretches of it still stand today at a height of 2 metres. The wall was made of stone about 4.5 metres high and 3 metres thick, with a ditch on the north side. A second ditch, or *vallum*, was later dug to the south. About every 1.5 kilometres stood a small fort called a milecastle – a barracks for between 25 and 50 men. In total, as many as 5,000 troops might have been needed to guard, supply and to look after the entire wall's defences. There were also 17 major forts added to the wall at regular distances. These were really small military towns with headquarters, barracks for the troops to sleep in, workshops for weapons and tools, a hospital and a large granary for food supplies. One fort, at Birdoswald in Cumbria, had 1,000 people.

LIFE IN ROMAN BRITAIN

From AD 70 onwards for 100 years, Britain under Roman rule was peaceful and prosperous. But what other benefits did the Romans bring? Perhaps most importantly they brought a written language, Latin, and written numbers. The history of Britain was now recorded on paper and many of the first accounts have been passed down by Roman writers. The Romans were also highly organized: they introduced a ten month calendar, and fixed hours of the day. They also built a huge network of roads, including Fosse Way and Watling Street.

Below: The Romans enjoyed public baths and the most famous in Britain are located at Bath in Avon. Aquae Sulis, as Bath was called, fell into Saxon hands in AD 577. Roman baths had **1** an exercise area (*palaestra*); **2** changing room (*apodyterium*); **3** cool bath (*frigidarium*); **4** warm bath (*tepidarium*); **5** hot room (*caldarium*); **6** underfloor heating system (*hypocaust*).

Right: **The important public buildings in Roman towns: 1** forum (market place); **2** temple; **3** circus (stadium); **4** baths; **5** theatre. The town wall defences had four main gates **6**.

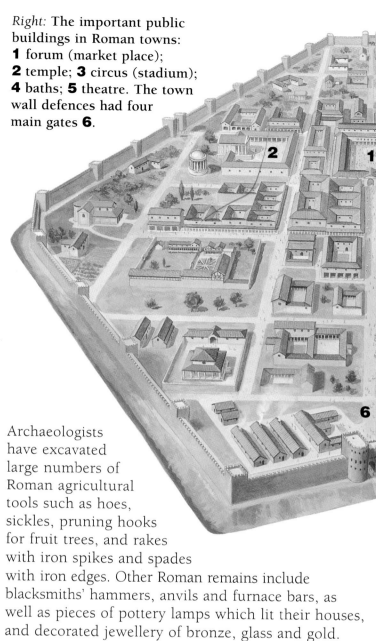

Archaeologists have excavated large numbers of Roman agricultural tools such as hoes, sickles, pruning hooks for fruit trees, and rakes with iron spikes and spades with iron edges. Other Roman remains include blacksmiths' hammers, anvils and furnace bars, as well as pieces of pottery lamps which lit their houses, and decorated jewellery of bronze, glass and gold.

ROMAN TOWN LIFE

The roads were vital military and trade routes in Roman Britain, linking the fortified Roman towns of London, York, Chester, Lincoln and St Albans. The Romans built new towns or converted Celtic bases introducing proper drains and straight streets that intersected one another at right angles like streets in a modern American city. At the centre of the town was the forum or market place, with a basilica or town hall, and a temple and public baths close by.

The public baths were places for people to meet together to gossip, to do sports or discuss business, rather than simply to wash. The baths were cheap and children got in free. The Romans also built theatres and amphitheatres in several British towns such as St Albans. In these huge arenas, a variety of different shows were put on to amuse the people such as gladiators fighting each other to the death, cock-fighting and bull-baiting.

ROMAN COUNTRY LIFE

Many Britons did not change their way of life under Roman rule. In the countryside, they continued to live in round timber-framed houses and farm much as they had done before the invasion, supporting their families. Because life in the countryside was largely unchanged, archaeologists call the inhabitants of Roman Britain Romano-British (rather than Roman) and that is the name given to things they made and built.

An important change in the British countryside was the Roman villa. Not unlike the stately homes of later centuries, these were large, luxurious houses surrounded by a big estate. They often had mosaic floors and painted walls, and some had glass windows. There would be several bedrooms, living rooms and a large kitchen. Some had central heating (*hypocausts*) with hot water running under the floors.

Above: **The Chi-Ro mosaic at Lullingstone in Kent shows the Christian sign: two Greek letters Chi and Ro – CHR – which stands for *Christos*, or Christ, in Greek. Christianity was brought to Britain by the Romans.**

Below: **A Roman coin found at Richborough, in Kent, dated AD 410. A Briton cowers before a fully armed Roman soldier on horseback. Richborough, in Kent, was Julius Caesar's chief port and military base.**

DECLINE OF THE EMPIRE

The Romans had to keep soldiers in Britain all the time to guard it against attack. From about AD 280 onwards, Saxon pirates (from what is now Germany) began raiding the shores of Britain. In the north, at the least sign of weakness in the Roman defence the Picts were ready to pour over Hadrian's Wall.

To guard against the Saxon raids, the Romans built a chain of forts along the shores from Norfolk to the Isle of Wight. The forts were under the command of an officer known as the Count of the Saxon Shore. The forts had massive walls, several of which still stand today. Burgh Castle in Norfolk has a fine example of such a wall. These forts held off the raiders until AD 367 when the Picts, the Saxons and warriors from northern Ireland joined forces. These invaders broke through Hadrian's Wall, and killed the Count of the Saxon Shore. But the Romans gradually restored order and made treaties with some of the northern tribes.

THE END OF ROMAN RULE

Two things combined to bring about the end of Roman rule in Britain. One was civil war between rival generals fighting to become emperor. The other was the increasing number of attacks on Rome by barbarian tribes from northern Europe. Slowly, legions of troops were withdrawn from Britain to protect other parts of the Roman empire. The last legion left in AD 406. Four years later, when the Romano-British appealed for help against other foreign invaders, the emperor could only reply: "Take steps to defend yourselves". Roman coins stopped being used by AD 430; Hadrian's Wall and other forts were neglected and villas abandoned; nobody repaired the roads; and 400 years of Roman rule in Britain slowly disappeared.

ROMAN CHRISTIANITY

Christianity was probably brought to Britain by Roman soldiers or civilian settlers from Gaul some time before AD 200. The influence of Roman Christianity led to the building of crosses and later churches. Saxon and British pagan gods and goddesses were slowly replaced. In AD 287 Alban, a Romano-Briton living at Verulamium, sheltered a Christian fleeing from persecution, and was put to death. (Verulamium is now known by its present name of St Albans.)

The Emperor Constantine made Christianity Rome's official religion in AD 324, by which time England already had three bishops, at Lincoln, London and York.

Left: A Roman pot made in about AD 200 shows men fighting. One holds up a finger to show he has lost. Some pots were made of bronze or iron and others of terracotta (clay). Most pottery was made for table use as platters, bowls or drinking cups.

ST PATRICK AND THE IRISH

Ireland's first great leader was Cormac, who ruled over Meath and Connacht from AD 275 to 300. He made himself *Ard-Rí* (high king), and set up a national assembly at Tara Hill, in Meath. Even more powerful was Niall of the Nine Hostages, who was high king from AD 380 to 405. At around this time a 16-year-old Romano-British boy, Patrick, was carried off to pagan Ireland and made a slave. He escaped and trained as a Christian priest. About 30 years later he went back to Ireland as a bishop and a missionary. There were already a few Christians in Ireland, but Patrick's preaching converted almost all the island. Many legends grew up about Patrick, for instance he is supposed to have banished all the snakes from Ireland. (In fact snakes never reached Ireland after the Ice Age. Ireland became an island at a time when Britain was still attached to the European mainland.) Patrick is the patron saint of Ireland.

Left: **The empire is dismantled. The Romans left in AD 406 and the Romano-British abandoned their country villas. Local farmers took away the valuable materials.**

- AD 324 Christianity becomes official religion of Roman empire

- AD 325 British bishops attend Council of Nicaea, first world-wide council of Christian Church

- AD 366 Picts raid as far south as London

- AD 367 Roman general Theodosius drives the Picts north beyond Hadrian's Wall

- AD 401 St Patrick sold into slavery in Ireland by pirates

- AD 406 Last Roman legion leaves Britain

- AD 407 Romano-Briton Constantine proclaims himself emperor

- AD 410 Emperor Honorius tells Romano-Britons that Rome can no longer defend them

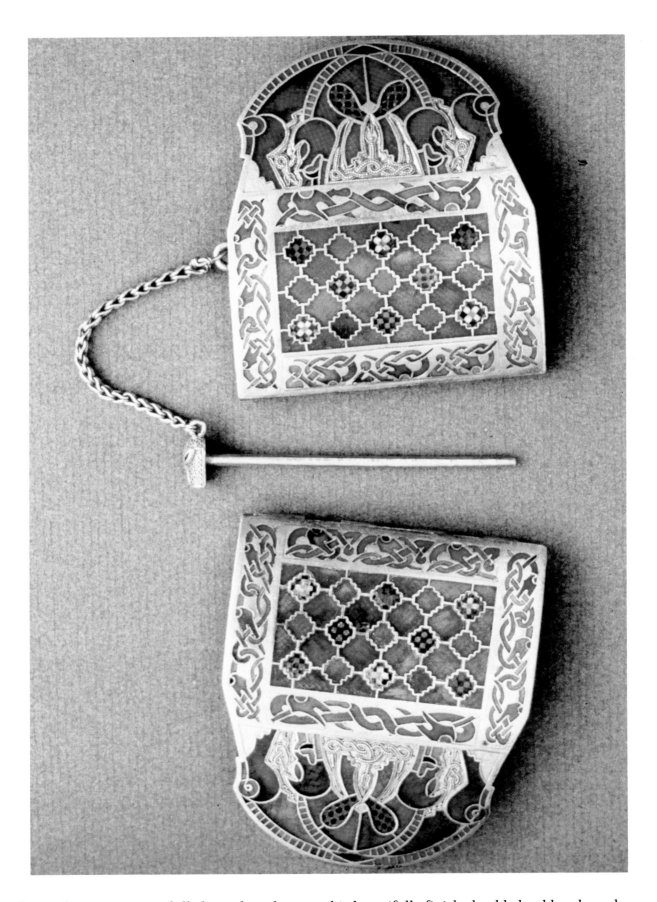

The Anglo-Saxons were skilled metal workers, as this beautifully finished gold shoulder clasp shows.

THE ANGLO-SAXONS
(440 – 1066)

THE ROMAN EMPIRE SPLIT in two – the Western Roman empire and the Eastern (Byzantine) empire. In AD 476 the Western Roman empire collapsed, and the years after this are often known as the Dark Ages. This is partly because so little is known about what happened at that time, and partly because the end of Roman law and order also led to the loss of classical culture, science and learning. The Dark Ages began in Britain much earlier than in the rest of Europe, when the last of the Roman legions left in AD 406. The soldiers were recalled to defend their empire, which was under threat from barbarian invasion, and they were never to return.

By that time Britain was already being attacked by Saxon pirates. The attacks grew stronger and more frequent. For a time the Romano-British people fought them off. Stories of that grim struggle are contained in the legends of King Arthur. But it was the pirate raiders who eventually won. Saxons, Jutes and Angles invaded Britain from northern Germany. From the Angles comes the word Angleland – England.

Later invaders were the Northmen, the fierce Vikings who settled in northern and eastern England and left their mark in place names containing old Norse words like *by*, a village, or *thwaite*, a clearing.

The Anglo-Saxons

EVEN BEFORE THE ROMANS left Britain in AD 406, England was being raided by Saxon pirates as well as by Jutes and Angles attacking from northern Germany, Denmark and what is now Holland and Belgium. The Picts from Scotland also broke through Hadrian's Wall and raided England.

Some Romano-British chiefs fought off these raiders with their own armies. But others invited mercenaries (paid soldiers) to help them fight their enemies. According to legend, the first German mercenaries to come to Britain and wage war on the Romano-British were Hengist and Horsa. The Anglo-Saxons (as we call the Saxons, Angles and Jutes) drove off the Picts, but instead of going back to their homeland they took over the Romano-British kingdoms by force.

- **450** Treasure buried at Mildenhall, Suffolk (found 1942)

- **476** Goths conquer Rome: end of Western Roman empire

- **477** Saxons arrive in England in force

- *c.* **500** Saxons defeated at Badon Hill by Britons under King Arthur

---

Below: **This map shows the borders of the various Anglo-Saxon tribes in England after the fall of the Roman empire. The Romano-Britons fled to Cornwall, while Wales and most of Scotland remained independent.**

THE DARK AGES AND KING ARTHUR

The years following the collapse of the Roman empire in AD 476 are often known as the Dark Ages, partly because there is so little written history of the time to shed any light on what happened in this period. In many ways it was like a return to life in the Iron Age, before organized Roman rule.

At the time of the fall of the Roman empire there was certainly a Romano-British tribe leader called Arthur who fought the Saxons from about 470 to 500. He lived in a castle called Camelot (it may have been in south Somerset) and he was probably a *dux bellorum*, or commander-in-chief of an army. His most famous victory was at Badon Hill. But the legends of Merlin the magician, the sword Excalibur, Guinevere, Lancelot and the Knights of the Round Table are exciting stories but not history. The Round Table at the Great Hall in Winchester is a Tudor reconstruction.

LIFE UNDER THE ANGLO-SAXONS

The Anglo-Saxons built simple wooden houses and barns and made towns into centres for trade and manufacturing. Craftworkers made pottery and glass, and metal workers included skilled jewellers. Most people were farmers, growing barley, oats and wheat for food, and flax for making linen for clothing. Sheep were kept for their wool as much as for their meat, and the Saxons also kept cattle, pigs and goats.

Under each tribal king there were three classes: noblemen; churls, who were freemen or yeomen, many of them owning land; and slaves. A slave could be bought for the price of eight oxen.

Left: **This is a picture for the month of March from an Anglo-Saxon calendar showing the Saxons working the land.**

From about 450 to 650 the Saxons created new kingdoms such as East Anglia (the kingdom of the East Angles), Kent, Sussex, Wessex, Northumbria and Mercia (present-day Midlands). The ancient Britons fled to Cornwall and Brittany in northern France (from where this region gets its name). Mercia was ruled by King Offa from 757 to 796. A strong ruler with a strong army, he is best known for Offa's Dyke, a defence stretching from the Severn estuary to the Irish Sea to keep out the Welsh. Almost 180 kilometres of earthworks 1.5 metres deep were built with wooden barriers and forts at the top. It can still be seen today. The Anglo-Saxons spoke Old English, which has developed into present-day English.

CELTIC AND ROMAN CHRISTIANS

The Romano-Britons were Christians whereas the Anglo-Saxons were pagans who worshipped their own gods and goddesses. St Patrick's followers Columba and Aidan converted the Anglo-Saxons after the Romans had left. They brought Christianity to Scotland and the north of England. There are Celtic monasteries at Iona in Argyll, Scotland and at Lindisfarne on Holy Island off the Northumberland coast. At Tintagel, Cornwall, lies the oldest known monastery in Britain, built by Celtic Christian monks in 470. In 597 Augustine, a missionary sent from Rome by Pope Gregory I to convert England, arrived in Kent and set up a Roman Christian church at Canterbury, where the cathedral would be built.

During the Dark Ages, Celtic and Roman Christians argued fiercely about the form their Church should take. In 664 King Oswy of Northumbria, who had supported Aidan, called a synod (conference) at Whitby, in Yorkshire. There the Celtic Church leaders under the Abbess Hilda decided to follow the Church of Rome and accept the Pope as their leader like the rest of Europe. They also decided the date of Easter and issues such as the style of a monk's haircut.

Left: **When Saxon soldiers reported that it was safe to land in Britain, whole families arrived. They beached their boats and waded ashore with their sheep and cattle.**

Above: **This elaborate Saxon helmet was crafted of iron, bronze and silver in about 625. It may have belonged to a king of the East Angles.**

15

MONKS AND LEARNING

Much of what we know about Britain comes from the writings of monks. One of the most important sources is the *History of the English Church and People*, completed in Latin in 731 by the Venerable Bede. He was a monk at the great monastery of Jarrow, near Newcastle, where he taught and wrote. Because he set up a school there for 600 monks, he is referred to as the father of English learning. Bede's *History of the English Church and People* was later translated into Anglo-Saxon by Alfred the Great.

In the monastery of Whitby, Caedmon, a monk who was perhaps the first English (or Saxon) poet, wrote *The Creation*, the earliest surviving English poem. Caedmon is thought of as the founder of English poetry. The other major work of this time is the *Anglo-Saxon Chronicle*, begun in the 800s by monks at Winchester, who recorded important events in England in the Anglo-Saxon language.

THE VIKINGS ATTACK

In the late 700s Northmen, or Norsemen, pirates from Scandinavia, began attacking the Anglo-Saxons. These Northmen were known as Vikings, from a Norse word meaning pirate or sea raider. The monks who wrote the *Anglo-Saxon Chronicle* called them "the heathen" or "the force".

The Vikings sailed in longships, sleek and fast all-weather vessels. They were disciplined fighters, but in their raids they slaughtered, burned and robbed. They carried off the most beautiful women, and took men to sell as slaves. They conquered Northumbria, East Anglia and Mercia. Only Wessex held out against them.

KENNETH MACALPIN, KING OF THE SCOTS

The early inhabitants of Scotland formed a number of tribes. By the 600s these tribes had united to form two kingdoms: Pictavia (land of the Picts), who occupied most of the northern part; and Dalriada (land of the Scots), who had moved to Scotland from Ireland.

In 843 Kenneth MacAlpin (son of Alpin), King of the Scots, claimed the throne of Pictavia through his grandmother, who was a Pictish princess. From his time onwards all the land north of the Clyde-Forth line was united and is now Scotland.

Right: **In the Dark Ages, monks were the only scholars. They copied books to send to other monasteries.**

KING EGBERT

During this time, a new dynasty of rulers was begun by Egbert, King of Wessex, who reigned from 802 to 839. He became the first king who could claim to be ruler over all England. Egbert enlarged Wessex (which at this point consisted of Berkshire, Devon, Dorset, Hampshire, Somerset, Wiltshire) to include Kent, Sussex, Surrey and Cornwall.

Egbert defeated Offa's powerful kingdom of Mercia at the battle of Ellandun in 825 (at Wroughton in Wiltshire). After this victory the people of Mercia and Northumbria acknowledged Egbert as Bretwalda (Lord of Britain). Egbert's grandson was Alfred the Great.

ALFRED THE GREAT

The Vikings who invaded England in the mid-800s came from Denmark, so we also call them Danes. They conquered Northumbria, took York and East Anglia, and overran Mercia. They would have conquered the whole of England but for the efforts of Alfred the Great. Alfred was the youngest son of King Ethelwulf of Wessex. He had spent much of his youth in Rome where he was educated.

Above: **Egbert (775-839). After being banished for laying claim to the West Saxon kingship, Egbert later returned to become King of Wessex in 802, and first ruler of England.**

Below: **The Vikings, or Danes, were bold sailors and fearsome soldiers. Their main weapons were swords, axes and spears.**

ALFRED DEFEATS THE DANES

During his fierce resistence of the Danes, Alfred spent some months hiding in the Isle of Athelney, among the marshes of Somerset. It is from here that the legend arose of Alfred burning cakes and being scolded by a local swineherd who did not recognize him as king.

In 871 Alfred defeated the Danes at the battle of Ashdown on the Berkshire Downs. He sought a peace in which the Danes agreed not to attack Wessex in return for a payment called the Danegeld – meaning gold for the Danes. But after five years the Danes under King Guthrum again attacked Wessex. Alfred raised an army and defeated the Danes at the battle of Edington in Wiltshire in 878. He also forced the King Guthrum to sign the Treaty of Wedmore and be baptized.

THE DANELAW

A new frontier between Wessex and the Danish territory followed the line of Watling Street, the old Roman road which ran from London to Chester. Alfred allowed the Danes to settle in the lands to the east of Watling Street, in what was later called the Danelaw. The Danes have left us their words such as *loft* as in Lowestoft meaning farmhouse and *thorpe* as in Scunthorpe which means village. In 890, Alfred built a fleet of ships to defend the shores of his southern kingdom of England. He also founded several new fortified towns, called *burhs*.

Right: **By the Treaty of Wedmore in 878, Alfred let the Danes take over eastern England as the Danelaw.**

Danelaw

English Mercia

Wessex

- **540** Bubonic plague in Britain

- **563** St Columba founds Iona monastery in western Scotland

- **590** Gregory I, the Great, becomes Pope (to 604)

- **597** St Augustine founds a monastery at Canterbury

- **600** Saxons, Angles and Jutes control most of England

- **604** First church of St Paul, London

- **613** Northumbrians defeat Britons near Chester

- **624-625** Sutton Hoo ship burial

- **627** Bishop Paulinus converts Edwin of Northumbria to Christianity and becomes Archbishop of York

- **635** Lindisfarne monastery established. St Aidan Bishop of Northumbria

- **642** Oswald of Northumbria killed in battle against Penda of Mercia

- **650** Epic poem *Beowulf* written

- **664** Synod of Whitby: Roman form of worship chosen over Celtic

- **704** Ethelred of Mercia abdicates to become a monk

- **716** Ethelbald becomes King of Mercia (to 747)

- **731** Venerable Bede completes *History of the English Church and People*

- **750** Gregorian chants first sung in England

- **757** Offa becomes King of Mercia (to 796)

- **760** *Book of Kells* written in Ireland

- **772-775** Offa builds Offa's Dyke defence to keep out the Welsh

Left: The Alfred Jewel, set in gold and crystal with a miniature enamel portrait of the king. It has the Saxon words for "Alfred ordered me to be made". This may have been the decorated end of a bookmark, to be used by a priest or monk when reading the Bible. Alfred was a religious man and encouraged his people to go to church.

- **787** Vikings raid Wessex
- **794** Vikings raid Scottish isles
- **795** First Viking raid on Ireland
- **802** Egbert is King of Wessex (to 839); Mercia's dominance is challenged
- **834** Kenneth MacAlpin becomes King of the Scots
- **843** MacAlpin defeats the Picts and unites Picts and Scots
- **856** Ethelwulf dies; succeeded by Ethelbald (to 860), Ethelbert (to 865) and Ethelred (to 871)
- **869** Danes occupy East Anglia and kill St Edmund
- **871** Alfred the Great becomes King of Wessex (to 899)
- **878** Alfred defeats Danes; Treaty of Wedmore divides England between Danes (Danelaw) and Saxons
- **890** Alfred establishes navy
- **891** *Anglo-Saxon Chronicle* begun
- **900** England divided into shires
- **919** Danes triumph in Dublin
- **980** Danes begin almost yearly raids on Britain

Above: In Alfred the Great's time England was divided into many small kingdoms.

Right: A statue of Alfred the Great stands at Wantage in Oxfordshire, his birthplace. Alfred was devout and scholarly. He translated several works from Latin into Old English.

THE WESSEX KINGS

Three kings, Alfred, Edward the Elder and Athelstan made the Anglo-Saxon kingdom of England strong. Alfred's son, Edward the Elder, defeated the Danes several times in his 25 year reign, and ruled over all England south of the river Humber. The Danelaw settlers of East Anglia and the Midlands submitted to him, and the Welsh princes also acknowledged him as their overlord. Edward's son, Athelstan, defeated a coalition of Vikings, Scots and Irish Celts at the battle of Brunanburh (937).

But a succession of weak rulers lost these gains. The weakest was Ethelred II, who came to the throne in 978, aged ten. Ethelred was known as the *Unraed - redeless*, or evil-counselled. The word was later translated as "unready". The Danes began raiding again and inflicted a defeat over the Saxons at the battle of Maldon in Essex, in 991. Ethelred was ill-advised to use the Danegeld (as Alfred had done at first) to try to buy off the Danes with bribes. Eventually his kingdom shrank to just Wessex and Kent.

Ethelred then attacked the Danes who were living peacefully in Wessex, including Gunhilda, sister of the Danish King Sweyn. Infuriated, the Danes waged war until, in 1013, they proclaimed Sweyn King of England. Ethelred fled to Normandy in France, the home of his wife, Emma. Their marriage established the first dynastic link between England and Normandy.

THE DANISH KINGS

Sweyn died in 1014, one year after becoming King of England. Ethelred came back, but he died in 1016. His son, Edmund Ironside, and Sweyn's son, Canute, battled for the throne. They finally agreed to share the kingdom between them, but Edmund died suddenly, having ruled his portion for just seven months.

Canute now became king of all England. He was also king of much of Scandinavia including Denmark, Norway and southern Sweden, but wisely he chose Englishmen, for the Church and for his Court.

Right: **The Danes who moved to Britain were farming people. They lived in simple wooden houses and cleared the forests for land.**

KING CANUTE

Canute brought peace and prosperity to England. He supplied a firm, fair government and maintained an army. Canute said: "I have vowed to God to govern my kingdoms with equity, and to act justly in all things". Two of his sons succeeded him as kings from 1035 to 1042: Harold I, known as Harefoot, and Harthacanute. Neither king contributed to the country's development.

THE LAST SAXON KINGS

In 1042, Edward, son of Ethelred II and Emma of Normandy, became king. Although he was a Saxon he had been brought up in Normandy and learned Norman ways. He was so devout that his people called him Edward the Confessor. Westminster Abbey was begun during his reign in 1052. Edward died in 1066 after naming his brother-in-law Harold Godwinsson, Earl of Wessex, as his heir. The Witan, the Saxon council, agreed and he was crowned Harold II at Westminster Abbey on January 6, 1066, the last Saxon king of England.

Left: **Edward the Confessor (1042-1066) elder son of Ethelred the Unready and Emma, daughter of Richard, Duke of the Normans. Edward founded Westminster Abbey.**

Above: **King Canute was surrounded by courtiers who tried to win his favour by flattery. There is a story that, to prove he was not taken in by their flattery, he commanded the tide to turn back – and got wet. Clearly even a king was less powerful than God and the forces of nature.**

- **1005** Malcolm II becomes King of Scotland (to 1034)

- **1013** Danes control England. Sweyn proclaimed King of England

- **1016** Canute, son of Sweyn becomes King of England

- **1034** Duncan I is King of Scotland

- **1035** Canute dies; succeeded by son, Harold I (Harefoot)

- **1040** Harold I dies; succeeded by half brother Harthacanute (to 1042). Macbeth kills Duncan I in battle, and becomes King of Scotland (to 1057)

- **1042** Edward, Ethelred II's son, becomes king (to 1066)

- **1057-1058** Duncan's son Malcolm kills Macbeth, and becomes Malcolm III King of Scots

- **1064** Harold Godwinsson shipwrecked in Normandy; forced to swear allegiance to William, Duke of Normandy, before William will release him

- **1066** Edward dies; Harold Godwinsson crowned last Saxon king of England

A beautiful book cover drawn by monks at Kells in Ireland. At the time of the Norman invasion, these monks lived in a monastery with beehive-shaped huts, a central stone chapel and a five-storey round tower.

THE NORMANS
(1066 – 1154)

IN THE 600 YEARS SINCE the Saxon pirates began to settle amid the ruins of the old Roman province of Britain, their descendants had made England one of the wealthiest and best-governed lands in western Europe. The Danes had also finally settled peacefully in the country. All was about to change, however, because the Anglo-Saxon king, Edward the Confessor, had no son to take his place. The storm clouds were gathering. Once again the Northmen threatened. Harald Hardrada of Norway, aided by Tostig, the renegade Earl of Northumbria, was waiting to pounce. So too were William, Duke of Normandy, who was Edward's brother-in-law, and named heir Harold Godwinsson, Earl of Wessex, who was Tostig's brother.

William won the contest, and for the next hundred years England was ruled by Norman kings. The Normans brought about a major change – they ended England's isolation. Henceforth England was very much a part of Europe. Indeed, until 1558, English monarchs owned a part of France – at times the major part.

Scotland and Ireland retained their independence under the Norman kings. Wales already had links with the Saxon kings, and within a few years the Normans overran southern Wales. But for centuries northern Wales remained independent of the Normans.

The Normans

THE NORMANS WERE originally Vikings who had settled in northwest France in the early 900s, by the River Seine. In 1066 an army of up to 7,000 men crossed over the English Channel in hundreds of boats.

CONTENDERS FOR THE CROWN

This invasion was led by William, Duke of Normandy, who claimed that he was the rightful King of England, even though Harold Godwinsson had already been crowned king and accepted by the Witan. King Harold led the English army to oppose the Norman invasion. But he and many of his men were weary. Three weeks earlier they had fought and beaten Harald Hardrada, a Norwegian contender for the throne, at Stamford Bridge in Yorkshire, and then had a six-day forced march back to London. Now Harold's forces assembled on the Sussex downs, near the town of Battle.

Above: **The charge of the Normans at the battle of Hastings. The Normans were more heavily armed than their Saxon opponents.**

Below: **Part of the famous Bayeux Tapestry telling the story of William's conquest. The pictures are embroidered in different coloured wool.**

Left: **William I, the Conqueror (1066-1087) was the illegitimate son of Robert, Duke of Normandy. He defeated Harold, King of England, at the battle of Hastings in 1066 and was crowned king. He was a stern but efficient ruler.**

- **1066** Edward the Confessor dies; Witan offers throne to Harold II; Tostig and Harald Hardrada of Norway invade northern England; defeated at Stamford Bridge by Harold. William of Normandy invades Sussex; defeats and kills Harold at Hastings. Halley's Comet seen

- **1070** Malcolm III invades Northumbria. Lanfranc Archbishop of Canterbury. Hereward the Wake heads a rising in fen country

- **1071** William I subdues fen rebellion

- **1072** William raids Scotland. Normans conquer Sicily in the Mediterranean

- **1073** Lincoln Cathedral begun

- **1078** Tower of London begun. Pope Gregory VII sends legates to reorganize Church in England

- **1079** William's son Robert Curthose begins castle that gives Newcastle-upon-Tyne its name

- **1086** Domesday Book completed

- **1087** William dies at Rouen. William II becomes king. Robert becomes Duke of Normandy

THE BATTLE OF HASTINGS

The Saxons and Normans were closely matched because the battle of Hastings lasted eight hours, a long time for a medieval battle. The best-armed Saxons (the *thegns* and king's bodyguards) formed a shield-wall against the Norman knights and infantry. The opposing armies met at Hastings on October 14, 1066. The English fought on foot with Harold fighting between his two brothers. They fought off several attacks by Normans on horseback. The Normans then pretended to retreat and some of Harold's forces, thinking they had won the battle, chased after them breaking up their shield-wall. Norman archers then fired arrows over them with deadly effect. According to legend, Harold was pierced through the eye by a Norman arrow, and killed.

William of Normandy advanced to Dover, then to Coventry and finally to London. On Christmas Day 1066, he was crowned King of England.

WILLIAM THE CONQUEROR

The man who overthrew the Saxons, and known ever since as William the Conqueror, was the illegitimate son of Duke Robert of Normandy and a tanner's daughter, Arlette. William was only seven when Robert died. Life was hard for any young boy expected to be a duke. It was much worse for a son born out of marriage. By the time he was 20, William had put down one major rebellion by his barons, and he would have to overcome many more.

THE DOMESDAY BOOK

William subdued England by taking the land away from the Anglo-Saxon lords and giving it to his Norman barons. He ordered many wooden and later stone castles to be built to protect his rule, and also sent out men to record what was in his new kingdom. The survey, recorded in the Domesday Book, was carried out in the first seven months of 1086 and showed that the population was about one and a half million. Every manor and land holding was recorded. William could now check that none of his noblemen had seized other property, and exactly what rents and fees their land should bear. Domesday comes from the word *dom*, meaning assessment. It was so thorough that, as the monks of the *Anglo-Saxon Chronicle* commented: "There was not a single hide nor rod of land ... not an ox, a cow, a pig was left out".

Left: **The Domesday Book is normally associated with Winchester where it was most probably compiled. It was actually two books: the first volume of 382 pages describes most of the country while the second volume was called Little Domesday, and was possibly compiled by monks at Ely.**

FOCUS ON NORMAN CATHEDRALS

The Normans brought over their architects from the Continent, who helped plan big Romanesque churches and cathedrals such as at Chichester and Durham. Romanesque was a style of western European architecture from the 10th to 13th centuries which featured ribbed vaulting and rounded arches. Deep doorways had rounded arches supported on thick, strong pillars and with highly decorated mouldings. The windows were often bordered with a chevron or a V-shape. Norman builders had only simple equipment with which to build their great cathedrals and churches, but the results were spectacular.

Domesday Village Life

VILLAGE LIFE revolved around the parish church because it was the only public building. The church and churchyard were used for fairs and games as well as for religious services and festivals such as Christmas, Whitsun and Easter. Sundays and Mondays were usually days of rest.

Most village people were *villeins*, who owned a few plough oxen and a small piece of land called a small-holding. They had to farm on the lord of the manor's land for certain amounts of time, and then at other times they could cultivate their own strips of land and tend to their livestock. Below villeins were the *bordars* who owned even less land (about two hectares) and had no livestock.

There were often one or two manors in a village and the barons owned all the large open fields, with some of the peasants being allowed to own much smaller strips of land. Any meadow or woodland was also owned by the barons. Manors varied greatly in size, ranging from many square kilometres to just a few hectares.

Farming was mainly hard manual work – sowing, weeding and harvesting were all done by hand. Only ploughing was aided by oxen. Sheep were the most important livestock, and often those belonging to villagers outnumbered those owned by the manor. Sheep were raised for their meat, for their wool (which could be sold by the owners), and for cheese made from their milk. At harvest time the lord of the manor would

Right: **An artist's impression of what a typical baron's manor would have looked like. The manor was a fortified home and it would have included a castle 1 for a lookout and protection. The baron himself would have lived in the large thatched building 2 inside a defensive picket fence called a bailey 3. The farm buildings 4 include barns, a blacksmith's shop and the bailiff's (farm manager) house. The villeins' houses 5 are grouped away from the baron's castle, around the parish church 6. There are three fields for farming: one for wheat 7, one for barley or oats 8 and one left fallow 9. This baron also has a deer park 10, a vineyard 11, and an orchard 12.**

provide pork, chicken, cabbages, eggs, cheese and apples for those gathering the crops.

In the autumn many farm animals were killed and their meat preserved in salt. This saved on precious winter fodder and also meant the villagers had a source of nourishment during the long winter months. They ate fish on Fridays and Holy Days as the Church did not allow them to eat meat on these days. The manor also ran the water-mill for grinding the manor's and the villagers' corn. There were also fisheries on the rivers, with part of the catch paid to the lord of the manor. Hunting was reserved for the Norman lords who created areas of countryside in which deer and boars could roam.

Above: **A house belonging to a tenant called a bordar. He was one of the lowest tenants in the feudal structure of land ownership and loyalty to the lord of the manor. This house has a timber frame filled in with wattle and daub (which is mud and plaster on a wicker mesh). It is built close to a wood and would have a run for pigs reared in the woods and fed on acorns. After sheep, pigs were the most important livestock, and the Domesday Book often described woods by the number of pigs that could be kept in them. Women worked as hard in the village as men, helping them in the fields, making baskets, plucking geese for arrow-feathers, stitching sheepskin for saddle-bags and churning butter – all duties performed for the manor house. At home, women would look after their children, house and garden.**

The Feudal System

UNDER WHAT IS CALLED the feudal system, which the Normans brought with them from France, all the land in England was owned by the king. He allowed others to hold some of it in return for certain services. The Domesday Book reveals what was owned by the king and through him, by his barons. These barons had private armies, under the command of knights, who were meant to be ready to fight for the king whenever he wanted them to do so. The barons built castles for defence and lived in manor houses.

HOW FEUDALISM BEGAN

After the collapse of the Roman empire, around the year AD 476, law and order had crumbled in Europe and barbarians invaded from all sides. The feudal system grew out of this lawlessness. It began in France, in about AD 750, and soon spread across Europe.

Fearing for their lives, people banded together under the protection of strong leaders or kings. But no leader was strong enough on his own to resist attack or control fighting between local barons, so the king granted land to certain powerful barons, in return for their promising to help him fight his enemies and pay him taxes.

HOW THE FEUDAL SYSTEM WORKED

The feudal system was based on exchanging land for services rather than for rent. The term comes from the Latin for fief, *feudum,* which means any land given away. At the top were the barons and Church institutions who held land given to them by the king and were called tenants-in-chief. In return for this land they were expected to pay the king taxes and provide him with knights to help him fight his enemies. William tried to ensure the barons' estates were scattered about the country so their power was diluted.

The barons kept some land for themselves and also allowed their knights to hold some of their land. Knights were trained warriors. In exchange for land, each knight had to promise to follow his baron to war or guard his castle for 40 days in a year, and provide a certain number of soldiers.

Left: William I made all landowners swear loyalty only to him. This meant they could not swear loyalty to powerful barons who might then build up private armies against the king. William also introduced the practice of knight service, whereby each knight had to follow the baron to war or guard his castle, for 40 days each year. In turn, the baron pledged allegiance to the king.

Below the knights in the feudal system came yeomen, or farmers, who were all free men. They usually lived in a village near the manor house and had to work a few days a week for the baron. At the lowest level were the peasants, known as serfs, who provided the baron with crops in return for protection. Serfs belonged to the baron, as property. They could be bought or sold, as could their children. They could not leave the village or get married without the baron's permission. They did not own their land. This series of arrangements was the basis of what is called the feudal system.

Right: The feudal system created a definite hierarchy, from the powerful at the top to the poorest at the bottom. First came the clergy, then the knight and his family, who were loyal to a baron. The middle class of merchants, lawyers, and yeoman farmers did not owe any services to a baron – they were free, as were craftworkers and shopkeepers. At the bottom were footsoldiers and the serfs.

FOCUS ON THE TOWER OF LONDON

As soon as the Normans moved into an area they would build a wooden fort, usually on a high earth mound with the garrison below protected by high wooden ramparts. The site would be carefully chosen because it overlooked the neighbouring countryside or it dominated a river or important overland route.

No castle could be built without the king's permission – another way of keeping the feudal system working and the barons in check. The most famous castle was the White Tower, built in London to protect the city from enemies coming up the Thames. The White Tower started out as a simple timber-and-earth castle built a few months after the victory at Hastings. By 1100 it was a large 28 metre stone tower with rooms for the royal family, surrounded by wooden buildings for the army and administrators. Today, the White Tower is known by its more famous name: the Tower of London – once the main residence for all English kings from William II to Henry VII. It was also to become a royal mint, a prison, a place of execution and home for the Crown Jewels and Royal Armoury. The Royal Armoury was moved to Leeds in 1996.

- **1089** William II campaigns to take Normandy from his brother

- **1090** Most of Wales comes under Norman rule. Ely and Norwich cathedrals begun

- **1092** William takes Cumbria from Scots

- **1093** Anselm of Bec becomes Archbishop of Canterbury. Malcolm III of Scotland killed while invading England: Donald Bane succeeds him. Durham Cathedral begun

- **1094** Revolt in northwest Wales. Duncan II, son of Malcolm III, drives out Donald Bane, but is later killed

- **1095** Anselm quarrels with William and goes to Rome.

- **1096** First Crusade begins. Normans conquer south Wales. William lends Robert funds for a crusade in return for keeping Normandy as a loan

- **1097** Edgar, son of Malcolm III, deposes and succeeds Donald Bane (to 1107); he accepts William as his overlord. Revolt by the Welsh

- **1099** William holds his first court at Westminster. He conquers Maine in north France

- **1100** William II killed while hunting; succeeded by Henry I (to 1135). Henry marries Matilda, daughter of Malcolm III of Scotland

- **1101** Robert of Normandy, back from the crusades, invades England, but is bought off

- **1106** Henry I defeats and captures Robert at battle of Tinchebrai, and gains Normandy

- **1107** Synod of Westminster: Henry gives up his right to choose bishops and abbots, and is reconciled with Anselm

- **1109** Anselm dies. Henry at war with France

WILLIAM II – THE RED KING

William the Conqueror died from injuries he suffered following a riding accident in 1087. He left Normandy to his eldest son, Robert, and England to his younger but more tough-minded son, William. William II was known as Rufus because of his ruddy complexion (Rufus means red in Latin). William II continued his father's strong rule but he was also a cruel king. He taxed his subjects, including the Church, as much as he could. Several times his barons rebelled in support of Robert of Normandy, a gentler man whom they thought would be easier to deal with. William suppressed these revolts with the aid of the *fyrd*, the old Saxon part-time army. He also fought off two invasions from Malcolm III of Scotland. Scotland and Ireland kept their independence under the Norman kings.

William II was fond of hunting stags and while out hunting in the New Forest he was killed by an arrow. It may have been an accident, but some say that Walter Tyrell, who fired the arrow, was acting on orders from William's younger brother, Henry.

Above: **William II, Rufus, (1087-1100) was born in 1066. He had long flame-red hair, and was hated by his people. He was shot by an arrow while hunting in the New Forest.**

Above: **Henry I (1100-1135) was born in 1068. He seized the throne on the death of Rufus. A strong king, it was said that in his time no man dared to harm another.**

Above: **Ten thousand Norman soldiers were stationed throughout England.**

Left: **With some 70 years of Norman rule and relative peace, towns began to grow. Traders and craftworkers settled in the bigger towns, such as London and Winchester.**

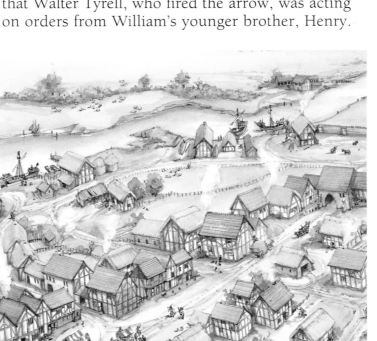

HENRY I

Henry seized the throne and took possession of the royal treasury at Winchester the day after William's death. Robert of Normandy did not accept Henry I as king and the two fought on both sides of the Channel until, in 1106, Henry defeated Robert at the battle of Tinchebrai in Normandy. Robert was imprisoned in England for 28 years until his death. Henry I became known as the Lion of Justice.

THE *CURIA REGIS*

King Henry set up the *Curia Regis*, or King's Council to settle land and other disputes between the king and his tenants. This was the beginning of the Civil Service, the body of officials who help the government run the country.

Henry, who was often absent in Normandy, needed an efficient government to operate in England in his absence. He created a class of loyal administrators from the servants of his royal household, including the chamberlain, who looked after the royal bedchamber; the marshal, who controlled the royal stables; the treasurer; and the steward, who looked after Court officials called ushers. Henry's chancellor, or secretary, issued writs for the sheriffs, or shire-reeves, who administered the counties. The chief officer of the state was the justiciar, who was the equivalent of today's Lord Chief Justice, but also acted as regent, or stand-in, when the king was overseas.

Above: In 1120, the *White Ship*, carrying Henry I's son, William, struck some rocks and sank in the English Channel. William was drowned.

THE *WHITE SHIP* DISASTER

Henry I had made himself popular with his Saxon subjects by marrying Edith (also known as Matilda), the daughter of Malcolm III of Scotland and of Margaret, a Saxon princess, herself sister of Edgar Atheling, a Saxon claimant to the throne. In 1120 Henry I's only son, William, and Henry's daughter Adela, were drowned returning from Normandy to England in a vessel called the *White Ship*. Henry was so grief-stricken that, it is said, he was never again seen to smile.

FOCUS ON NORMAN CRAFTWORKERS

Craftworkers such as stone masons and metal workers lived in the towns and sold their goods there. Stone masons carved stone columns and blocks, as well as decorative gargoyles, sometimes with the faces of people they knew! They carved their own special marks on cathedrals, churches and castles to identify

their work. The main crafts were cloth making, leatherwork, carpentry and metalwork. For hundreds of years wool was the main British export to Europe, where it was dyed in vats and woven into cloth. Goldsmiths were also busy and safehouses were provided to keep their priceless ornaments out of the reach of robbers.

Henry had lost his only legitimate son and heir to the throne, so he now tried to persuade his barons to swear to stand by his eldest daughter, Matilda.

Henry's daughter Matilda had been married to Henry V of Germany (who died in 1125). In 1126 the barons agreed to accept her as their next ruler. For greater security Henry I married her to Geoffrey Plantagenet, Count of Anjou.

MATILDA AGAINST STEPHEN

Despite their promises to Henry I, many Norman barons were still reluctant to see his daughter Matilda – or any woman – become the next monarch. Many barons did not like Geoffrey of Anjou because he tried to weaken their power. There was also another contender for the throne: Henry I's nephew, Stephen of Blois, son of William the Conqueror's daughter Adela and the French Count of Blois. He was more likely to let the barons have their own way. In the end the rival claims of Matilda and Stephen of Blois seemed to be decided when Stephen was the first to arrive in London after King Henry died in 1135.

Aided by his brother Henry, Bishop of Winchester, Stephen quickly won the support of the Church, and only three weeks after Henry died he was crowned king. Matilda, however, did not give up her claim to the throne.

STEPHEN'S WEAK REIGN

The Normans had provided England with 60 years of firm rule by three strong kings. Stephen, however, was both good natured and weak. Unchecked by a firm king, the Norman barons avoided paying the taxes they owed to the Crown and built castles where they liked, raiding and robbing at random. In total the barons built 100 new baronial castles in defiance of the king. Stephen's disputed claim to the throne also plunged the country into years of civil war. A number of barons went over to Matilda who was supported in her fight for the throne by her half-brother Robert, Earl of Gloucester.

Right: **An impressive Norman castle overlooking its own village, is visited by the king. The lord of the manor or baron was expected to entertain the king and his followers.**

Above: **Matilda was the only daughter of Henry I. Some nobles accepted her as queen in 1141, but most continued to support the weaker Stephen of Blois.**

Above: **Stephen of Blois (1135-1154) was the son of William I's daughter Adela. A weak king, he gained only the contempt of his barons. He was the first English king to allow jousting tournaments.**

- **1110** Henry I betrothes his eight-year-old daughter Matilda to the Holy Roman Emperor, Henry V, and increases taxes for her dowry. Bad weather ruins the crops. Earliest known miracle play performed at Dunstable, Bedfordshire, about this time

- **1114** Henry leads an army into Wales and makes peace. Chichester Cathedral is begun

- **1120** Prince William drowned in the *White Ship* off Harfleur.

- **1121** Henry marries again, to Adela of Louvain

- **1123** Rahere, Henry's jester, founds Augustinian priory of St Bartholomew, London

- **1124** First Scottish coinage

- **1126** Henry persuades barons to accept his daughter Matilda as his heir

- **1128** Widowed Matilda marries again, to Geoffrey Plantagenet, son of Fulk, Count of Anjou. David of Scotland founds Holyrood Abbey, near Edinburgh

- **1129** Fulk goes to Palestine: Geoffrey takes over rule of Anjou, Maine and Touraine

- **1131** Tintern Abbey founded

- **1133** St Bartholomew's Fair first held at Smithfield (the "smooth field"), London; held once a year for over 700 years

Left: **The layout of the castle would include: 1** a spiral staircase; **2** baron's bedroom; **3** great hall; **4** chapel; **5** kitchen and store rooms.

Robert was the illegitimate son of Henry I, but rather than claim the throne for himself he chose to support his half-sister.

THE SCOTS ATTACK

The Scots under King David joined in the fray and invaded northern England in 1138. They were repelled by an English army hurriedly gathered together by the brave Archbishop of York, Thurstan. His troops carried the banners of St Cuthbert, St John of Beverley and St Wilfred, all much revered in the north. The men of the north, led by Thurstan's clergy, fell on the Scots at Northallerton and killed 12,000 of them. This bloody slaughter is known as the battle of the Standard.

MATILDA TAKES POWER

In 1139, Matilda landed at Portsmouth with Robert and they won many campaigns. In 1141 they captured Stephen at Lincoln Castle and imprisoned him at Bristol Castle. Matilda was made queen, and was acknowledged as Lady of the English by Stephen's own brother, Henry, the Bishop of Winchester. But she imposed many taxes on the English people and once again made the barons hostile to her. Her reign lasted only eight months. Bishop Henry deserted Matilda and rejoined Stephen. Robert was captured and exchanged for Stephen. On Stephen's release the war intensified and Matilda was besieged in Oxford Castle. She escaped in 1142 by disguising herself in a white robe and fleeing through the snow. Eventually she went to Normandy, and never returned.

- **1135** Henry I dies in Normandy. Stephen of Blois, his nephew, crosses to England and seizes the throne. Foundation of Fountains Abbey in Yorkshire

- **1136** Stephen gives Cumberland to David of Scotland, who accepts Stephen as king. Matilda claims the throne

- **1137** Geoffrey of Monmouth writes his largely fictional *History of the Kings of Britain*. Stephen wins campaign in Normandy against Geoffrey of Anjou

- **1138** Robert, Earl of Gloucester, begins civil war in support of Matilda. David of Scotland supports her, but is defeated at battle of the Standard

- **1141** Battle of Lincoln: Matilda's forces capture Stephen. Stephen's supporters defeat Matilda's army at Winchester, and capture Robert of Gloucester. Stephen and Robert exchanged

- **1142** Matilda escapes from Oxford Castle

- **1144** Geoffrey of Anjou captures Rouen, and controls Normandy

- **1147** Matilda leaves England

- **1149** Matilda's son Henry returns to England; knighted by David I of Scotland

- **1151** Geoffrey of Anjou dies; his son Henry succeeds him.

- **1152** Eleanor marries Henry of Anjou. Synod at Kells; Pope acknowledged as supreme head of the Church in Ireland

- **1153** Henry of Anjou lands in England. Treaty of Wallingford; Stephen agrees Henry shall be his heir. Death of David I of Scotland; succeeded by grandson Malcolm IV (to 1165)

- **1154** Nicholas Breakspear elected as Pope Adrian IV (only English pope). Death of Stephen

THE BARONS REBEL

With the death of Robert in 1147 Matilda lost her only close ally and so she abandoned her claims to the throne. Stephen was confirmed as king, but he still proved quite incapable of controlling the barons. The country remained in disorder. Stephen tried to gain the barons' support with extravagant gifts, but they realized that he was a weak ruler and that they could do as they liked, which they did.

HENRY OF ANJOU

Order was not restored during Stephen's reign until 1153, when a powerful contender for the throne landed in England. His name was Henry, son of Matilda (Henry I's daughter) and of Geoffrey Plantagenet, (Count of Anjou). Henry of Anjou had first come to England when he was 11 years old to be educated in Bristol Castle by Robert of Gloucester who was Matilda's half-brother.

Henry's marriage, in 1152, had surprised Europe. His bride was Eleanor of Aquitaine, ruler in her own right of a large part of France as the heir to the Duke of Aquitaine. Henry's possessions in France were already larger than all England, and now, with his wife, he controlled more than half of France.

In 1153 Henry landed in England to claim his right to the throne. Although he could not defeat Stephen decisively, at Wallingford in Oxfordshire he forced Stephen and the barons to accept his terms to end the civil war. Stephen was to keep the throne, but acknowledge Henry as his heir. Stephen, the last of the Norman kings, died in 1154, and Henry II was crowned King of England.

Above: **The four Norman kings. William I and William II are on the top row; Henry I and Stephen are below. The first three kings created strong Norman rule, but Stephen threw it away. Until his reign, Norman rule had helped to develop Britain's economy and end Viking raids.**

Left: **Geoffrey Plantagenet, Count of Anjou, was one of the first people known to have borne a coat-of-arms. It featured the three lions which still appear on the royal arms of England.**

THE PLANTAGENETS
(1154 – 1399)

THE PLANTAGENETS RULED ENGLAND for almost 250 years. These were years of strife and violence, but they also saw the beginnings of English democracy in the birth of Parliament. It was Plantagenet kings who fought the Hundred Years War against the French, initially winning most of the battles but losing the war and most of England's French possessions. The name Plantagenet was a nickname for the founder of the dynasty, Geoffrey of Anjou, who wore a sprig of broom, *planta genista*, as a badge. But the name does not appear to have been used by the royal family itself until the mid-1400s so some historians prefer to call Henry II and his sons Angevins, men from Anjou.

Geoffrey Plantagenet, Count of Anjou, whose son began 250 years of Plantagenet rule in Britain.

Henry II

HENRY OF ANJOU, the son of Matilda and Geoffrey of Anjou, became Henry II, the first Plantagenet King of England, in 1154. He immediately set about ruthlessly destroying the castles of those barons who had opposed him during Stephen's reign. He also wanted more control over the Church, which had a powerful hold over ordinary people during these times.

THOMAS à BECKET

In 1155 Henry appointed his friend, a priest Thomas à Becket, as Chancellor, the chief minister of England. Later, in 1162, Henry persuaded Becket to become Archbishop of Canterbury. He thought that as both Archbishop and Chancellor Becket would do his bidding and help keep the Church in check. But Becket "put God before the king" and defended the rights and possessions of the Church. Henry set out his Church reforms in the Constitutions of Clarendon in 1164 – including the trial of clergy in the Crown's courts, not the Church's own courts. Becket and Henry were in such bitter conflict that twice Becket had to flee to France. When he returned the second time in 1170, Henry is said to have cried out in anger: "Who will rid me of this turbulent priest?" Four knights took Henry at his word, went to Canterbury and brutally murdered Becket at the foot of the altar steps in the cathedral. This aroused horror in Europe and Becket was made a saint.

Above: **Henry II (1154-1189) was one of the most powerful rulers of the Middle Ages. A man of great humour but violent temper, he brought England a time of peace and prosperity.**

Left: **On December 29, 1170, Thomas à Becket was murdered on the steps of the altar of Canterbury Cathedral for having opposed the king. Many miracles were soon reported at his tomb. He was made a saint three years later.**

TIME CHART

● **1154** Henry II King of England (to 1189). Henry appoints Thomas à Becket Lord Chancellor

● **1162** Thomas à Becket appointed Archbishop of Canterbury. Henry raises Danegeld for the last time

● **1163** Oxford University established

● **1164** Constitutions of Clarendon: clerics condemned by the Church to be punished by lay courts. Becket goes into exile

● **1170** Henry has his son crowned king to ensure succession. Becket is murdered in Canterbury Cathedral

● **1171** Henry invades Ireland and the Irish princes submit

● **1172** Synod of Cashel: Irish Church reformed along English lines. Henry absolved of murder of Becket

● **1173** Henry's family rebel in France. Barons in England join them. Henry crushes revolt in France and imprisons Queen Eleanor. Becket made a saint

Below: **In 1173 Henry II ruled more of France than the French king, Louis VII.**

THE INVASION OF IRELAND

England's long and troubled involvement in Ireland began in the reign of Henry II. Henry took advantage of the fact that Irish clan chiefs were fighting each other to claim the title of *Ard-Rí*, or High King. In 1166 he sent a force led by Richard de Clare, Earl of Pembroke, who was also known as Strongbow, to support the King of Leinster in Ireland. In 1171 Strongbow invaded Ireland, claiming the authority of the Pope to convert the Irish Celtic Church to the Roman Church. Irish kings, nobles and bishops submitted to his forces in the same year.

HENRY II'S SONS

Henry II had four strong-willed and unruly sons: Henry, Richard, Geoffrey and John. Henry, the eldest, was known as the Young King because his father had him crowned during his own lifetime to protect the succession. Henry II gave each of his three elder sons lands from his French possessions: the Young King had Normandy, Maine and Anjou; Richard had Aquitaine; Geoffrey had Brittany; but John received no territories to rule and so people at the time nicknamed him Lackland.

The four sons were encouraged by their mother Eleanor, to rebel against the king. She had already fallen out with Henry II in an unhappy marriage. Henry and Geoffrey both died before their father. Henry II fought against Richard and John and kept Eleanor imprisoned for much of their married life. Henry's sons never succeeded in overthrowing him.

THE CRUSADES

Since the Norman times Anglo-Norman knights had become involved in the crusades. The crusades were a series of military expeditions undertaken by European Christians over 3,000 kilometres away in the Middle East. Their aim was to recover the Holy Lands, where Christianity began, from Muslim occupation. There were eight major crusades from 1095 to 1270, most of which were failures, though a Christian kingdom of Jerusalem was briefly established. During the Middle Ages, many men and women made journeys, called pilgrimages, to Jerusalem and other holy places in Palestine where Jesus had lived and died.

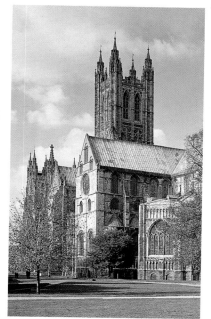

Left: **The Archbishop of Canterbury is the head of the Church of England. The first archbishop was St Augustine, who founded an abbey in Canterbury in 597. Archbishop Lanfranc laid the foundations for the Cathedral from 1070-1089. Thomas à Becket was murdered in the cathedral in 1170 and his tomb there became a centre of pilgrimage.**

FOCUS ON A MEDIEVAL MARKET

Most medieval towns had fairs and markets. Markets were usually held once a week, when farmers from local villages would bring their produce and livestock to sell. There were stalls for butter, salt and fish, as well as shops selling pies for a penny. Metal, leather and woodwork would also be for sale. Beggars and pick-pockets mingled with the crowds looking at the many craft and food stalls while jugglers, musicians and dancing bears entertained passers-by.

This picture shows a stone cross from the late 14th century in the market square at

Chichester in West Sussex. Official business would be done in the market hall at the centre of the square. Many such halls survive today, for example, in Chipping Campden in Gloucestershire and Chipping Norton in Oxfordshire (chipping means selling). Some larger medieval towns had annual fairs where merchants and traders from other parts of the country and overseas exchanged goods. St Giles Fair, held in Oxford, dates back to medieval times.

Richard I and the Crusades

Above: **A knight of the crusades.**

THE CHRISTIAN CHURCH had lost control of the Holy Lands to the Arabs in the 7th century. The Arabs were Muslims and followed Mohammed, founder of the religion of Islam. At first they let Christian pilgrims visit the holy places. But when Muslim Turks invaded the region they began to attack the Christian pilgrims.

In 1095 Pope Urban II called on Christians to liberate Jerusalem from the Turks. Up to 25,000 people, from knights to paupers, travelled to Constantinople, and went on to capture Jerusalem in 1099 in the First Crusade.

A famous legend tells of Blondel, a minstrel who tirelessly searched for, and found, the lost king. Richard was rescued only when his long-suffering subjects paid an enormous ransom - but they warmly welcomed him back to London. Soon, however, he left for Normandy to defend his French lands. Richard was mortally wounded by an archer while

Right: **Saladin, the great Muslim general and sultan of the Saracens. He united the Muslim kingdoms and from 1187 led them in a *jihad* (holy war) against the Christian crusaders – among them Richard the Lionheart, King of England.**

THE THIRD CRUSADE

Nearly 100 years later English knights were among the main participants in the Third Crusade. The great Muslim leader, Saladin had recaptured Jerusalem from the crusaders in 1187. Richard I came to the throne in 1189 as a soldier already admired for his skill and courage. His bravery earned him the name *Coeur de Lion*, the Lionheart.

That year Richard responded to the Pope's call to try to win Jerusalem back from the Muslim Turks. He came within sight of Jerusalem, but never recaptured it from the Muslims. He did, however, secure a five-year peace treaty with Saladin. This allowed European pilgrims to visit the holy places again. During negotiations, Saladin sent Richard, who had become ill, fresh fruit and snow water to help him recover.

RICHARD: THE ABSENT KING

On his way home from the Holy Lands, Richard was captured, handed over to his enemy, the Holy Roman Emperor Henry VI, and held prisoner.

Left: Richard I, (on the right) wearing the red cross of the crusaders. He led an army of knights to the Holy Land in 1189 on the Third Crusade.

besieging the castle of Chaluz, in France, in 1199. Richard spent only seven months of his ten-year reign in Britain – and that was to raise money for the Third Crusade by selling Church and state lands and charters of self-government to the towns.

IMPACT OF THE CRUSADES

The crusades may have been a military failure for Europe, but returning crusaders brought back with them valuable spices, such as nutmeg and cinnamon, along with sugar, cotton and Oriental tapestries. They also brought back Arabic ideas about science, medicine, philosophy and art.

Below: A battle between Muslims and Christian knights. The crusaders sewed big crosses onto their clothes, having taken up the call of the Pope to "wear Christ's cross as your badge. If you are killed your sins will be pardoned". Some knights who were also monks formed a full-time regiment in Jerusalem called the Knights of St John, or the Knights Hospitallers.

- **1174** Henry II does penance at Canterbury for Becket's murder. William of Scotland invades Northumberland and is captured. Henry crushes English revolt and makes peace with his sons. Treaty of Falaise: William of Scotland freed after paying homage to Henry

- **1176** Assize of Northampton: Henry establishes judicial rules. Eisteddfod held at Cardigan

- **1178** Henry establishes Central Court of Justice

- **1179** Grand Assize of Windsor curbs power of feudal courts

- **1180** Wells Cathedral begun

- **1186** Henry makes peace with Philip II of France

- **1187** Henry and Philip of France agree to go on the Third Crusade

- **1188** Richard, third son of Henry, does homage to Philip II

- **1189** Philip and Richard force Henry to acknowledge Richard as heir. Death of Henry: Richard I succeeds him (to 1199). Massacre of Jews at Richard's coronation

- **1189-1192** Richard and Philip of France lead Third Crusade but fail to take Jerusalem

- **1191** Civil war in England between Richard's brother John and William Longchamp

- **1192** Leopold of Austria captures Richard as he travels to England

- **1193** John claims the throne

- **1194** Richard is freed and returns to England; John flees to France

- **1199** Richard killed at siege of Chaluz; John succeeds him (to 1216)

The Magna Carta

KING JOHN, RICHARD'S BROTHER, was a tough, energetic man. Like many other Plantagenets, he was given to violent rages and cruelty. One of his early acts as king was to order the murder of his nephew, Arthur, whom he had imprisoned at Rouen in France. This young prince, as son of John's older brother Geoffrey, had a good claim to the throne.

Arthur's murder and John's behaviour provoked the barons of Anjou and Poitou into fighting against John. He lost most of his French lands and also angered the Pope by refusing to accept his choice of Archbishop of Canterbury. When John took the clergy's lands, Pope Innocent III banned nearly all Church services in England.

KING JOHN AGAINST THE BARONS

John continued to confiscate Church property, so in 1213 the Pope declared that John was no longer the rightful king of England, and granted Philip of France the right to depose him. As John had already angered his English barons by taxing them harshly and abusing feudal rights, it was not long before the English barons joined forces and rebelled against the king.

In June 1215 John was forced to meet the barons in a meadow beside the River Thames at Runnymede. There John put his seal to a document the barons had drawn up to confirm their rights against the king. This document was the famous Magna Carta, or Great Charter. It established certain curbs on royal abuses of power and laid the foundation for British democracy.

Above: **The Children's Crusade in 1212 involved possibly up to 50,000 French and German children who tried to reach the Holy Land. Most were turned back or were sold as slaves.**

- **1201** John grants a charter to Jews

- **1203** Arthur of Brittany, John's nephew, murdered

- **1204** Philip of France conquers Normandy from John

- **1205** Dispute over new Archbishop of Canterbury: John nominates John de Grey, Bishop of Norwich

- **1206** Pope Innocent III rejects de Grey's nomination, supports election of Stephen Langton as Archbishop of Canterbury

- **1207** John rejects Langton. Port of Liverpool founded

- **1208** Pope puts England under interdict, or exclusion. Llewelyn the Great seizes Powys

Below: **The English succession. Claimants to the Crown are underlined.**

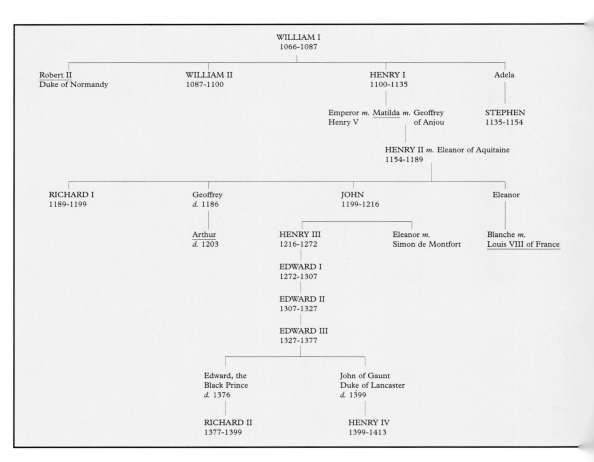

WHAT THE CHARTER SET OUT

Four original copies of the Magna Carta exist, one each in Lincoln and Salisbury Cathedrals and two in the British Museum. Most of the 63 clauses in the Magna Carta pledged the king to upholding the feudal system of the barons, but some also protected the rights of freemen, those citizens not tied to feudal lords. Clauses which have had great influence included the following: in all important matters the king must seek the barons' advice; no special taxes could be raised without the barons' consent; no freeman (those not tied to feudal lords) should be imprisoned or exiled, or deprived of property, except by the law of the land; and (one of the most important clauses) "to none will we sell, to none will we deny or delay right of justice". This ensured the basic right of free justice for all regardless of the seriousness of the crime or the individual's wealth or position.

After all the trouble with Rome, the Church was to be formally guaranteed certain long sought-after rights including freedom from state control, and the right to elect archbishops, bishops, abbots and other senior Church representatives.

EFFECT OF THE CHARTER

The effect of the Charter was that the king could continue to rule, but must keep to the laws of the land, and could be forced to do so. The Magna Carta was in force for only a few weeks before John persuaded the Pope to revoke it. Civil war broke out and John died in 1216. The Magna Carta was reissued in a revised form and, in 1225, became the law of the land.

Above: **King John's great seal which was attached to the Magna Carta. It showed the King's agreement so turning the Charter into law.**

Right: **A page from the Magna Carta. There are four copies of the Magna Carta: one each in Lincoln and Salisbury Cathedrals, and two in the British Museum.**

- **1209** London Bridge completed (stands until 1832). Some scholars leave Oxford for Cambridge (the beginning of Cambridge University)

- **1213** Philip II of France accepts Pope's mandate to conquer England. John accepts Langton as Archbishop of Canterbury; papal interdict is lifted. English ships destroy French fleet

- **1214** French defeat English and allies at battle of Bouvines. Barons threaten revolt. John takes crusader vows, and in return Pope excommunicates the barons

- **1215** John agrees to Magna Carta. Pope annuls Magna Carta; civil war resumes

- **1216** Louis of France invades England. John dies: succeeded by son Henry III, aged 9 (to 1272). William Marshal becomes regent. Magna Carta reissued

- **1217** William Marshal defeats the French at the battle of Lincoln; French leave England

Rivals for the Throne

Above: Henry III (1216-1272) became king at the age of nine but did not rule until 1234. Simon de Montfort and the English barons rebelled against his favouritism and promotion of foreign men at Court.

Henry III came to the throne aged only nine as John's eldest son. In his youth the country was well governed for him by William Marshal, Earl of Pembroke, and then by Hubert de Burgh, who was the Justiciar. When he grew up Henry III came under the influence of foreign barons and courtiers: first Peter des Roches from Poitou, Bishop of Winchester, and then des Roches' nephew (or perhaps son), Peter des Rivaux. Henry married Eleanor of Provence in 1236, and her many uncles from Savoy were given large estates and positions of power. Chief among them was Peter of Savoy, to whom Henry gave an estate near London, by the Thames; the Savoy Hotel and Theatre now stand on this site.

Although Henry III was a pious, sensitive man, he was completely without any ability to govern by himself. His inept and spendthrift ways upset the English nobles (those original Norman barons who came to England during the Norman Conquest).

SIMON DE MONTFORT

One of these nobles was Simon de Montfort, who came to England in 1229 to claim the earldom of Leicester, which he inherited through his grandmother. De Montfort quickly became a favourite of Henry, and of the king's sister Eleanor, whom he married. Henry's misrule and his reliance on foreigners made the barons take up arms against him. They assembled a Great Council in Oxford in 1258, and with de Montfort as their leader they forced the king to swear to the Provisions of Oxford, in return for financial help to cover his debts. These Provisions said that the king was to rule with the advice of a council of barons.

WELSH RESISTANCE

The conquest of Wales was carried out by powerful barons known as the Lords Marchers, because they guarded the marches, or frontiers, between Wales and England. The wild northern regions of Wales remained largely independent and it was in North Wales at this time that the Welsh archers developed the longbow, which became one of the most formidable weapons of its day.

Above: Simon de Montfort, leader of the dissatisfied barons, as shown in a window of Chartres Cathedral.

Below: Caernarfon Castle was built as a royal residence. The Eagle Tower is about 22 metres in diameter. The central gate had five double doors.

Below: English bases in North Wales. Massive castles were built at key sites to control the Welsh.

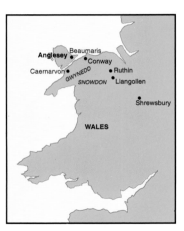

Beaumaris
Anglesey
Conway
Caernarvon
GWYNEDD
SNOWDON
Ruthin
Llangollen
Shrewsbury
WALES

Above: Two knights fight each other in a mock battle, or joust, at a tournament. Each knight had his coat-of-arms on his shield, on the crest of his helmet and on his horse's trappings.

LLEWELYN THE GREAT

One of the leading princes of Wales in the early 13th century was Llewelyn the Great, prince of Gwynedd in North Wales. Llewelyn was also accepted as leader by the people of South Wales. In the early part of the reign of Henry III, Llewelyn was driven back from South Wales by the Regent, William Marshal, Earl of Pembroke. But Llewelyn increased his territory to include Gwynedd, Clwyd, Powys and part of Dyfed. His younger son, David, became Prince of Gwynedd from 1240 to 1246.

- **1219** Henry III's Regent William Marshal dies; succeeded by Justiciar Hubert de Burgh

- **1224** The king recovers royal castles held by the barons. Louis VIII of France declares war

- **1225** Henry reissues Magna Carta and Charter of the Forests, in return for grant of general tax

- **1227** Henry declares himself to be of age to rule; but Hubert de Burgh retains power

- **1228** Death of Stephen Langton. Llewelyn the Great besieges Montgomery; Henry relieves city. Sixth Crusade: Jerusalem taken

- **1229** Llewelyn nominates his son David as his successor. Henry tries to take an army to France to recover his lands, but de Burgh fails to provide shipping

- **1230** Henry's French campaign fails

- **1231** England and France make a truce

- **1232** Henry dismisses de Burgh. Peter des Roches, Bishop of Winchester, becomes adviser to the king

Below: Longbow archers prepare to fire their arrows. A good archer could shoot ten arrows a minute accurately over a distance of 180 metres.

LLEWELYN THE LAST

In 1246 the throne passed to David's nephews Llewelyn ap Gruffydd (the Last) and his brother Owen. Threatened by claims on Wales from Henry III and others, the brothers united and fought with such determination that, by the Peace of Woodstock in 1247, Henry was forced to recognize them as rightful rulers, so long as they paid homage to him. Llewelyn later declared himself Prince of Wales, up to that time the English had only known him as Lord of Snowdon. In 1282 he died in a rebellion against Edward I and earned the title Llewelyn the Last.

DE MONTFORT RULES ENGLAND

In 1261 Henry persuaded the Pope to absolve him from his oath under the Provisions of Oxford, and won over many barons who now disliked de Montfort's high-handed ways. De Montfort, who had gone abroad, returned to lead a rebellion which restored the Provisions of Oxford. Louis IX of France was then asked to act as judge, and decided in Henry's favour. At this, de Montfort resorted to arms, and in 1264 defeated and captured Henry III at the battle of Lewes, on the Sussex Downs. De Montfort ruled England in the king's name and summoned a parliament which gave the barons greater control over the king.

THE BEGINNINGS OF PARLIAMENT

The term parliament comes from the French word *parleyment*, or talking place. Parliament as a royal council of the English kings came into existence during the reign of Henry III. But the idea of a king's council went back to the Anglo-Saxon Witan, and later the *Curia Regis*, or King's Council, of the Norman king, Henry I. The king usually only called the council when he wanted loans or advice. It was made up of bishops and nobles who held land granted to them by the king.

Simon de Montfort's Parliament was different because when he called an assembly (with the king still as prisoner) in 1265 he did not invite just the barons. He also summoned the elected representatives of the counties, called knights of the shire, and two burgesses from each city or large town. For the first time ever, all classes of people were included, except villeins and serfs.

Left: Edward I (1272-1307) was nicknamed "Longshanks" because he was very tall and had long arms and legs. He was a skilful general and a strong and respected leader. He was also devoted to his queen, Eleanor.

This was to become the beginning of a separate council from the king's council of lords – the House of Commons. The first Act of Parliament to be recorded was the Statute of Merton in 1275. It allowed landlords to enclose common land and also declared that children born out of marriage were considered illegitimate.

While Parliament was meeting, some barons quarrelled with de Monfort, and Henry I's son, Edward, defeated and killed de Montfort at the battle of Evesham in 1265. During his lifetime de Montfort was so popular with the English people that he was known as Good Sir Simon. Henry III took control of the kingdom again until his death in 1272.

EDWARD I: THE LAWGIVER

Edward I, who was 33 when he came to the throne in 1272, was brisk, capable, and an experienced general. His love of order led him to reform the government.

The many laws passed in Edward's reign have earned him the nickname of the Lawgiver. He was the first English king to use Parliament as an instrument of government to reform the law of the land. Among his early reforms were three Statutes of Westminster, all of which dealt with local government and the ownership and inheritance of land. The Statute of Wales marked the end of Wales as a separate country; but left Welsh common law, language and customs intact. Edward also built impressive castles in North Wales from 1283 to 1307, including Caernarfon which is still standing today.

Below: **The Middle Ages, or medieval period as it is also known, was a time of wars across the borders in Scotland and Wales, and violence in England with barons struggling against the king and against each other. Castles were built and walled towns had to be well guarded with soldiers on sentry duty day and night.**

- **1233** Revolt of Richard Marshal, Earl of Pembroke, allied with Llewelyn. Richard defeats royal forces near Monmouth

- **1234** Henry III makes peace with Richard. Richard murdered in Ireland

- **1237** Barons insist on nominating three of Henry's counsellors

- **1240** Llewelyn the Great dies; succeeded by son David (to 1246)

- **1241** Henry leads expedition to Wales. Peter of Savoy, uncle of Queen Eleanor is royal adviser

- **1242** Henry defeated by Louis IX of France. Barons refuse to pay for French war

- **1245** Building of Westminster Abbey is begun

- **1246** Welsh prince David dies; succeeded by Llewelyn the Last (to 1282) and his brother Owen

- **1257** Llewelyn assumes the title Prince of Wales

- **1258** Provisions of Oxford: barons take control of Henry's government

- **1261** Pope absolves Henry from the oath to observe the Provisions of Oxford

- **1262** Llewelyn attacks England

- **1263** Simon de Montfort returns as leader of the barons; Henry accepts the barons' terms

- **1264** Battle of Lewes: de Montfort defeats and captures Henry

- **1265** De Montfort's Parliament. Battle of Evesham: Henry's son Edward defeats and kills de Montfort

- **1266** Roger Bacon invents the magnifying glass

- **1267** Henry recognizes Llewelyn as Prince of Wales

WAR WITH SCOTLAND

In Scotland, the barons asked Edward to choose a successor to Alexander III, Edward's brother-in-law, who had died without an heir in 1286. Edward I selected John Balliol as ruler of Scotland but treated him as a puppet king. The barons rebelled and in 1296 Edward invaded Scotland and captured Balliol. For ten years after this Scotland was without a king. Edward tried to rule it himself, but he was defied by William Wallace, who led an uprising and made himself master of Scotland. Wallace was an extraordinary general who managed to inspire half-armed peasant foot soldiers to take on the might of mail-clad knights. However, Edward reconquered the country and captured Wallace, who was put to death in 1305.

ROBERT BRUCE AND BANNOCKBURN

Within months of William Wallace's death, Robert Bruce became the great champion of Scotland. He was crowned King of Scotland at Scone in 1306, but an English army was quickly on the scene and Bruce suffered two heavy defeats. After a spell in hiding, Bruce defeated an English army twice as strong as his own at the battle of Bannockburn in 1314. This battle ensured that Scotland would stay independent of England.

In 1320 at the abbey of Arbroath, in Angus, an assembly of Scottish lords drew up a declaration of independence. It affirmed loyalty to Robert Bruce. Edward II agreed to a truce with Scotland. First the Treaty of Northampton brought peace to the two countries of England and Scotland. Then the Treaty of Brigham conceded to the Scots that the laws of Scotland were to be respected as independent of those of England. It also confirmed that Scotland itself was to be independent of England, with a distinct border, and that no Scottish subject could be forced to attend an English court.

EDWARD II

The first Prince of Wales became King Edward II in 1307. He was the fourth son of Edward I but his older brothers had all died when he was a boy. Edward therefore relied very much on his friends and favourites, and they in turn influenced his decisions in matters of state, to the fury of the barons. Edward's favourites included Piers Gaveston, whom a group of lords seized and beheaded in 1312. Later, Edward became fiercely loyal to Hugh Despenser and his son, also named Hugh. When the younger Hugh married Edward's cousin, the barons rebelled.

EDWARD III

Edward was only 14 years old when he came to the throne of England. His mother, Isabella of France, and her lover, Roger Mortimer, Earl of March, had ordered Edward II's murder in 1327, and had secured Edward III's succession with Parliament's support. For three years real power lay with this couple. But in 1330 Edward III rebelled against them and took charge of the government.

Right: **Springtime sowing in the countryside in the mid-1300s. Although this was a period marked by royal murders and fighting between barons, as well as war in France, ordinary people got on with their lives. All but 10 percent of the population lived and worked on the land. The earth was ploughed in rough strips from March onwards. The sower scattered the seeds by hand in the furrows of the ploughed ground, not stopping to cover it. Bird scarers used slings and other distractions to stop birds from taking the seeds. The summer months were for haymaking, and the corn was harvested in early September. From 1350 the Black Death was to cut the work force by more than one third.**

Above: **The battle of Bannockburn in 1314 was a humiliating defeat for the English and a triumph for Robert Bruce. After eight years of war with England, he finally became the undisputed King of Scotland. It is said that when in hiding, he found the courage to fight on from watching a spider trying again and again to climb its web.**

THE HUNDRED YEARS WAR BEGINS

The Hundred Years War between England and France was a series of wars, interspersed with truces. Edward III started the war in 1337, when Charles IV of France died without a direct heir. Edward wanted to secure his claim to the French throne through his mother, Isabella of France. Philip of Valois, who took the French throne, was anxious to regain Gascony, the last major English territory in France. Edward was spurred on by the ideas of chivalry and honour and also knew that if he could unite his restless barons in an overseas quest for honour they were less likely to start trouble at home.

- **1269** Prince Edward goes on crusade. First toll roads in England

- **1272** Henry III dies: Edward I, though absent, proclaimed king (to 1307)

- **1274** Edward I arrives in England and is crowned king. Llewelyn the Last refuses to take oath of allegiance to Edward

- **1275** Edward holds his first Parliament. First Statute of Westminster; wool duties granted to the Crown

- **1277** Edward begins campaign in Wales against Llewelyn, who submits with Treaty of Conway

- **1282** Llewelyn's brother, David, begins a revolt against the English. Edward marches into Wales. Llewelyn killed in battle

- **1283** Welsh revolt collapses. David is executed. Edward begins building castles in Wales

- **1284** Statute of Wales, Welsh government organized

- **1291** Scots ask Edward to choose between 13 claimants to the Scottish throne

- **1292** Edward awards Scottish throne to John Balliol (to 1296), making Scotland a fief of England

- **1296** Edward invades Scotland (Balliol abdicates) and declares himself King of Scotland

- **1297** Wallace leads revolt in Scotland

- **1298** Edward defeats Wallace at Falkirk

- **1301** Edward makes his son, Edward, Prince of Wales

- **1305** Wallace executed

- **1306** Robert Bruce claims Scottish throne (to 1329)

- **1307** Death of Edward. Succeeded by son Edward II (to 1327). Bruce defeats English

Right: The Hundred Years War was not one long war but a series of short ones. It began in 1337 and ended in 1453 (actually 116 years). English longbowmen and pikemen fought French knights on horseback and crossbowmen. Knights who were given land in feudal times had to raise and equip an army if needed. Knights wore heavy armour and rode horses. Foot soldiers wore helmets and tunics.

FOCUS ON THE ORDER OF THE GARTER
Edward III founded the Order of the Garter in 1349 to carry on the medieval ideals of knighthood and chivalry. Legend has it that a countess accidentally dropped her garter while dancing with Edward III. The King picked it up and rebuked his sniggering courtiers with the quip *Honi soit qui mal y pense* (French for Warning be to him who thinks ill of this). This is now the motto of the Order. The garter is the highest order of knighthood.

EDWARD'S VICTORIES

Another cause of the Hundred Years War was the wool trade. The weavers of Flanders depended on English wool, and England's wool was their only source of income apart from farming. But the aristocratic rulers of Flanders were pro-French and attempted to curb the English wool trade. Edward III made a treaty with the Flemish weavers in 1338 to reinforce his claims against Philip VI who had already seized Gascony.

In the early years of the war the English won two major battles. The naval battle of Sluys in 1340 gave them control of the English Channel, and made an English invasion of France relatively easy. When the invasion began Edward had a major land victory at Crécy in 1346, on the banks of the Somme. This battle was won by Edward's longbowmen, whose arrows mowed down the French.

THE BLACK DEATH

During Edward III's reign, the greatest disaster befell Europe. In only twenty years the Black Death (bubonic plague carried by rats from Asia) killed about one third of Europe's population. The disease got its name from the spots of blood that formed under the skin and turned black.

The Black Death came to England in 1348, through Melcombe Regis, the port of Weymouth. Within a few weeks it had spread to London and Bristol, where at one stage the living were hardly able to bury the dead. Within a year almost every part of England and Wales had been affected. The death toll was half the country's population at that time.

- **1308** Edward II marries Isabella of France

- **1311** Privy Seal office is established

- **1314** Scots defeat English at the battle of Bannockburn

- **1320** Declaration of Arbroath: Scots lords state to the Pope their loyalty to Robert I (the Bruce)

- **1323** Edward and Robert agree truce

- **1324** French invade Gascony

- **1327** Edward deposed and; Edward III becomes king (to 1377). England regains Gascony

Below: Black rats on board merchant ships carried the bubonic plague in their blood and their fleas transmitted it to people.

Left: European streets in the Middle Ages were filthy places. Open sewers ran down the middle and there were rats and rubbish everywhere. Human waste was thrown out of windows with a cry of *"Gardez-loo"* to warn passers by to get out of the way. Disease spread because of dirt and rats.

- **1328** Edward III makes peace with Scotland. Philip VI becomes the first Valois King of France

- **1330** Edward arrests Roger Mortimer, Earl of March, and begins personal rule

- **1336** Trade with Flanders is halted. French attack Isle of Wight and Channel Islands

- **1337** Philip VI seizes Gascony: start of Hundred Years War. Edward claims French Crown

- **1338** French fleet sacks Portsmouth. Edward lands at Antwerp: makes alliance with German emperor. Flemish weavers make trade treaty with England

- **1340** English naval victory at Sluys wins control of English Channel. Parliament appoints auditors of the king's expenditure

- **1343** France and England make truce

- **1346** Edward defeats French at Crécy

- **1347** Edward captures French port of Calais

- **1348** Black Death reaches England. Edward founds the Order of the Garter

- **1350** Black Death reaches Scotland. Extension of Windsor Castle begins

- **1351** Statute of Labourers curbs wages

Below: **The effigy of the Black Prince that lies on top of his tomb in Canterbury Cathedral. He was a brilliant general. During the last years of his life illness made him bedridden and unable to control his armies.**

Many villages were abandoned because of the plague. One of these deserted villages has been reconstructed by archaeologists at Cosmeston, near Penarth in South Wales.

The Black Death also halted Edward III's campaign against Scotland, but Scottish rejoicing at this was soon dashed when the plague struck there too. Scotland, Ireland and Wales, however, suffered less severely than England. The Black Death lasted on and off for over 150 years.

THE BLACK PRINCE

Edward III's eldest son, Edward, Prince of Wales, was as fine a soldier as his father, and is known as the Black Prince because of the colour of his armour. In 1346 he distinguished himself by his bravery at the battle of Crécy when he was only 16. The French may have lost over 10,000 men against less than 200 English deaths. Here he won the three plumes and the motto *Ich dien* (German for I serve) used by princes of Wales ever since. A truce was made in 1348 but Philip VI died in 1350 and Edward attacked France again.

In 1356 Edward the Black Prince won his greatest victory as a commander at Poitiers, where he captured the French king, John II. This monarch was ransomed for 3 million gold crowns and the Duchy of Aquitaine. While fighting in Spain the Black Prince caught an infection which made him ill and he died in 1376, one year before his father.

Richard II

When Richard succeeded Edward III he was only 10 years old and inherited the cost of the Hundred Years War which left the Crown deeply in debt. Richard II was too young to rule, so the country was governed for a decade by his uncles: John, Duke of Lancaster, generally known as John of Gaunt, and Thomas of Gloucester. Their rule was not popular and the introduction of heavy taxes led to the Peasants' Revolt in 1381.

Above: **Richard II (1377-1399) was a lover of art not of warfare and suffered from being unfairly compared with his father, the Black Prince, who was a great soldier.**

Below: **Richard II met with the rebels at Smithfield during the Peasants' Revolt in 1381.**

LABOUR UNREST

The immediate effect of the Black Death had been a loss of a third of the labour force, and a rise in workers' wages which amounted to about 50 percent for craftworkers and agricultural workers, and 100 percent for women farm workers. Employers had little choice but to pay, but a Statute of Labourers in 1351 fixed the price of labour to be on the same scale as it had been before the Black Death. Labourers resented this law. The Statute was a failure.

- **1353** Edward III transfers the wool staple (market) from Bruges in Flanders to England

- **1356** Edward Balliol gives up throne of Scotland to Edward. Black Prince defeats and captures John II of France at Poitiers

- **1357** Treaty of Bordeaux between England and France

- **1360** France cedes Aquitaine, Ponthieu and Calais

- **1363** Statute of Apparel prevents people wearing dress above their station in life

- **1364** Hostage for payment of John II's ransom escapes: John returns to captivity, and dies

- **1366** Statutes of Kilkenny: Irish Parliament forbids the English overlords to marry the Irish and bans Irish language, laws and customs

- **1375** Peace with France: England left with only Calais, Brest, Bordeaux and Bayonne. Robin Hood appears in ballads

- **1376** The Good Parliament: first to elect a Speaker. Black Prince dies

- **1377** Edward dies: succeeded by 10-year-old Richard II (to 1399); regency council rules

- **1380** Wyclif translates Bible

- **1381** Peasants' Revolt

- **1387** Geoffrey Chaucer starts *The Canterbury Tales*

- **1388** Lords Appellant control government

- **1389** Richard II assumes rule

- **1393** Great Statute of Praemunire reasserts supremacy of State in Church affairs

- **1395** Irish chiefs submit to Richard

THE PEASANTS' REVOLT

The Peasants' Revolt of 1381 was led by Wat Tyler, a tiler (though some say a blacksmith), and Jack Straw (possibly a nickname). This open rebellion was sparked off by the imposition of a poll tax of one shilling per head.

More than 20,000 peasants from Kent and Essex marched on London. Here they killed the Archbishop of Canterbury who was also the Chancellor, whom they blamed for imposing the unfair taxes. They also burned John of Gaunt's palace, the Savoy. Richard II, still only 14 years old, faced a mob at Mile End and promised: "You shall have from me all you seek." Tyler and his men of Kent remained armed while the rest dispersed. A few days later, in the king's presence, Tyler was killed by the Lord Mayor of London, William Walworth.

FOCUS ON GEOFFREY CHAUCER

The poet Geoffrey Chaucer was born around 1340 and was squire to Edward III. He travelled to Italy on the king's business where he read books by Dante and Boccaccio. Chaucer wrote for Richard II's court, but his poems were read by a wider audience and were very popular. The most famous is a long poem called *The Canterbury Tales* which follows a group of pilgrims (some shown here) who tell each other stories on the way to Becket's shrine at Canterbury. It was the first important book written in English rather than Latin.

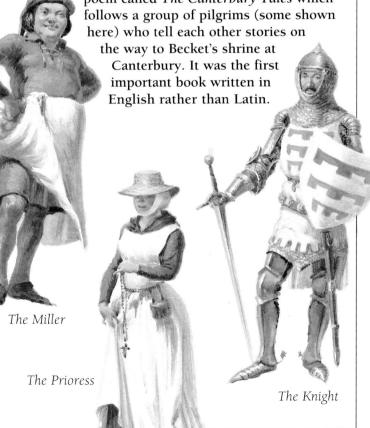

The Miller

The Prioress

The Knight

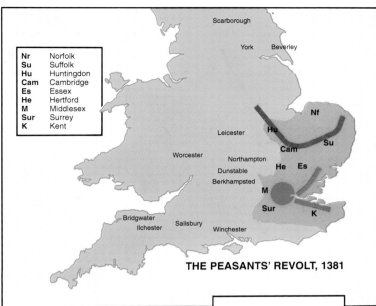

Nr	Norfolk
Su	Suffolk
Hu	Huntingdon
Cam	Cambridge
Es	Essex
He	Hertford
M	Middlesex
Sur	Surrey
K	Kent

THE PEASANTS' REVOLT, 1381

Above: **A map of the Peasants' Revolt of 1381, showing the main areas of rebellion.**

- Main counties in revolt
- Bishop Dispenser's tour of suppression
- Peasants' advance on London

RICHARD II LOSES CONTROL

When the king's uncle John of Gaunt went off to Spain to pursue a claim to the throne of Castile, there was armed conflict between the king's men and the Duke of Gloucester who, in 1387, had set up a ruling council known as the Lords Appellant. In 1389, Richard took control of the government from the Duke of Gloucester, declaring "I am now old enough to manage my own affairs". For eight years the king's rule was peaceful and prosperous.

But when Richard's wife, Anne of Bohemia, died of the plague in 1394 he was left heartbroken and without purpose.

Richard turned into a tyrant, revenging himself in 1397 on the Lords Appellant. The Earl of Arundel was beheaded. The Duke of Gloucester, Richard's uncle, was murdered. Two others, Henry of Bolingbroke and the Duke of Norfolk, who had quarrelled, were banished. Soon afterwards John of Gaunt died, and Richard seized his estates. This was too much for John's son Henry of Bolingbroke. He returned from exile, swiftly gathered a large body of supporters, defeated the king's forces and took Richard prisoner to the Tower of London. By general consent Richard was deposed, and Henry succeeded to the throne as Henry IV in 1399.

Henry V (1413-1422) was a great soldier who won a famous victory over the French at Agincourt in 1415.

LANCASTER AND YORK
(1399 – 1485)

T HE PLANTAGENETS were a fierce and quarrelsome family, and never more so than when disputing the right to the throne. Henry of Lancaster, son of John of Gaunt and grandson of Edward III, battled hard to become Henry IV, the first of the Lancastrian kings.

Much of Henry V's short reign was spent across the English Channel pursuing claims to France (England still held Calais and parts of Bordeaux) in the final stages of the Hundred Years War.

A complicated series of local civil wars involving various noble families who claimed the Crown marked the reign of Henry VI. A strong claim was put forward by Richard, Duke of York. The fighting that followed became known as the Wars of the Roses, from the red and white roses on the badges of the two conflicting families, Lancaster and York. In the end Henry Tudor, great-great-grandson of John of Gaunt, won the throne.

Scotland saw its throne pass to the Stewarts, a gallant and ill-fated family. Wales lost its independence and was gradually integrated with England, while the long struggle by the English to conquer Ireland continued.

Henry IV

HENRY IV had to struggle to hold the Crown, which he had seized by force. In 1400, a rising of Richard II's supporters was quickly crushed. Then Richard died in prison, probably murdered. But that was only the start of Henry's troubles. For the next five years, he had to face one rebellion after another.

THE LOLLARDS

In the late 1300s a religious movement had started in England which attacked many of the beliefs and practices of the Church of Rome. Its followers were known as Lollards, from a Flemish word meaning mutterer. They originally followed the teachings of John Wyclif, but later became more extreme. The Church saw them as heretics, and opponents of the established order of government.

To combat Lollardy, Henry IV's Parliament passed the cruel law *De Heretico Comburendo* (1401), which condemned heretics to suffer death by burning. Henry IV was the first English king to put men to death for their religious beliefs. Many followers of John Wyclif were burned at the stake.

OWEN GLENDOWER

Owen Glendower was the last independent Prince of Wales who ruled lands in North Wales. A feud with his neighbour, Lord Grey de Ruthyn, led to rebellion against England. Henry IV declared Glendower's lands forfeit, and gave them to Grey. Glendower raised an army and the Welsh backed him in what became, from 1402 to 1413 a national rebellion.

Above: **Henry IV (1399-1413) was the first British king whose native language was English. He spent much of his reign fighting rebellions, as well as a major national uprising in Wales.**

Right: **A breech-loading cannon of the 15th century. This cast bronze weapon fired solid balls which could knock down the thickest castle walls. Early cannons were not accurate and sometimes killed their loaders. The use of artillery (firearms) in battle and siege spread quickly throughout Europe. But English forces still relied on their longbowmen and knights on horseback to gain victory as at the battle of Agincourt in 1415.**

- **1399** Henry Bolingbroke seizes the throne as Henry IV

- **1400** Conspiracy by Earls of Huntingdon, Kent and Salisbury to kill Henry fails. Richard II dies in captivity. Henry campaigns in Scotland. Owen Glendower rebels in Wales

- **1401** Henry marries Joan of Navarre

- **1402** Henry enters Wales in pursuit of Glendower

- **1403** Revolt by the Percies: Henry kills Henry Percy (Hotspur) at Shrewsbury

- **1404** Glendower controls Wales, takes title Prince of Wales

- **1406** Prince James of Scotland captured by English on way to France. Robert III of Scotland dies; succeeded by captive James I (to 1420)

- **1409** Glendower's rebellion collapses

- **1410** St Andrew's University, Scotland, founded

- **1411** Henry, Prince of Wales, tries to control government. He is dismissed by Henry IV

Left: A 15th-century farmhouse. Yeomen or free farmers became increasingly prosperous in this period particularly if they had large flocks of sheep. Farmhouses like this one are still lived in today.

Below: Owen Glendower led Wales against England from 1400 to 1409. Defeated, but never captured, his final fate is unknown.

Henry IV was already troubled by uprisings in England, and Glendower had considerable success. For some years he virtually ruled Wales. But a successful campaign led by Henry's son, the future Henry V, broke the rebellion by 1409. Glendower's territory and castles were taken from him, but he evaded capture and disappeared.

THE CAPTIVE KING OF SCOTLAND

The Stewarts were in many ways an unlucky family. Most of the Stewart rulers came to the throne young, so the country was ruled by nobles in their name. Five of them died violent deaths.

Yet it was a Stewart, James VI of Scotland, who would unite the thrones of England and Scotland as James I of England in 1603, and the Stewarts (spelled Stuarts from then on) reigned until 1714. Queen Elizabeth II is herself descended from a daughter of James I of England (and James VI of Scotland).

The last years of the reign of Robert III of Scotland, in the early 1400s, were dominated by his brother the Duke of Albany, who was governor of the land. He was suspected of murdering Robert's heir, David. To safeguard his second son, James, Robert sent him to France by sea in 1406. English sailors captured the ship and James, who was 10 years old, was taken to London, where he remained a captive for 18 years, until 1424.

Robert went into deep mourning at the news of his son's capture, and died soon afterwards. The prisoner James was proclaimed King of Scotland. In captivity James wrote a long allegorical poem called *The Kingis Quair* (The King's Book). He also became a musician and an athlete.

FOCUS ON PILGRIMS

People of Christian faith in the Middle Ages went on pilgrimages for different reasons. Many went to seek forgiveness for their sins, or as a result of promises they made to God in return for His help. Others went seeking a miracle cure for an illness (just as people still go today to visit Lourdes in France). They visited famous shrines, monasteries and cathedrals around Britain, such as Becket's tomb at Canterbury. But many also travelled overseas, as far away as Jerusalem in the Holy Land.

The medieval pilgrim began his journey with a blessing by a priest, and on his return trip he would wear on his hat the badge of the shrine visited. The ones shown here are from Canterbury Cathedral. Along the way he would find hospices set up specially for pilgrims. Peasants, nuns, knights and merchants journeyed together. Pilgrimages were one of the few reasons many people had in the Middle Ages to travel long distances at home or overseas.

Henry V

DURING THE FINAL YEARS of Henry IV's reign much of the government passed to his son Henry, though the ailing king resisted any suggestion that he should abdicate. When Henry V came to the throne in 1413, he began by declaring a general pardon for his enemies and revived Edward III's old claim to the throne of France, which was occupied by Charles VI, who had suffered from fits of madness for the past 20 years.

The Dukes of Burgundy and Orleans were rivals for power in France. Henry allied himself with the Burgundians. The prospect of a war in France did much to unite the warring factions in England. Henry said to his father: "By your sword you won your crown, and by my sword I will keep it."

HENRY'S FRENCH CAMPAIGN

Henry's military campaign in France began by capturing the town of Harfleur at the mouth of the River Seine. From there he set out with about 5,000 men, 4,000 of them archers, to march east to Calais. The English found their way barred by a French army more than three times as strong. Attempts to negotiate a clear road to safety failed, and Henry resolved on battle. The French unwisely chose a narrow front between two woods, giving them no room to manoeuvre.

THE BATTLE OF AGINCOURT

Once again, against huge odds the English longbow won the day. This was the battle of Agincourt, fought on October 25, 1415; it was over in three hours, with the loss of almost 10,000 French dead and 2,000 captured, and only a few hundred English killed or wounded. Henry returned to England a hero. He had led the battle from the front, wearing his jewelled crown over his helmet. But Henry's army was too weak to attempt taking the French capital, Paris.

Right: **The battle of Agincourt, 1415. A small English army defeated a much larger French one. The English strength was its archers, whose longbows showered the enemy with arrows. The wet weather also bogged the heavily armoured French knights in the mud.**

Right: **Henry V (1413-1422) is chiefly remembered for his victories against the French, including the battle of Agincourt in 1415. He was a chivalrous soldier and sensible ruler; but his gains in France were lost on his death.**

DEATH OF HENRY V

Henry led a much larger expedition to France in 1417. Within three years he was master of Normandy. His ally, the Duke of Burgundy, was murdered by supporters of Charles VI's heir, the dauphin. This united the dauphin's opponents, who supported Henry V's claim to the French throne. Following the Treaty of Troyes in 1420, Henry was accepted as Regent of France, and as King Charles's heir. To cement the agreement Henry married the French King's daughter, Catherine of Valois. But two years later while on another campaign, Henry died of dysentery, a common disease among armies at that time.

Below: **It might take up to an hour for a knight to be fully dressed for battle. His esquire, or attendant, would strap or lace the leg armour on to the belt first, then came the breastplate and backplate and finally the gauntlets and the helmet.**

Left: **Full suit of plate armour**

Helmet

Joints in armour allowed some limb movement

Breastplate

A suit of plate armour could weigh 20 to 25 kg

Flexible chain mail underneath

Gauntlet

- **1413** Henry V becomes King of England (to 1422)

- **1415** Invasion of France: Henry captures Harfleur. Battle of Agincourt. Henry founds last monastery before Reformation at Twickenham

- **1417** Henry invades Normandy

- **1420** Treaty of Troyes: Henry to be Regent of France during life of Charles VI, and succeed him. Henry V marries Charles's daughter Catherine. Scottish Regent Albany dies; succeeded by son Murdoch (to 1425)

- **1422** Henry V dies suddenly; succeeded by infant son Henry VI (to 1461). Henry VI's uncles become regents: Humphrey of Gloucester in England; John of Bedford in France

- **1424** James I of Scotland is released, marries Joan Beaufort, and is crowned in Scotland

- **1428** James I calls for election of representatives of sheriffdoms to Scottish Parliament. English lay siege to Orleans in France; Joan of Arc hears "voices"

- **1429** Joan of Arc leads French to relieve city of Orleans. English defeated at Patay. Charles VII crowned King of France at Rheims

- **1430** Burgundian troops take Joan of Arc; hand her over to the English. Statute states shire-knights eligible for Parliament

Above: **A French archer loading a crossbow. The crossbow with its bolt, bowstring and stirrup (*see below right*) was powerful but much slower to load than the English longbow. English archers could fire 10 arrows a minute and their steel-tipped arrows could pierce armoured knights.**

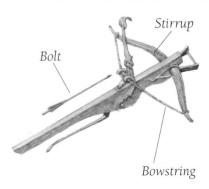

Stirrup

Bolt

Bowstring

Above: **Henry VI (1422-1461) went mad and had to submit his kingdom to a protector, Richard, Duke of York, from 1461 to 1470. He briefly claimed the throne again but was murdered in 1471.**

- **1431** Humphrey of Gloucester crushes Lollard uprising in Abingdon. Henry VI crowned King of France. Joan of Arc burned as a heretic in France

- **1433** Tattershall Castle, Lincolnshire, built with a million bricks

- **1436** Scots defeat English near Berwick

- **1437** Richard, Duke of York, captures Pontoise; Earl of Warwick becomes Regent of France. Murder of James I of Scotland: succeeded by son, James II, aged six (to 1460): Earl of Douglas is regent. Henry VI declared of age, but the Council of State holds power

- **1438** Truce between England and Scotland

- **1439** Congress of Calais: fruitless bid for Anglo-French peace. Henry Beaufort, great-uncle of Henry VI, controls the government. Regent Douglas dies. England makes truce with Burgundy

- *c.* **1440** Johannes Gutenberg invents printing from movable type

HENRY VI

Henry V left his English throne to his baby son, Henry, who was nine months old. Two months after becoming king of England, the baby Henry VI was proclaimed King of France on the death of his mad grandfather, Charles VI. His uncle, Humphrey Duke of Gloucester, was made regent in England. Another uncle, Duke John of Bedford, a skilled and experienced general, ruled France on his behalf. The French claimant to the throne, the dauphin Charles, controlled the country south of the River Loire, but England's hold on the northern region seemed secure.

JOAN OF ARC

In 1428 the demoralized French forces were given unexpected inspiration. Joan of Arc, a young peasant girl from Domrémy on the eastern border of France, heard voices and saw visions which commanded her to free her country from the English. One of the voices was that of the Archangel Michael, who appeared to her in a flood of light and told her to go to the help of the king. Joan went to the dauphin and said: "Gentle dauphin, I am sent to tell you that you shall be anointed and crowned in the town of Rheims, and you shall be lieutenant of the heavenly king who is the King of France".

During the siege of Orleans, Joan of Arc walked unseen through English lines one night during a storm and raised her banner from the battlements of the city to rally the French troops. Under her command the dauphin, Charles, marched to Rheims, where he was crowned King of France. Joan's voices then became silent, and she planned to return home. But she was captured by the Burgundian forces, who were still allied to England, and handed over to the English.

Above: **Map of France showing the main battles of the Hundred Years War, 1337–1453.**

Above: **Joan of Arc (1412-1431) was aged only 17 when she led the French to victory against the English at Orleans.**

Above: **Joan of Arc was tried and found guilty of heresy and sorcery by the Inquisition in 1431. She was burned at the stake by the English in the market place in the French city of Rouen.**

Left: This was a period of great splendour in clothes for the rich. For men and women in the 1400s, an upper garment with long flowing lines was the most important piece of clothing: for men it could reach the knee, ankle or calf; for women it had long wide sleeves. Both men and women wore long hose, or stockings. For men these could be worn with leather soles attached, or with shoes or boots. Shoes had very long points. Turban-style hats were popular for men. Women favoured elaborate headwear.

THE HUNDRED YEARS WAR ENDS

Joan of Arc was sold to the English who tried her for witchcraft and heresy, and burned her at the stake. An English soldier saw her die and said: "We are lost; we have burned a saint." In 1435 the valiant Duke of Bedford died, and in the same year the Burgundians finally broke their alliance with the English, and made a treaty with France.

Charles reorganized his army, learning from Joan's inspired victories that the once invincible English archers could be defeated by surprise attacks. Improved French artillery then pounded to ruins English fortresses. By 1453 the English had been almost completely driven out of France, and Henry VI had lost all his father's military conquests. The Hundred Years War was over.

HENRY VI: THE SCHOLAR KING

Henry VI's years as a child king saw bitter conflict between leading nobles competing for influence. When he came of age the situation had not improved; he was a gentle, pious and scholarly man, dominated by the powerful men around him.

When the Duke of Suffolk arranged Henry's marriage to the forceful French princess Margaret of Anjou, he signed a secret treaty ceding Maine to France. The English were furious when they found out. When the Hundred Years War ended in defeat for England, it was said that the Lancastrians, who had seized the throne by force, were unlucky for the country.

THE STRONG MAN OF SCOTLAND

James I of Scotland was released by the regents of Henry VI in 1424, after 18 years in captivity. He took back to Scotland an English bride, Joan Beaufort, granddaughter of John of Gaunt. But he found the land had been badly governed by his cousin Murdoch, son of the late regent, Albany. Within a year he had Murdoch and his sons executed. Within four years James had reorganized the Scottish government, strengthened Parliament, reformed the law courts and curbed the more rebellious of the Highland chiefs. Three of these chiefs he hanged; the rest he released after a short time in prison.

The Printing Revolution

THE CHINESE INVENTED a printing process using wooden blocks in the 6th century AD, and also produced a form of paper to print on. But printing by machines did not appear in Europe until the 1450s. By that time German-born Johannes Gutenberg had invented a printing press with separate pieces of metal type that could be moved around and could print individual letters. This printing method was slow, but the quality was the same for each copy and much easier to read than handwriting. For the first time many copies of a book could be made easily.

CAXTON AND THE FIRST BOOKS

The first book printed in English was produced in the 1470s by William Caxton. Before this, books were copied by hand in universities and monasteries, making them precious and rare. Only priests and nobles could afford to buy them.

William Caxton was born around 1422 in Kent, but moved to Bruges, in what is now Belgium, where for 30 years he was a rich merchant. At the age of 50 he moved to Cologne, in Germany, to learn the printing techniques of that country. In Bruges he set up his first press around 1474. There he produced the first book ever printed in English, a history of the legendary city of Troy, which he had translated himself.

In 1476 Caxton returned to England, encouraged by King Edward IV, and set up the first English press at Westminster, near London. With support from Richard III and Henry VII, Caxton later produced nearly 100 books, including Chaucer's *The Canterbury Tales* (in 1478). Many were printed in English rather than in the usual Latin and French, and some were his own translations of foreign books.

Above: **A page from a book called *Legenda aurea*, printed by William Caxton at his press in Westminster. The picture is a woodcut of St Jerome. Before the first printing presses, there were only about 30,000 to 40,000 books in Britain. By the time of Caxton's death in 1491 there were over nine million.**

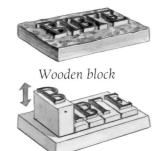

Wooden block

Movable metal type

Above: **Block printing required a carver to cut the letters in reverse in one solid piece of wood, which could be used for only one job. Gutenberg introduced metal type which could be broken up and reused.**

Below: **In the Middle Ages books were not made of paper but of dried animal skins, on which scribes copied out text. The sheets were then stitched together by hand and bound between leather-covered boards.**

In Caxton's time there were often several different English words for one thing and many dialects, or regional variations, of English were spoken. Caxton chose one dialect for his books, and so helped establish a common language throughout the country. Caxton's type of printing press was used for 350 years, until the power-driven press.

HENRY VI AND PLANTAGENET FEUDS

While Henry VI was still a boy, the security of his throne came under threat from feuding uncles and cousins. Chief among them were the Beauforts, the descendants of John of Gaunt and his mistress, Katherine Swynford. The second Beaufort son, Henry, became Bishop of Winchester and was the richest man in the kingdom. Henry Beaufort competed for power with Humphrey, Duke of Gloucester, during Henry VI's minority, and influenced the feeble King when he came of age. These rivalries were to break out into what became known as the Wars of the Roses.

Above: **A printing press. The press was screwed down by hand and this squeezed the paper and type together. The invention of movable metal type meant that books could be produced** more quickly and efficiently. Printing was introduced into England by William Caxton in 1476. It helped to spread and establish a common English language instead of local dialects.

Left: At first printing was carried out by rubbing an inked woodblock onto a sheet of paper. But Gutenberg invented movable metal type and adapted a wine press to apply pressure evenly over a whole sheet of paper. The ink was spread on a metal plate and then dabbed on the type with a leather-covered tool.

Wars of the Roses

THE WARS OF THE ROSES were a series of conflicts for the English throne between families within the Plantagenet line. The main rivals were the House of York and the House of Lancaster, and these warring houses each had an emblem – the red rose of Lancaster, and the white rose of York – which gave its name to these wars.

The conflict between Lancaster and York was made worse by the barons, who were no longer fighting in France. Henry Beaufort's nephew John, Duke of Somerset, was the commander of Henry V's forces in France. After John's death, his brother Edmund, who became Duke of Somerset, led the English forces in the last battles of the Hundred Years War, and was a possible heir to the throne. Edmund's sister, Joan, married James I of Scotland. Several of the Beauforts died without children and others were killed in the Wars of the Roses.

Above: **The Wars of the Roses get their name from the badges of the two families involved: the red rose of Lancaster and the white rose of York. When Henry VII married Elizabeth of York he combined the two to form the Tudor rose (shown here).**

Right: **A map of England showing the movements and battles of the Yorkist and Lancastrian forces during the Wars of the Roses. The rivalry between the two great families ended with victory for Henry Tudor who was a Lancastrian.**

Below: **The crown of Edward IV, who became undisputed king during the Wars of the Roses after the battle of Tewkesbury in 1471.**

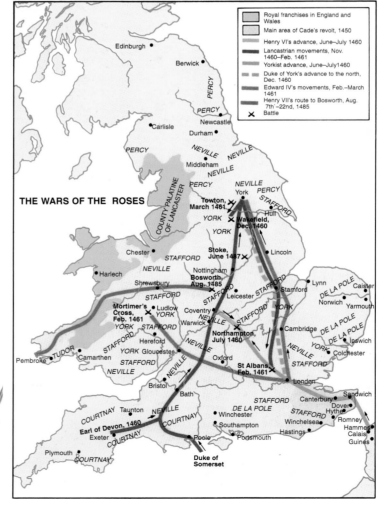

- **1440** English recapture Harfleur from the French. Douglas's sons murdered by order of councillors after dining with James II of Scotland

- **1441** Henry VI founds King's College, Cambridge

- **1444** William de la Pole, Duke of Suffolk, negotiates truce with France

- **1445** Henry VI marries Margaret of Anjou

- **1447** Parliament called at Bury St Edmunds, Suffolk. Humphrey of Gloucester arrested and dies in captivity

- **1449** English sack Fougères, Brittany: war with France resumes. Richard of York becomes Lord Lieutenant of Ireland; Edmund, Duke of Somerset, leads English in France

- **1450** Duke of Suffolk accused of selling the realm to France, and is murdered on way to exile. Jack Cade's Rebellion: 30,000 rebels from Kent and Sussex control London for a few days

- **1451** French capture Bordeaux and Bayonne, leaving England only Calais

- **1453** Henry VI becomes insane: York is regent

- **1454** Henry recovers; infant son Edward becomes Prince of Wales

- **1455** Wars of the Roses begin. Battle of St Albans: Yorkist victory. Henry VI captured. York becomes Lord Protector

- **1456** Queen Margaret dismisses York

- **1459** Civil war renewed: Lancastrian victory at battles of Bloreheath and Ludford

- **1460** Battle of Northampton: Yorkists capture Henry VI again. He agrees to York's succession

Above: **The Lancastrian King Henry VI at his Court as shown in an illuminated manuscript. In 1453 Henry suffered the first of several periods** of insanity. **Richard, Duke of York became Protector because Henry was unable to carry out his duties as King of England.**

This left John's daughter, Margaret Beaufort, as the Lancastrian heir. She married Edmund Tudor, Earl of Richmond and was the mother of the future king, Henry VII.

YORK VERSUS LANCASTER

For some years after he married, Henry VI had no heir. There were two obvious candidates for the succession. Richard, Duke of York, was descended through his father from Edward III's youngest son, Edmund, and through his mother from Edward's second son, Lionel. He had a better claim to the throne than the king himself. The other candidate was the Lancastrian Edmund Beaufort, Duke of Somerset. Like Henry VI, Edmund was descended from Edward III's third son, John of Gaunt, but like all Beauforts he was barred from the throne. But he was still a favourite of King Henry and his queen, Margaret of Anjou. York, an honest and competent man, did not press his claim.

FIGHTING BEGINS

In 1453 King Henry went mad. During the same year his wife gave birth to a son, Edward. Law and order had almost completely broken down and unruly groups of soldiers, returned from fighting in France, roamed the countryside. York was made

Lord Protector. Somerset was blamed for defeats in France towards the end of the Hundred Years War, and was sent to the Tower. Almost as suddenly as he went mad, King Henry VI recovered. But Queen Margaret still controlled the king, and she now influenced the dismissal of York as Lord Protector and the release of Somerset.

York still did not openly claim the Crown, but he decided to fight against the hostile Margaret. His army met that of Margaret, Henry and Somerset at St Albans. Somerset was killed, Henry VI was captured and York briefly became Lord Protector again. After a few years of uneasy peace fighting broke out again and the Lancastrians won. York was killed.

WARWICK THE KINGMAKER

After the death of the Duke of York in 1460, the Yorkist leadership passed to his son, Edward, who was only 19 years old. One of the most powerful nobles, Edward's cousin Richard Neville, Earl of Warwick, became the power behind the throne during the Wars of the Roses. His intrigues gave him the nickname of the Kingmaker. Warwick Castle today provides a spectacular reminder of this turbulent period.

Above: **Warwick Castle, the base for Richard Neville, an** **important leader in the Wars of the Roses.**

Left: **Edward IV (1461-1483) was the first Yorkist king. He was a very tall, handsome and strong leader who brought a period of peace and prosperity to England. During his reign the arts also flourished.**

EDWARD OF YORK

In the 1460s the civil war became more intense with each side seeking vengeance for the killing of its own supporters. After several battles, Edward of York entered London and was proclaimed king as Edward IV. Soon afterwards, the battle of Towton crushed the Lancastrians. Despite this, the Lancastrian cause was kept alive by Queen Margaret, who still favoured Edmund Beaufort. Edward IV's marriage to Elizabeth Woodville brought her family to prominence and angered Warwick, who had hoped to arrange a French marriage for the king.

In 1469, Warwick rebelled and captured Edward. Warwick and Edward were reconciled but only briefly, and then Warwick had to flee to France. There, as a price for French help, he allied with his old enemy Queen Margaret. Warwick returned to England and won massive support; Edward in turn had to flee. Warwick restored King Henry VI to the throne, but his second reign lasted only a few months.

EDWARD'S VICTORY

Edward returned to England with troops from Burgundy. At the battle of Barnet (1471) Warwick was killed. At Tewkesbury, a few weeks later, the Lancastrians were finally crushed and many of the great barons killed. Henry VI's son Prince Edward was killed during the battle by Edward IV and his brothers. Yorkist Edward's battle cry had always been: "Kill the nobles and spare the commons!" Edward IV was then undisputed king. Henry VI was put back in the Tower and died shortly after, probably murdered.

Below: **The battle of Bosworth Field in Leicestershire. Henry Tudor, who lived in exile in France, invaded England to claim the Crown by force. On August 22, 1485, Richard III was hacked to death by Henry Tudor's forces. In this picture, Henry kneels as he is crowned with a golden coronet. Legend says that the coronet was found on the battlefield from under a gorse bush.**

- **1460** James II of Scotland killed by exploding cannon at Roxburgh: succeeded by James III, aged eight (to 1488)

- **1460** Battle of Wakefield: Lancastrian victory. Richard of York killed

- **1461** Battle of Mortimer's Cross: Richard's son, Edward, Duke of York, defeats Lancastrians. Second battle of St Albans: Margaret rescues Henry VI, defeats Earl of Warwick. York assumes the Crown as Edward IV (to 1483). Battle of Towton: Lancastrians defeated. Henry flees to Scotland

- **1462** Warwick crushes Lancastrians

- **1463** Edward again defeats Lancastrians: Margaret flees to France

- **1464** Edward crushes more Lancastrian rebellions. Yorkists capture Henry. Edward marries Elizabeth Woodville

- **1466** Lord Boyd kidnaps James III and becomes governor of Scotland

EDWARD IV: FIRST YORKIST KING

Edward IV proved the strong and efficient ruler England badly needed. Popular demand called for the reconquest of the lost lands in France. He obtained funds through Parliament to finance an invasion but he also accepted money from the French not to invade, thus giving him two sources of income. He pursued a peaceful foreign policy which encouraged trade and kept taxes low. Also a ruthless king, Edward called another Parliament to condemn his treacherous brother George, Duke of Clarence, who died in the Tower.

EDWARD V: THE PRINCE IN THE TOWER

Edward IV had two young sons, and his rule and succession seemed secure. But at the age of 40 he was taken ill, and died within ten days. His 12-year-old son, Edward, succeeded him in 1483. But under the protectorship of his uncle, Richard, Duke of Gloucester, the reign of this young boy lasted just eleven weeks and one day.

Above: **Richard III (1483-1485) was the last Yorkist king. He was an energetic and competent king but made many enemies.**

- **1467** Scottish Parliament bans "fute-ball and golfe"

- **1469** Warwick changes sides, captures Edward IV, but lets him go

- **1470** Warwick forced to flee to France: he and Queen Margaret unite. Warwick lands with an army, restores Henry VI to the throne. Edward flees to Flanders

- **1471** Edward lands in Yorkshire with Flemish troops: resumes Crown. Battle of Barnet: Warwick killed. Battle of Tewkesbury: Prince of Wales killed. Margaret captured and Henry VI murdered in the Tower

- **1473** Edward sets up Council of the Marches to keep order in Wales

- **1475** William Caxton prints first book in English at Bruges. Edward plans to invade France, but is bought off by Louis XI

- **1476** Caxton prints first book in England at his press in Westminster. James III of Scotland subdues rebellion by John, Lord of the Isles

- **1483** Edward dies; succeeded by son Edward V, aged 12. Richard, Duke of Gloucester, is Regent: he declares Edward illegitimate and takes the throne as Richard III (to 1485). Edward and his younger brother disappear

- **1484** Heralds' College is founded. Richard III makes peace with Scots

- **1485** Henry Tudor, Earl of Richmond, invades England. Battle of Bosworth: Richard is killed and Wars of the Roses end. Henry Tudor takes throne as Henry VII

Right: **A famous painting by Sir John Millais in the late 19th century. It shows the two young princes, 12-year-old Edward V and his 9-year-old brother Richard, who were sent to the Tower of London by their uncle** Richard III and never seen again. Richard III was so loathed by his enemies that after his death at the battle of Bosworth, he was buried without ceremony and later his bones were thrown out and his coffin used as a horse trough.

RICHARD III

Richard, Duke of Gloucester, was renowned for his generalship, his abilities as an administrator, and his loyalty to the late king, Edward IV. Richard's strength was in the north but he was hated in the south. The Woodvilles, relatives of Edward's queen, Elizabeth, and Lord Hastings, one of Edward IV's generals, opposed his claim to the throne.

On Edward IV's death in 1483, Richard acted quickly: he accused Hastings of treason, and had him executed within the hour. Richard took Edward V and his young brother to the Tower "for safety"; they were never seen again. He told Parliament that Edward IV's marriage to Elizabeth Woodville (who also disputed Richard's claim) was invalid because Edward had previously made a marriage contract with someone else; the little princes were thus illegitimate. As a result, within three months of Edward IV's death, Parliament asked Richard to accept the Crown. At first Richard appeared to hesitate, but after some persuasion he accepted afterall.

The playwright William Shakespeare was later to portray the king as an evil hunchback in his play *Richard III*. But today many historians question whether he was so evil. In 1485 Henry Tudor, the last Lancastrian claimant to the throne, crossed from France and landed at Milford Haven in west Wales. He met Richard at the battle of Bosworth. Richard was deserted by many of his followers and killed. Henry Tudor was generally welcomed as Richard's successor and became Henry VII. The following year he married Edward IV's daughter, Elizabeth of York, thus ending the Wars of the Roses.

THE TUDORS
(1485 – 1603)

THE BEGINNING OF THE Tudor period in British history also signalled the end of the Middle Ages. The old feudal ways of life had largely disappeared and a new aristocracy drawn from the ranks of the growing middle classes was emerging. This was a period of great exploration and expansion in overseas trade, which gave the country a new source of wealth. The ideas of the Renaissance, which revived an interest in the art and learning of ancient Greece and Rome, marked the beginnings of modern culture and science. These ideas were spread by the use of the printing press. The Protestant Reformation, which began in Germany in an attempt to correct some of the worst features of the Roman Catholic Church, was adopted in England at first as a political move, and later as a matter of faith. The Tudors finally united Wales and England, so that one set of laws and rights applied to both countries. They also tried to complete the conquest of Ireland by settling English colonists in large estates there which were called plantations. Scotland suffered years of violent conflict.

Henry VIII with Jane Seymour and his three children; Mary (*far left*), Edward (*left*) and Elizabeth (*far right*).

Henry VII

Above: **Henry VII (1485-1509) was religious, hard-working and clever. He restored peace, justice and prosperity after years of conflict and civil war.**

THE LANCASTRIAN HENRY TUDOR defeated the Yorkist King Richard III at the battle of Bosworth Field in 1485, and became King Henry VII. This marked the end of the series of civil wars known as the Wars of the Roses which had been fought between two leading families called Lancaster (who had a red rose badge) and York (who wore a white rose badge).

Many nobles had been killed or their power weakened. Henry VII made sure this continued by getting rid of their private armies and by executing many for treason against the Crown. He then took over their estates. Henry also married a Yorkist princess to help bring the two families together.

YORKIST THREATS

Despite Henry VII's victory in the Wars of the Roses, he was still forced to watch constantly for threats to his throne from the few remaining Yorkist supporters. These supporters were often aided by foreign powers. France and Scotland in particular were traditional enemies of England. Richard III's younger sister, Margaret, the Duchess of Burgundy, twice found youths prepared to pretend to be claimants to the throne.

LAMBERT SIMNEL

The first pretender to the throne was Lambert Simnel, the son of an Oxford joiner. Yorkists tried to pass Simnel off as the missing Edward, Earl of Warwick, who had been imprisoned in 1485.

Below: **The Tudor succession. Lancastrian Henry VII consolidated the power of the Tudor dynasty by marrying Elizabeth of York.**

TIME CHART

- **1485** Henry Tudor defeats Richard III, becomes king (to 1509). Yeomen of the Guard founded. Edward, Earl of Warwick, son of Duke of Clarence, imprisoned

- **1486** Henry VII marries Elizabeth of York, daughter of Edward IV

- **1487** Lambert Simnel, pretending to be Earl of Warwick, proclaimed "King Edward VI" in Dublin. Simnel captured in England. Henry sets up special court of his council (later called Court of Star Chamber) to deal with offences the Common Law had proved unable to suppress

- **1488** Scottish rebels murder James III: son, James IV, becomes king

- **1489** First gold sovereigns minted

- **1491** Perkin Warbeck persuaded to impersonate Edward IV's son Richard of York

- **1492** Peace with France: Henry VII allows himself to be bought off. Warbeck finds support in Flanders

- **1494** Aberdeen University founded. Henry sends Sir Edward Poynings to Ireland to end Warbeck support. Statute of Drogheda (Poynings' Law) restates Henry's power

- **1495** Warbeck goes to Scotland: Sir William Stanley executed for supporting him

- **1496** James IV invades Northumberland in support of Warbeck. Anglo-Dutch treaty

- **1497** John Cabot discovers Newfoundland for Henry VII. Warbeck captured in Devon

- **1498** Warbeck imprisoned in the Tower of London

- **1499** Warbeck tried for treason and executed

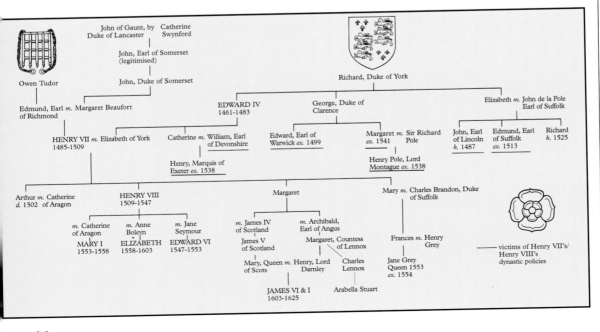

The Irish, who had long been supporters of the Yorkist cause, rallied to Simnel. Lord Kildare, Lord Deputy of Ireland, had him crowned Edward VI in Dublin by the archbishop. Margaret of Burgundy supplied money and arms to support his cause and he sailed for England in 1487. However, Henry VII defeated him at Stoke in Nottinghamshire. Simnel was captured and made a servant in the royal kitchens where he lived for almost 40 years.

PERKIN WARBECK

The second claimant was Perkin Warbeck, son of a Flemish tax collector. Warbeck was supported in turn by the King of France, Duchess Margaret, the Holy Roman Emperor, and James IV of Scotland. He posed as Richard, Duke of York, who had been murdered with his brother Edward V in the Tower.

Warbeck claimed that he was spared when his brother was killed. Margaret supported him as her long lost nephew. He stayed with her in Flanders and eventually landed in England but was caught and hanged in 1499. Henry punished Flanders for harbouring Warbeck; he expelled all Flemings from England and moved England's wool market base from Antwerp to Calais. Another Yorkist claimant, Edmund de la Pole, known as the White Rose of England, was also supported by Margaret. He was executed in 1513.

IRELAND UNDER POYNINGS

To limit Irish support for Perkin Warbeck and the Yorkist cause, Henry VII sent Sir Edward Poynings to Ireland as Lord Deputy. Poynings called an Irish Parliament, which passed the Statute of Drogheda, also called Poynings's Law: no Irish Parliament could meet without the English king's consent, and no bill could be considered there without his permission. All bills placed before the Irish Parliament had to be passed by the English Privy Council beforehand. Also, all laws passed in England should also be the law in Ireland. This ended home rule in Ireland for centuries.

Below: **A royal judge hearing cases around England. Henry VII tightened his grip on government by restoring Henry II's system whereby royal judges travelled from town to town to administer the common law.**

- **1501** Arthur, heir to Henry VII, marries Catherine of Aragon. Palace of Holyrood House, Edinburgh, is begun

- **1502** Death of Prince Arthur

- **1503** Henry's daughter Margaret marries James IV, King of Scots. Arthur's brother, Henry, betrothed to his widow, Catherine

- **1504** First English shilling issued. Battle of Cnoc Tuagh: Lord Kildare, Lord Deputy of Ireland, defeats his rival Ulrich Burke

- **1507** Walter Chapman and Andrew Myllar set up first Scottish printing press

- **1509** Henry VII dies; succeeded by son Henry VIII. Henry marries Catherine of Aragon

- *c.* **1509** English morality play *Everyman* first performed. Parliament grants Henry VIII customs revenue for life

- **1511** Henry joins the Holy League with Spain and the Pope against France

- **1512** Henry sends an unsuccessful expedition to capture Guienne in France

- **1513** Battle of Spurs: English defeat the French at Guingates (Thérouanne). Battle of Flodden: James IV of Scotland killed; James V, aged two, succeeds

- **1514** Henry's sister, Margaret, Queen Regent of Scotland, marries Archibald Douglas, Earl of Angus. Anglo-French truce: Henry's sister Mary marries Louis XII. Thomas Wolsey becomes Archbishop of York

- **1515** Duke of Albany becomes Protector of James V: Margaret flees to England. Wolsey becomes Chancellor. Work starts on Hampton Court

- **1517** May Day riots: London apprentices attack foreign traders. Albany goes to France, and is not allowed to return home

Henry VIII

Above: **Henry VIII (1509-1547) had been a great supporter of the Roman Catholic Church, but his divorce from Catherine of Aragon caused a break with the Pope which led to the Reformation of the English Church.**

HENRY VIII BECAME KING IN 1509 at the age of 17. A short time before that he was betrothed to Catherine of Aragon, youngest daughter of the Spanish rulers Ferdinand and Isabella. She had been married to Arthur, Henry's elder brother, to strengthen an alliance between England and Spain. But Arthur died suddenly, so Henry VII decided his younger son should marry Catherine because he was worried that he may have to return her dowry. The marriage was at first forbidden by the Church because the couple were too closely related, but Henry VII persuaded the Pope to allow it.

THE RENAISSANCE

The Renaissance is the modern name for the revival and spread of learning that took place from the 1400s onwards. It began in Italy, and spread throughout Europe. The works of ancient Greek and Roman writers and philosophers were widely read. Artists developed new styles of painting, including the use of perspective, or the illusion of distance. The speed with which these new ideas spread was due to the use of printing presses which began at this time. The Renaissance came to England in the reign of Henry VII, who invited Italian scholars and artists to his court. It found its greatest expression in literature: the Tudor period was a time of great poetry. It was also a time of major musical activity, especially the composition of Italian-style madrigals for groups of singers.

Left: **Henry VIII loved entertainments. At one banquet he provided "24 great beeves, 100 fat muttons, 91 pigs and 14 dozen swans". He played several musical instruments, enjoyed dancing and composed songs; it has been claimed that he wrote the famous song *Greensleeves*. Henry was well educated and he enjoyed discussing religion, art and other Renaissance subjects.**

- **1517** Martin Luther publishes his 95 Theses in Germany, starting a movement later known as the Reformation

- **1518** Wolsey is made papal legate. Peace of London between France and England. Royal College of Physicians founded

- **1519** Henry VII's chapel at Westminster Abbey completed

- **1520** Field of Cloth of Gold: Henry meets Francis I of France. Holy Roman Emperor Charles V visits Henry: Treaty of Calais

- **1521** Diet of Worms: Luther condemned as a heretic. Pope Leo X gives Henry title of Defender of the Faith. Albany returns to Scotland

- **1523** Thomas More becomes Speaker of the House of Commons

- **1525** Peace between England and France. William Tyndale translates New Testament into English

- **1526** Peace between England and Scotland

- **1527** Henry asks the Pope to end his marriage to Catherine of Aragon

- **1529** Wolsey stripped of power. Thomas More becomes Lord Chancellor

- **1530** Death of Wolsey

- **1531** Clan Donald and the Macleans rebel: pacified by James V. Clergy agree to acknowledge Henry as their "protector and only supreme head"

- **1532** More resigns as Lord Chancellor

- **1533** Henry marries Anne Boleyn. Act of Restraint of Appeals forbids appeals to Rome. Thomas Cranmer now Archbishop of Canterbury; declares Henry's marriage with Catherine void; Pope excommunicates Henry

- **1534** Act of Supremacy: Henry VIII makes himself Head of the Church in England

- **1535** Thomas More executed on a charge of treason. Thomas Cromwell made Vicar-General. Miles Coverdale makes first translation of Bible into English

- **1536** Catherine of Aragon dies. Anne Boleyn executed; Henry marries Jane Seymour. Small monasteries dissolved. Pilgrimage of Grace: northern revolt against religious changes. Act of Union unites Wales with England

- **1537** Jane Seymour gives birth to a son, Edward: she dies

- **1538** James V of Scotland marries Mary of Guise

- **1539** Henry orders the dissolution of larger monasteries

- **1540** Henry VIII marries Anne of Cleves, but soon divorces her and marries Catherine Howard. Thomas Cromwell executed for treason. War with France

FRENCH AND SCOTS DEFEATED

In 1511 Pope Julius II asked Henry VIII, the King of Spain and the Holy Roman Emperor to help him drive the French out of Italy. Henry agreed, hoping to reconquer some of England's former territories in France. His first expedition failed, but in 1513 he led a second expedition and at Guingates (Thérouanne) he won a short battle known as the Battle of Spurs after the speed at which the French fled. In that year the Scots invaded England to aid France. At Flodden Field, in Northumberland, the Scots faced an English army half its size but led by an experienced general, Thomas Howard, Earl of Surrey. English cannon, arrows and tactics won the day. The Scots lost King James IV and 10,000 men.

HENRY, DIVORCE AND THE CHURCH

After 18 years of marriage to Catherine of Aragon, Henry VIII had no male heir, only a daughter, Mary, born in 1516. No queen had ever ruled all England, and the Wars of the Roses showed the damage that could be caused by disputes over the succession to the throne. In 1527 Henry decided to divorce Catherine, who was unlikely to bear more children, and find a wife who could give him a son and so secure the Tudor dynasty.

Henry ordered Cardinal Wolsey to ask the Pope to grant a divorce. The Pope refused, and Wolsey fell from power. So that Henry could grant himself a divorce, he decided to separate the Church in England from the authority of the Pope, a move

Above: **Henry VIII met the French king in 1520 at the Field of Cloth of Gold – so called because of the luxurious display, by both kings, of pavilions and tents made and furnished with satins, velvets and cloths of gold.**

carried out by a series of Acts of Parliament. Meanwhile Henry had married a lady of the court, Anne Boleyn. In 1533 the new Archbishop of Canterbury, Thomas Cranmer, declared Henry's marriage with Catherine invalid (using the original argument that he could not marry his brother's widow) and his marriage with Anne legal. Anne soon produced a child, but it was another girl, Elizabeth. Once again Henry was disappointed, and, not having a son, he turned against Anne.

In 1536 a charge of adultery was brought against Anne. She was accused of treason, tried and beheaded. Henry then married Jane Seymour, who produced the longed-for son which they named Edward.

HENRY CLOSES THE MONASTERIES

English monasteries were in decline in the 1500s, and many of them were badly run. Henry's first attack against them came from Wolsey, who obtained papal permission to suppress 40 of the smaller monasteries.

- **1541** Henry VIII takes the title of King of Ireland. Wales gets representation in the English Parliament

- **1542** Catherine Howard executed. England and Scotland at war. Scots lose battle of Solway Moss. James V of Scotland dies; daughter Mary succeeds

- **1543** Henry marries Catherine Parr

- **1544** English army invades Scotland, occupies Edinburgh. Boulogne captured

- **1545** Scots win battle of Ancram Moor. The *Mary Rose*, refitted in 1536, sinks in the Solent

- **1546** Peace with France. Cardinal Beaton, a Scottish statesman, assassinated

- **1547** Henry VIII dies; succeeded by Edward VI, aged nine; Duke of Somerset appointed Protector

- **1548** Heresy laws abolished in England

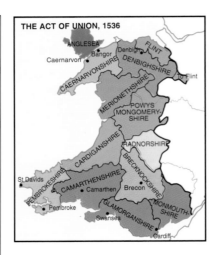

Above: **The administrative regions of Wales after the Act of Union in 1536. Wales was now completely absorbed into the English system of government.**

In 1536 Henry ordered nearly 400 of the remaining small ones to be dissolved, and took over their land and property. The rest of the smaller monasteries were then dissolved and the monks pensioned off.

This move was so beneficial to Henry's finances that in 1539 Henry decided to dissolve the larger monasteries. Monasteries that resisted were destroyed and their monks brutally killed. Henry gained still more wealth by selling off the monastery lands to rich nobles, but the charity and care which the monks had given to the poor and needy was a great loss.

UNION WITH WALES

In 1536 Henry VIII decided that Wales should be united with England. By the Act of Union it became part of England. An Act in 1541 gave Wales the right to send members to the English Parliament in Winchester. The Welsh shires were created by the Tudors, and English law was extended to Wales, with English as the official language of the law courts.

HENRY, KING OF IRELAND

Having made himself Supreme Head of the Church in England, Henry VIII decided to extend his powers to Ireland, where the English owned large estates including most of Leinster and Meath.

Right: **In 1536 Henry closed all the smaller monasteries and confiscated their property to help his finances. In 1539 all the larger monasteries were closed. In just ten years Henry VIII closed all of England's 800 monasteries.**

Right: **Hans Holbein the Younger's painting of Sir Thomas More (third on the left) and his family. More, once Henry's friend and Lord Chancellor, was to accept the King as supreme authority over the Church. He was later canonized by the Catholic Church.**

In 1541, an Irish Parliament was called in Dublin and gave Henry the title of King of Ireland. More than 40 Irish chiefs and Anglo-Irish nobles surrendered their lands to the King and received them back as vassals, the same terms by which English barons held their lands. Henry tried but failed to force Protestantism on Catholic Ireland.

HENRY'S FAILURES IN MARRIAGE

After Jane Seymour's death, Henry's chief minister, Thomas Cromwell, arranged a marriage with a German princess, Anne of Cleves. The marriage was to ally England with the Protestant princes of northern Germany – an alliance on which Cromwell was very keen. Henry had never met Anne, but as part of the marriage arrangements he received a portrait of her. One story has it that when Anne arrived she was so plain that the disappointed Henry described her as "the Flanders mare". However, there is no reason to believe the painting falsely flattered her face.

The marriage was soon dissolved, and Henry married Catherine Howard, a beautiful young noblewoman. Catherine was unfaithful to him, and Henry had her beheaded.

Henry's last marriage was to a widow, Catherine Parr, who knew how to manage him, and who outlived him. Henry died in 1547. He left behind a son, Edward VI, who was a sickly child of only 10 years of age, and two unmarried daughters, Mary and Elizabeth. This meant that the succession to the throne was far from secure.

FOCUS ON THE MARY ROSE

The *Mary Rose* was Henry VIII's greatest warship. It could carry 200 crew, 185 soldiers and 30 gunners. There were some 140 cannon and hand guns. But it capsized and sank before Henry's eyes a few kilometres from Portsmouth Harbour during an engagement with a French invasion fleet on July 19, 1545.

The wreck was located in about 12 metres of water in 1971 by Alexander McKee and raised in 1982 with the current Prince of Wales in attendance. Among the artefacts recovered were cannons, longbows, gold coins and sail maker's and barber-surgeon's tools. The remains are now housed in Portsmouth alongside HMS *Victory* in an exciting display of Britain's maritime history.

THE REFORMATION

Although Henry VIII had broken ties with the Pope, he still supported the beliefs and customs of the Roman Catholic faith. During the reign of his son Edward VI, England was to move steadily away from Catholicism and towards the Protestant religion, in the movement later known throughout Europe as the Reformation. The Reformation had started in Germany in 1517 when Martin Luther protested against certain elaborate practices of the Roman Catholic Church. Forty years later, half of Europe was Protestant.

EDWARD VI

Edward was only nine when he came to the throne, and the government was in the hands of his uncle, Edward, Duke of Somerset, who had the title Protector. Somerset abolished the laws against heresy, removed images and altars from the churches, and introduced an English-language *Book of Common Prayer*, which was compiled by Thomas Cranmer. By an Act of Uniformity in 1549, the use of this Prayer Book was made compulsory. In another change, priests who had previously had to live as single men were now allowed to marry.

LADY JANE GREY

In 1550 the Duke of Northumberland took over from Somerset as Protector and persuaded Edward to name Lady Jane Grey as his heir to the throne. Lady Jane, the grand-daughter of Henry VII, was married to Northumberland's son Guildford Dudley. Edward agreed to Lady Jane Grey becoming his successor because he feared that the Crown would otherwise pass to his sister, Mary, who was a devout Catholic and who would make England a Catholic country again.

Edward died in 1553 but his death was kept secret and Lady Jane was proclaimed queen. But less than two weeks later Mary's claim to the throne was recognized and Lady Jane and her husband were imprisoned.

Above: Edward VI (1547-1553) was reserved, courteous, intelligent, and intellectual. But he became seriously ill and died, probably of consumption, aged only 15 years of age.

● **1549** First Prayer Book in English; made compulsory by Act of Uniformity. Clergy allowed to marry. Fall of Duke of Somerset (executed in 1552), succeeded by Duke of Northumberland as Protector. Images and altars in churches ordered to be destroyed

● **1553** Edward VI dies; Lady Jane Grey proclaimed queen. After nine days, Jane deposed: Mary Tudor becomes queen. Duke of Northumberland executed. Sir Thomas Wyatt leads rebellion. Sir Hugh Willoughby and Richard Chancellor's voyage in search of a northwest sea passage to Asia

● **1554** Wyatt, Lady Jane and her husband Guildford Dudley executed. Mary I marries Philip II of Spain

● **1555** Catholic Restoration begins. Bishops Latimer and Ridley among Protestants burned

At first Mary refused to execute Lady Jane Grey, Dudley and Northumberland, for attempting to secure a Protestant succession. But a rising in their favour led by Sir Thomas Wyatt made Mary realize they would always be a danger to her while they lived. They were beheaded in the Tower of London on February 12, 1554.

MARY I

Mary I came to the throne in 1553. She had been unhappy ever since Henry VIII had divorced her mother, Catherine of Aragon. Her greatest wish now was to undo the Reformation and restore England to the Roman Catholic faith. Mary's husband, the devoutly Catholic Philip II of Spain, encouraged her plans. Opposition to the Church of Rome was strong and could only be crushed by harsh measures. Mary began by stopping all clergy from reading the *Book of Common Prayer*. In Mary's five-year reign 275 Protestants were put to death for refusing to convert back to Catholicism.

Right: **Mary I (1553-1558) was strong-willed, a shrewd politician and believed passionately that it was her duty to return England to the Catholic Church.**

Above: **A chained English Bible in a church. During the Reformation the use of the English Bible and the *Book of Common Prayer* was made compulsory by the Act of Uniformity of 1549. It was also forbidden to remove these books from churches so they were chained up to keep them safe.**

Left: **The coronation procession of Edward VI in 1547 as it moved down Cheapside from the Tower of London (visible to the left) to Westminster Abbey (to the right). London south of the Thames had hardly been developed, but both Henry VII and Henry VIII had spent lavishly on royal residences in London.**

- **1555** John Knox returns from exile to Scotland

- **1556** Archbishop Cranmer burned at the stake. Cardinal Pole, papal legate, becomes Archbishop of Canterbury. Earl of Sussex becomes Lord Deputy of Ireland

- **1557-59** War with France

- **1558** French recapture Calais. Mary, Queen of Scots, marries dauphin Francis of France. Mary I dies; succeeded by sister Elizabeth I (to 1603). Acts of Supremacy and Uniformity re-enacted

- **1559** Dauphin Francis becomes Francis II of France: Mary, Queen of Scots assumes title Queen of France

- **1560** Church of Scotland established. Mary of Guise (wife of James V and mother of Mary Stuart) deposed as Scottish regent. Reformation imposed in Ireland

- **1561** Mary returns to Scotland after husband's death

Left: The burning in Mary's reign of two leading Protestant bishops, Latimer and Ridley, in 1555. Archbishop Cranmer, who was himself later burned at the stake, is shown praying to God to give them strength. At the final moments Ridley said to Latimer: "We shall light such a candle as shall never be put out".

Among the victims were nobles and clergy such as Archbishop Cranmer. Mary has since acquired the nickname "Bloody Mary".

Mary died broken-hearted in 1558. Her husband did not love her and lived abroad and she had no child or heir. The loss of Calais – England's last foothold in France – in 1558 was the final blow for this unhappy queen. "When I die," Mary said, "Calais will be written on my heart."

Elizabeth I

HENRY VIII'S YOUNGER DAUGHTER, Elizabeth, ascended the throne in 1558, with no opposition. She restored the Protestant religion and gradually established the Church of England.

Elizabeth I was a remarkable woman. She spoke five languages besides English: Greek, Latin, French, Italian and Spanish. She was a talented musician, a graceful dancer and a fine archer. She was also a very skilled politician, calculating and extremely clever. Elizabeth said of herself that she had "the body of a weak and feeble woman, but the heart and stomach of a king, and a king of England too".

FOCUS ON THE GREAT TUDOR PALACES

There are many fine Tudor manors, houses and palaces all over England – from the black-and-white half-timbered houses of Chester, to the Great Houses of Hardwick Hall, and especially Hampton Court Palace (*below*). Five wives of Henry VIII lived in the splendid Hampton Court situated beside the Thames, and it is said to be haunted by the ghost of Catherine Howard, Henry's fifth wife. The palace was offered to Henry in 1526 by Cardinal Wolsey who wanted to keep in favour with the king. Tournaments were held in the Tiltyard Gardens, and the Clock Court, Great Hall and Gate House are all of Tudor origin. Bess Hardwick, one of the richest people in Elizabeth I's reign, was actively involved in the designs of her great house, Hardwick Hall, Derbyshire in 1597. Now that the barons' wars were over, these palaces were built without castle-style fortifications.

Above: **This portrait was painted when Elizabeth was 56 years old, just after England's victory over the Spanish Armada in 1588.**

GOOD QUEEN BESS

Elizabeth's reign lasted for 45 years. She remained unmarried and independently powerful, and dominated her male advisors. She died without an heir. Her court celebrated her as Gloriana, and the ordinary people referred to her as Good Queen Bess. Her enemies were mostly Roman Catholics, who were badly treated and often went in fear of their lives. Her reign also witnessed the execution of Mary Stuart and the dramatic attack of the Spanish Armada.

MARY, QUEEN OF SCOTS

Mary Stuart became Queen of Scotland when she was just a week old on the death of her father, James V. She was brought up as a Catholic in France, and was married at the age of 16 to the dauphin of France. When he became king in 1559, she became Queen of France as well as of Scotland. Through her descent from Henry VIII's sister, Margaret, Mary was also Elizabeth's heir and so she had a claim to the English throne too.

Mary was celebrated as the most beautiful woman of her time, an accomplished and graceful child of the French court. She was also a clever politician – almost as dominating as Elizabeth of England.

MARY'S DECLINE AND FALL

In 1561 Mary's husband died and she returned to Scotland. The Scots were mainly Protestants and disapproved of Mary's religion and of her foreign ways. She next married her cousin, Henry Stuart, Lord Darnley, who was a jealous man. Darnley helped murder Mary's secretary, David Rizzio, suspecting him of being the queen's lover.

Mary, in turn, was determined on revenge. Soon after their son James was born, Darnley was strangled and the house where he was staying blown up. Suspicion fell on James Hepburn, Earl of Bothwell, and increased when Mary married him. The Scottish lords did not like Bothwell. Scottish opposition to Mary forced her to give

Right: **The execution of Mary Stuart, in February 1587. Elizabeth had kept her prisoner for 18 years. Finally she became too great a threat as a focus for Catholic plots to be allowed to live.**

Left: **The sinking of a great Spanish galleon by English ships in 1588. The Spanish Armada was beaten by the skill of the English fleet and violent storms.**

the Channel. Eventually the Armada took shelter in Calais harbour, but Drake sent in fireships. To escape the danger of their whole fleet catching fire, the Spaniards hurriedly raised anchor and sailed out to another confused battle. Both sides had run short of cannon fire, and with no further supplies available, the Armada was forced by bad weather to escape into the North Sea.

The Armada returned home after sailing round the British Isles. It lost 44 ships out of 130. Many surviving ships had to be scrapped. This did not end the conflict between Spain and England which continued because Elizabeth could not bear to hold peace talks with Spain. It was left to her successor, James I, to make peace in 1604.

ELIZABETH'S COURT

The court around Queen Elizabeth glittered like the queen herself. Hers was an age when, it seemed, every gentleman aspired to be a poet or a musician, or both. For example, Sir Philip Sidney, the brave soldier who died fighting the Spanish at Zutphen, in the Netherlands, was a fine poet.

up the throne in favour of her baby son, James VI. Mary fled to England, throwing herself on Elizabeth's mercy. But Elizabeth made her a prisoner. Mary was considered a ringleader in a series of Catholic plots against Elizabeth.

Mary was charged with involvement in the Babington Plot and was tried and found guilty. Elizabeth eventually allowed Mary's execution.

PHILIP II PLANS AN INVASION

Under Elizabeth I, England became Protestant again. Philip II of Spain was determined to dethrone her. He wanted to restore England to the Catholic faith that his wife Mary I had so rigorously tried to reinstate. Elizabeth had angered Philip by supporting the Dutch in their war of independence against Spain. British seamen, were also raiding Spanish colonies and plundering treasure ships. Philip planned an invasion.

THE ARMADA

In 1588 an Armada, or fleet, of 130 Spanish warships set sail up the English Channel, to pick up soldiers from Dunkirk in France and land them on the English coast. The English prepared an emergency fleet led by experienced sailors Lord Howard of Effingham, Francis Drake, John Hawkins, and Martin Frobisher. The English fought a running naval battle with the Spanish in

Left: **Rich Elizabethan men wore embroidered jackets, fur-lined robes, and short padded trousers called breeches. Noble women wore wide skirts stiffened by hoops and padding and lace ruffs around the neck.**

Elizabeth's reign saw a flourishing of plays and poetry. The Globe Theatre, since restored in 1996, could hold nearly 3,000 people.

The outstanding playwright was William Shakespeare, but at the time he was one of many highly regarded dramatic poets. Others had more than one occupation. Playwright Christopher Marlowe, murdered in a tavern brawl, is thought to have been a secret agent; Edmund Spenser, who wrote *The Faerie Queene*, helped in the plantation (settlement) of Ireland.

England led the way in the writing of music for keyboard instruments, and much traditional church music was written at this time. Two outstanding musicians were Thomas Tallis and his pupil William Byrd.

Towards the end of Elizabeth's reign madrigals (love poems sung by several voices without musical accompaniment) were introduced into England. Thomas Morley edited a collection of madrigals in honour of Elizabeth, called *The Triumphs of Oriana*, but it was not published until after the Queen's death.

Above: **Sir Philip Sidney, Elizabethan poet, courtier, diplomat and soldier, was idolized by the English people. He has been called the "jewel of Elizabeth's court".**

- **1562-64** Elizabeth I sends forces to France to help the Huguenot (French Protestants) in their revolt against the Catholic government. John Hawkins becomes the first English slave trader

- **1565** Mary, Queen of Scots marries her cousin Lord Darnley. Royal Exchange, London, founded. John Hawkins brings back sweet potatoes and tobacco

- **1566** Darnley and others murder David Rizzio, Mary's secretary

- **1567** Darnley murdered; Mary marries Bothwell. Mary abdicates; succeeded by son James VI, aged one. Earl of Moray becomes Regent: Mary held prisoner

- **1568** Mary escapes to England and becomes prisoner of Elizabeth

- **1569** Rebellion in north of England: Durham Cathedral plundered

- **1570** Pope Pius V declares Elizabeth a usurper and heretic

- **1572** Duke of Norfolk and Earl of Northumberland executed for treason. Francis Drake attacks Spanish harbours in the Americas

- **1573** John Hawkins begins to reform the Navy

- **1575** MP Peter Wentworth claims freedom from arrest for Members of Parliament for discussing key areas of government

- **1576** James Burbage opens first theatre at Shoreditch

- **1577-80** Drake's voyage round the world. Drake returns from voyage and is knighted by Elizabeth

- **1583** Sir Humphrey Gilbert claims Newfoundland for England. Edinburgh University founded

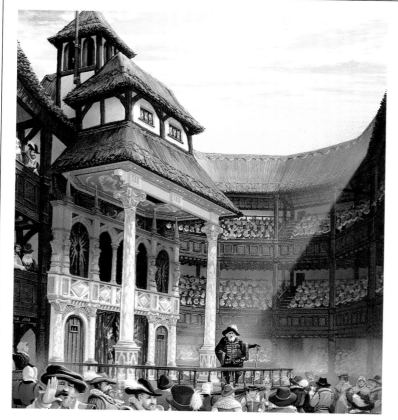

FOCUS ON THE THEATRE

England's first theatre was built at Shoreditch. It was based on the enclosed courtyard of big inns, where actors used to perform. The theatre was built by actor-manager James Burbage. The building was simply called 'The Theatre'. It was open to the sky, like the later Globe Theatre where Shakespeare acted. Other theatres, such as the Blackfriars and the Whitefriars, had roofs.

Exploration

WHEN THE ITALIAN EXPLORER Christopher Columbus approached Henry VII in 1492 for funds to pay for his voyages of discovery, Henry, known for his financial caution, turned him down. Columbus was eventually funded by King Ferdinand and Queen Isabella of Spain, who benefited greatly from his discoveries in America.

Five years later Henry VII did finance John Cabot's expedition. Cabot was a sailor from Genoa, Italy, who was based in Bristol. His voyage led eventually to the founding of the first British colony in America, at Newfoundland (in present-day Canada). Later a rich cod-fishing trade developed there. Henry VII was pleased with the results and gave Cabot a pension of £20.

THE RISE OF THE NAVAL POWERS

From the end of the 15th century, Portugal, Spain, France, the Netherlands, and later England, started on a series of daring expeditions to claim new lands and wealth on the other side of the world.

The European powers intended to ship spices, precious metals, cotton and other materials back home. To do this they all needed strong navies. Henry VIII helped to establish a reliable English navy of 50 to 70 ships and about 8,000 sailors, as well as a network of dockyards. One of the new ships he had built was the *Mary Rose*, named after his favourite sister, but it capsized and sank before his eyes on July 19, 1545.

Above: **A galleon sets sail. A team of sailors unfurl the mainsail. Galleons were very large ocean-going ships, four times as long as they were wide. They had a special deck for cannons. They replaced earlier ships called carracks, which were broader, slower and less manoeuvrable.**

- **1584** Sir Walter Raleigh tries to establish a colony near Roanoake Island, Virginia (now North Carolina)

- **1586** Drake raids Santo Domingo and Cartagena in West Indies. Francis Walsingham uncovers Babington Plot, involving Mary, Queen of Scots. Mary condemned for treason

- **1587** Mary, Queen of Scots, executed. Drake partly destroys Spanish fleet at Cadiz. War with Spain breaks out

- **1588** Philip II launches "Invincible Armada" against England, but it is destroyed

- **1590** First Shakespeare plays performed

- **1592** Plague kills 15,000 Londoners

- **1593** Poet and playwright Christopher Marlowe murdered

- **1595** Hugh O'Neill, Earl of Tyrone, heads rebellion in Ireland

- **1595** Spaniards land in Cornwall, burn Mousehole and Penzance. Raleigh explores Orinoco River in South America

Left: **Elizabeth I knights Walter Raleigh in 1584. In the same year Raleigh sent ships to North America to explore the east coast.**

SIR FRANCIS DRAKE

Sir Francis Drake was an accomplished explorer and sea captain who served Elizabeth loyally and helped England become a major sea power. Between 1577 to 1580, he and his men on the *Golden Hind* made an epic voyage around the world, the first crew to do so. Elizabeth and others bought shares in the voyage, the object of which was to plunder the Spanish colonies as well as to explore a way by sea to Asia and its riches. Elizabeth gave Drake a knighthood on his return.

SIR WALTER RALEIGH

Walter Raleigh was a great soldier, explorer, and writer. The story of Raleigh removing his coat and placing it over a large puddle so Elizabeth could avoid getting wet may not be true. But he did become one of the Queen's favourites at Court. Elizabeth wanted colonies for England – chiefly to establish trading posts for merchants and so bring wealth to the country.

In 1584, Raleigh sent 100 colonists across the Atlantic to America to find gold and take possession of new lands. Queen Elizabeth was impressed with the venture and so he named the new land Virginia after her, because people called her the "Virgin Queen". Raleigh was also the first person to introduce tobacco and potatoes into England from the American colonies.

Compass

Astrolabe

Backstaff

Above: **The most important navigation instrument used in the 1500s was the compass, which showed in which direction the ship was travelling. The astrolabe and the backstaff used the sun to measure the distance north or south of the equator.**

- **1597** John Harington describes his new invention, the water-closet

- **1598** Battle of the Yellow Ford: Irish defeat the English

- **1599** Earl of Essex becomes Lord Deputy of Ireland; he concludes truce with Tyrone, but is arrested at home. Lord Mountjoy succeeds Essex as Lord Deputy of Ireland. East India Company founded

- **1601** Essex dabbles in plots, is tried for treason and executed. Spanish army lands in Ireland, but surrenders at Kinsale

- **1603** Mountjoy crushes Irish rebellion. Elizabeth I dies; succeeded by James I of England (James VI of Scotland). Amnesty in Ireland. Main and Bye Plots against James I: Raleigh is jailed for involvement

Below: **A cutaway view of a two-decker galleon.**
1 gundeck; **2** anchor cable; **3** cookhouse; **4** hold; **5** rudder; **6** captain's table.

Below: **Produce bought back from the Americas by Elizabethan explorers included potatoes and tobacco leaves.**

Charles II (1660-1685) had to flee to France when Civil War broke out, but returned on Cromwell's death.

THE STUARTS
(1603 – 1714)

ELIZABETH I'S HEIR WAS JAMES VI of Scotland, son of Mary Stuart, Queen of Scots. The family of Stuart had ruled Scotland for 232 years before James VI united England and Scotland under a common crown, though not yet in law. Eventful as those years had been, they were not so dramatic as the following 111 years during which the Stuarts ruled over England, Wales, Scotland and, in name, over Ireland. In that time the combined nation underwent two revolutions: the English Civil War 1642-1645 which ended with the execution of Charles I, and the Glorious Revolution of 1688. This was a bloodless affair, when the Dutch prince William of Orange was invited to become King of England in place of Catholic James II, and so secure the Protestant succession for the English throne.

At first the Stuart monarchs claimed to rule by divine right; eventually it was made plain that they ruled by the consent and invitation of Parliament. The death of Charles I brought a period known as the Commonwealth when England was ruled by Oliver Cromwell and Parliament. On Cromwell's death, Parliament called Charles II back from exile and in 1660 the monarchy was restored. By the end of the Stuart period England and Scotland were formally united, and Ireland was more controlled by the English than before.

Meanwhile, the British were expanding overseas. Many colonies, were set up in North America. The religious tensions at home drove some people abroad to escape persecution. The most famous group was the Pilgrim Fathers, who founded the Plymouth Colony in America in 1620. Elsewhere, British traders established settlements in southern Africa and India which would eventually develop into an empire.

James 1

THE NEW KING James I of England was, as he said himself, an "old and experienced king". He had already ruled Scotland for 25 years as James VI. The son of Mary Stuart and Lord Darnley, he believed in the divine, or God-given, right of kings to rule, and had managed the Scottish Parliament more or less as he liked. The English Parliament was far less easy to handle, insisting that the king could rule only by its consent. James supported the Protestant Church and was determined to enforce its practices.

THE GUNPOWDER PLOT

James I enforced an old law against Roman Catholics which stated that they had to go to Protestant churches, or be fined. A group of Catholics decided to start a revolution by blowing up the Houses of Parliament at a time when James was to be there. But one of the conspirators warned a relative, who was likely to be endangered by the plot: "Retire yourself into the country… they shall receive a terrible blow this Parliament, and yet they shall not see who hurts them."

Above: **James I (1603-1625) is said to have suffered from a stammer and dribbled. But he was an intelligent king who wrote against the evils of tobacco and introduced a new English translation of the Bible.**

The relative passed the information on to the authorities who searched the cellars of Parliament.

GUY FAWKES

Guy Fawkes, one of the conspirators, was caught red-handed guarding several barrels of gunpowder. The leader of the conspiracy was not, in fact, Fawkes but Robert Catesby. Fawkes endured hours of torture on the rack, but refused to incriminate anyone else. Fawkes and the other conspirators confessed under torture and were tried for treason and executed.

AUTHORISED BIBLE

When James I came to the throne there were five English translations of the Bible in use. He ordered a new translation. Fifty churchmen and scholars completed the task in seven years. The result was the Authorised Version, or King James Bible – which is still the most popular English version after more than 350 years. The beauty of its language has been a lasting influence on all English-speaking peoples. It also provided a major inspiration for the Puritan movement which later overthrew Charles I.

Left: **Guy Fawkes (*third from right*) with his fellow plotters. They stacked firewood and gunpowder under the Houses of Parliament, and planned to set fire to them when James I opened Parliament on November 5, 1605.**

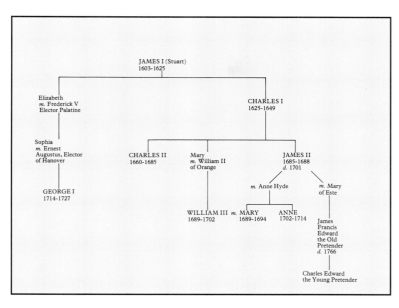

Left: The Stuart family tree. By 1603 James I's family name of Stewart was being spelled Stuart – the French way. This arose because James's grandfather had taken French nationality in 1537. James was a Protestant but he accepted Catholics and was prepared to allow his heir, Charles, to be engaged to the French Catholic princess, Henrietta Maria.

THE PURITANS

The Reformation of England had brought very few changes to the Church and many Catholic practices continued. The Church of England retained bishops, ceremony and vestments. But many people wanted a simpler, purer form of worship, with no bishops or elaborate religious ritual. They became known as Puritans. Some Puritans left England for America, where they could worship as they chose. But most remained determined to fight oppression rather than evade it. They were the dominant influence in Parliament in its later clash with Charles I.

LADY ARABELLA STUART

Lady Arabella Stuart was James's first cousin, and had a claim to the throne on Elizabeth's death. For this reason Elizabeth I and then James, were determined that she should marry only someone they could trust.

Arabella fell in love with William Seymour, later Duke of Somerset. He was a great-great-grandson of Henry VII and, in Henry VIII's will, had been made the next heir to the British throne after Elizabeth. James forbade this match, but the couple married secretly in 1610. A conspiracy against James I was hatched, but the couple were found out and imprisoned. Arabella and Seymour planned an escape, Seymour got away, but Arabella was recaptured and confined in the Tower, where she died, insane. Seymour later became a leading Royalist general in the Civil War.

Below: The title page of the Authorised Version, or King James Bible, showing its publication date: ANNO DOM. 1611. The Bible remains the most widely read book ever published in the English language.

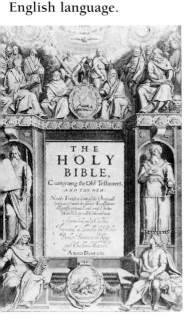

- **1603** James VI of Scotland becomes James I of England

- **1604** James enforces Act of Uniformity. James's first Parliament rejects his plan to unite England and Scotland, but James proclaims himself King of Great Britain, France and Ireland. Peace with Spain

- **1605** Gunpowder Plot: Guy Fawkes caught. Act of Uniformity proclaimed in Ireland

- **1606** Guy Fawkes and other plotters are executed for treason. James raises customs duties without consent of Parliament

- **1607** First permanent settlement in America at Jamestown, Virginia

- **1609** Plantations (settlements) plan for Irish lands from confiscated Irish estates to be granted to settlers from mainland Britain

- **1610** James's cousin Lady Arabella Stewart marries William Seymour: the couple are imprisoned

- **1611** James dissolves Parliament. Authorised Version of the Bible is published

- **1615** Lady Arabella Stuart dies. English fleet defeats Dutch fleet off Bombay

- **1616** Willem Schouten rounds Cape Horn. Walter Raleigh released from Tower. Navigator William Baffin searches for Northwest Passage to Pacific Ocean and discovers Baffin Bay

- **1617** Raleigh attacks Spanish colonies

- **1618** Thirty Years War starts

- **1618** Raleigh executed for treason

- **1619** Dutch ships bring first negro slaves to the colony of Virginia

The First Colonies

THE BEGINNINGS OF the British empire took place in Elizabethan times with Sir Walter Raleigh's unsuccessful attempt to set up a colony at Roanoke in North America. But James I distrusted Raleigh and finally had him executed. In 1607 three ships sailed into present-day Chesapeake Bay in Maryland where they built a fort at Jamestown (named after James I). Of the 104 colonists, almost half died that summer from malaria, typhoid and shortage of food. It was here that the Algonquin princess Pocahontas befriended Captain John Smith and saved him from being clubbed to death. She later came to London and attended the royal court. She died in 1617 on her way back to Jamestown. The colony itself eventually prospered and plantations of tobacco were established with the help of the local native American tribes. Later the colonists brought in black slaves from West Africa to work the fields.

THE PILGRIM FATHERS

On December 15, 1620 a very different colony was established farther north by just over 100 English Puritan farmers and craftsmen. These colonists became known as the Pilgrim Fathers. They were seeking a place where they could worship without persecution. They left Plymouth in a ship called the *Mayflower* and dropped anchor off Cape Cod in Massachusetts.

The colony flourished when native American farmers taught the settlers how to grow corn (maize). In the autumn of 1621 they held their first harvest supper. They feasted on geese, turkeys, duck, shellfish, watercress and wine and invited the native Americans to the first Thanksgiving Day. That day, towards the end of November, is now a national holiday in the United States. Families and neighbours meet together to share the traditional Thanksgiving meal of turkey, cranberry sauce and pumpkin pie.

THE EARLY SETTLERS

The first settlers' houses were built of wood, of which there was plenty in the surrounding forests. The roofs were made of thatch and later of thin sheets of hardwood called shingle. The first chimneys were made of stone and later of brick. The colonists' life was hard: they spun thread, wove cloth, and tanned leather for jackets and shoes, and made candles from fat or beeswax. Although there was plenty of land to grow crops and they were free from religious persecution life was tough for these first settlers so that even after ten years, their colony still numbered only about 300 people.

Left: **The Hudson Bay Company was started in 1670 especially to trade in furs. Here fur trappers trade with native Americans in northern Canada in the 1700s.**

Above: In 1636, Roger Williams established a permanent settlement at Providence, Rhode Island (the smallest state in the United States). Williams was a Puritan minister who was driven out of Massachusetts because he accused the Puritans of not being tolerant enough. Williams bought the land from two native American Narragansett chiefs. Setting up a new colony held many dangers – land had to be cleared, even in the harsh winter, and supplies were scarce. However, by 1643 there were four settlements in Rhode Island which united in 1663.

Left: The *Mayflower* took 102 Puritan colonists and 47 crew safely across the Atlantic. The ship was only about 30 metres long and 6 metres wide. The height of the space below deck was only one metre (high enough for a small child) and there were no portholes. Here the men, women and children rolled about and were sick as the ship was tossed around by the ocean swell for two months. The only water available for washing was sea water. Nevertheless, only one colonist and four crew died on the epic voyage.

- **1620** Pilgrim Fathers sail from Plymouth to colonize America. They arrive at Cape Cod and found the Plymouth Colony

- **1621** James I calls third Parliament: it votes money for English involvement in Thirty Years War. Great Protestation asserts the rights of Parliament; petition against Catholicism

- **1623** George Villiers, James's favourite, becomes Duke of Buckingham. Charles and Duke of Buckingham fail to negotiate Spanish marriage. First English settlement in New Hampshire

- **1624** James calls fourth Parliament. Marriage arranged between Charles and Henrietta Maria of France

- **1625** James dies: succeeded by Charles I. Charles marries Henrietta Maria. Parliament votes customs' duties for king for one year only

- **1626** Charles summons second Parliament which impeaches Buckingham and is dissolved. War with France. Charles collects taxes without Parliament's approval

- **1628** Charles calls his third Parliament: MPs present Petition of Right, and oppose king's collection of taxes

Charles I

ON JAMES I's DEATH IN 1625, his son Charles I inherited a difficult financial situation. Parliament believed that "the King should live of his own", meaning that money from taxes and Crown lands should pay all government expenses, and also the expenses of the Court.

It was usual for Parliament to vote a new sovereign money for life in the form of customs duties. However, James I had found expenses rising faster than income. This was partly due to inflation, caused by the arrival of gold and silver from the Americas. James resorted to a variety of methods to raise money, including creating the title of baronet and selling it to wealthy candidates.

Irritated at Charles's attempts to ignore them, Members of Parliament voted taxes to Charles for one year only. Charles had a constant struggle to find money by other means to finance himself. Finally he raised taxes without Parliament's consent, but this led to a bitter conflict with those wanting to protect the rights of Parliament.

Below: Charles I shown from three different angles by the Dutch portrait painter, Van Dyck, in 1635. Charles's reign was to end with the English Civil War of 1642-1646. The Parliamentary army, led by Oliver Cromwell, defeated the King's forces at Naseby and Charles was imprisoned. But when he was discovered plotting another campaign, he was tried and beheaded in 1649. The Bible he was given before his execution can be seen at Chastleton Hall in Oxfordshire.

- **1628** Charles I adjourns Parliament. Physician William Harvey publishes discovery of blood circulation

- **1629** Parliament reassembles to condemn Charles's actions: Commons bar door to King's officers. Charles dissolves Parliament and rules without it

- **1630** John Winthrop leads 1,000 Puritan settlers to Massachusetts, in America, and founds Boston

- **1631** English mathematician William Oughtred introduces multiplication symbol x

- **1632** Lord Baltimore receives charter for Maryland colony in America

- **1633** William Laud appointed Archbishop of Canterbury. Sir Thomas Wentworth becomes Lord Deputy in Ireland

- **1634** Wentworth calls Irish Parliament, imposes the 39 Articles on Ireland

- **1635** Charles raises Ship Money (an old tax, dating back to the Danish invasion) from inland towns

- **1636** Charles rules that the Scottish Church should be governed by bishops

- **1637** John Hampden tried and found guilty for refusing to pay Ship Money

- **1638** National Covenant in Scotland challenges King's power

- **1640** Short Parliament refuses funds requested by Charles, who dissolves it. Scots win victory: Charles agrees to truce and pays £850 a day to the Scots to stop further military advances. Long Parliament (to 1653). Strafford and Laud impeached

- **1641** Court of Star Chamber and High Commission abolished. MPs set out grievances in Grand Remonstrance. Strafford executed

Above: An ornate English chair of the period. Chairs in the later 1600s were upholstered for the first time, with rich fabrics for greater luxury. Furniture of the period was also elaborately carved, and had very ornamental designs.

Above: A fashionable lady and gentleman during the reign of Charles I. Lace, braid, muslin and embroidery were used to decorate clothes, and colourful plumes were worn in hats.

PARLIAMENT'S PETITION OF RIGHT

In the first four years of his reign Charles I called three Parliaments and disagreed with all of them. At the root of the problem were money and war: first against Spain, and then against France to support the Huguenots (the French Protestants). Parliament was all for the war, and voted funds for it – but at a price.

That price was embodied in the Petition of Right, presented to the king by the House of Commons in 1628. It demanded an end to: martial law; billeting of troops on people; imprisonment without trial; and forced loans and taxes (raised without the consent of Parliament). The king was forced to accept the petition.

KING AGAINST PARLIAMENT

The quarrel between the king and Parliament continued, because Charles refused to stop collecting his own taxes after the time limit set by Parliament. The Commons passed three resolutions condemning the actions of Charles and his ministers. When the Speaker of the House, Sir John Finch, tried to announce that the king had dismissed Parliament, the Members of Parliament held him in his chair while the resolutions were put to the vote, and the doors were barred against Black Rod, the royal messenger from the House of Lords. Today, the Commons slam their door in Black Rod's face whenever he comes to summon them to hear the Queen's Speech in the Lords at the opening of Parliament.

After this incident Charles did dissolve Parliament, and he ruled for 11 years without it. Like his father James I, Charles firmly believed in the doctrine of the divine right of kings, and rejected the role of Parliament to run the country.

The Civil War

THE ENGLISH CIVIL WAR OF 1642 to 1646, or Great Rebellion as some people called it, was sparked off by religion. Charles tried to impose bishops on the Scottish Church, and the Presbyterians refused to accept them. They signed a Covenant to resist, and raised an army. Charles made peace, but it did not last. He had to summon Parliament to obtain money to pay for his army, but dissolved it after just three weeks. Then the Scots invaded England, and Charles persuaded them to halt on payment of £850 a day. Desperate, he had to call Parliament again in 1640.

This Parliament began by impeaching Strafford and Laud, the king's hated ministers, for treason, and later had Strafford executed. They abolished two ancient courts – Star Chamber and High Commission – which Charles had used to raise money illegally. John Hampden and John Pym led Members of the Commons to insist on reforms. Charles tried to arrest them and three other Members for treason. He failed, and soon armed conflict broke out.

The opposing sides were the Parliamentarians, or Roundheads (they had their hair cut short), and the Royalists, or Cavaliers – because they wore long hair like the knights (*chevaliers* in French) of old.

Above: **The first major battle of the Civil War took place at Edgehill in 1642; the last took place at Worcester in 1651. Key battle sites: king raises his standard at Nottingham 1642; Edgehill 1642; Marston Moor 1644; Naseby 1645; surrender of Royalist headquarters at Oxford 1646; Preston 1648; Dunbar, 1650; Worcester, 1651.**
● **Royalist headquarters**
■ **Parliament's headquarters**

- **1642** Charles I tries to impeach five members of the Commons. Civil War begins (to 1646). Drawn battle of Edgehill

- **1643** Alliance between Scots and Parliament.

- **1644** Battle of Marston Moor: Oliver Cromwell defeats Royalists. Second battle of Newbury: Royalist victory

- **1645** Laud executed. Self-Denying Ordinance discharges MPs from civil and military office. Battle of Naseby: final defeat of Charles, who surrenders to the Scots.

- **1646** Surrender of Royalist headquarters at Oxford

- **1647** Scots surrender Charles to Parliament. Army, in conflict with Parliament, seizes Charles

- **1648** Scots try to help Charles: defeated by Cromwell at Preston

- **1649** Charles tried for treason and executed

Left: **In the English Civil War, it was Oliver Cromwell and his New Model Army of plainly dressed Roundheads who finally beat the king's splendidly clad Cavaliers.**

BATTLES OF THE CIVIL WAR

The king's main support was in the west; Parliament held the east, and London. The actual fighting took place in a relatively small part of the country. But the impact of the Civil War was felt everywhere, not least because family loyalties were split. Early battles were inconclusive: the king's forces had better cavalry under the command of his nephew Prince Rupert (who had fought in Europe in the Thirty Years War). But the Parliamentary army, with its musketeers and pikemen, proved steadfast on the whole against the cavalry attacks. They were also later trained to charge and proved so steady in attack that Rupert called these well-trained forces Ironsides. Led by Oliver Cromwell, the Ironsides defeated Rupert and the Royalist army at Marston Moor in 1644 and won all the north of England.

Parliament was so impressed it reorganized its forces into a New Model Army, based on Cromwell's Ironsides. This army grew to 20,000 men and was strictly disciplined, properly equipped, and regularly paid. It was led by General Fairfax with Cromwell as second-in-command. It defeated the king at the battle of Naseby in 1645, the last major battle of the Civil War. Charles escaped to Scotland but was handed over to Parliament by the Scots. Eventually, Parliament came to the conclusion that it could not trust the king and Charles became the only British monarch to be tried for treason and executed.

Above: **Even though Charles I had been defeated on the battlefield he still believed he should not give up any of his power. He tried to start another campaign by forming an alliance with Scotland and this led to his being tried for treason in 1649. It was Cromwell who pushed for Charles to be tried in a court of law.**

Above: **Charles I's son and heir, Prince Charles, fought against Cromwell in the Civil War. Trying to flee to France, he was nearly caught by Cromwell's soldiers at Boscobel in Shropshire, but hid in an oak tree until they had passed.**

Left: **Before the executioner's axe at Whitehall Palace on January 30, 1649 Charles I behaved with great courage. He wore an extra shirt in case anyone thought he shivered for fear rather than cold. His body was secretly buried in Windsor Castle.**

The Commonwealth

THE EXECUTION OF Charles I left England firmly in the hands of Parliament and its army. For the next 11 years the country did not have a king. This period was called the Commonwealth.

Cromwell had to defend the Commonwealth against Dutch, French and Spanish support for the young Charles II, as well as Scottish and Irish rebellions. Charles II was proclaimed king in Scotland, and the Irish also rallied to the Royalist cause. Cromwell took an army to Ireland, where he subdued the Royalists with great severity. Charles and an army of Scots marched into England, where they were defeated by Cromwell at Worcester. Charles escaped to France.

CROMWELL AND PARLIAMENT

The country was governed by the so-called Rump Parliament, made up of those Members of the Commons remaining when Cromwell and the army had forced through Charles I's trial and execution. It was this Parliament that had declared the Commonwealth and also abolished the House of Lords. Members of the Rump were mostly Puritans.

Oliver Cromwell, however, was the real power in the land. He turned the Rump out, and called a new Parliament, nominated by the Army and the independent Nonconformist Churches. It was nicknamed Barebone's Parliament, after one of its more extreme religious Members, Praise-God Barebone. This Parliament also failed to provide a strong government.

CROMWELL: LORD PROTECTOR

From 1653 Oliver Cromwell ruled as Lord Protector. He was offered the Crown by Parliament but refused to be King Oliver. As Protector, Cromwell made the country peaceful and also made it stronger abroad. He allowed some religious freedom, except for Catholics in Ireland. He put down the Levellers who believed in the abolition of distinctions of rank. Cromwell still tried to rule in partnership with Parliament, but they could not agree and so instead Cromwell used his army to enforce what he thought was right. To maintain his army he had to increase taxes which made him very unpopular. Cromwell died, probably of cancer, in 1658.

Above: During the Commonwealth many people wore plainer clothes with no trimmings or frills. Colours were often black, dark brown and grey. Women wore linen caps. Men and women wore grey or green woollen stockings and square-toed shoes.

Above: Oliver Cromwell was born in 1599. He studied law in London and sat in Parliament, where he opposed the king. He was a dedicated, religious man with a strong personality.

Above: **Charles II (1660-1685) was known as the Merry Monarch. His return marked the revival of entertainments discouraged by the Puritans. Theatres reopened, and hunting and gambling increased.**

- **1649** Commonwealth set up with Cromwell in charge. Irish rise in favour of Charles II

- **1650** Charles II crowned in Scotland

- **1651** Cromwell defeats Charles at Worcester: Charles escapes to France

- **1652-54** War with Dutch over shipping

- **1653** Cromwell turns out the Rump Parliament, calls a nominated Parliament. Cromwell becomes Lord Protector

- **1655** Cromwell dissolves Parliament: rule of the Major-Generals. Anglican services banned

- **1656-59** War with Spain: England captures Dunkirk from Spaniards

- **1656** Cromwell excludes opponents from second Parliament

- **1657** Cromwell refuses Crown

- **1658** Cromwell dissolves Parliament. Death of Cromwell: succeeded by son Richard

Charles II

CROMWELL WAS GIVEN a king's funeral. At this time no one was sure who should replace him – though most people wanted to return to having a monarchy. Before he died, Oliver Cromwell nominated his son to succeed him. Richard Cromwell was a weak and mild man and the Army, still the main power in the land, turned him out. Amid all the chaos, General George Monk, commander in Scotland, organized new elections, and a fresh Parliament recalled Charles II from exile to be king in 1660. Charles travelled from Holland with 100 ships, and timed his entry into London to coincide with his birthday. He was received with great popular acclaim.

THE CLARENDON CODE

After the upheavals and trauma of the Civil War and Commonwealth, people feared the Puritans both on religious grounds and also as a threat to the monarchy. Parliament therefore passed a group of Acts, which were known as the Clarendon Code, named after the king's chief minister, the Earl of Clarendon.

The Code compelled all clergymen and people holding office in local and national government to take Communion in accordance with the rites of the Anglican Church. People who did not attend Church of England services would be punished. Nonconformist prayer-meetings were limited to five people, and their clergy were barred from coming nearer than eight kilometres to a town.

Charles II is thought to have had some Catholic sympathies, but he knew that to keep his Crown he had to support the Church of England. So he went along with Parliament's rigid laws against Catholics and Puritans alike. Only on his death-bed did he convert to the Roman Catholic faith.

THE GREAT PLAGUE

The London that Charles II returned to in 1660 was the largest city in Europe with 500,000 inhabitants (Paris had 350,000). However, health and hygiene in the city had not improved since the time of the Black Death in the Middle Ages. The streets were just as dirty and full of disease and rats were everywhere. Many houses were built closely together and streets were very narrow. This meant that any epidemic would spread rapidly.

FOCUS ON THE GREAT PLAGUE

On June 7, 1665, Samuel Pepys noted in his famous diary that "this day, much against my will I did in Drury Lane see two or three houses marked with a red cross upon the doors". This was the tell-tale sign that the occupants had become sick with the plague. The Great Plague, from 1664 to 1665, was an outbreak of bubonic plague in the southeast of England which killed 68,596 people – almost 20 percent of London's population. There was no cure: bodies would be carried out at night in carts to special mass pits. Drivers rang handbells and called out "Bring out your dead!" They were paid well for a dangerous job. Pepys provides a gritty day-to-day account of the plague in his diaries.

- **1659** New Parliament called; quarrels with the Army and is dissolved. Rump Parliament returns, persuades Richard Cromwell to resign

- **1660** George Monk, commander in Scotland, marches to London. Monk rules as captain-general. Long Parliament recalled. Charles II promises amnesty. Army disbanded. Act of Indemnity

- **1661** Charles calls his first Parliament

- **1662** Charles marries the Portuguese princess Catherine of Braganza; sells Dunkirk to France

- **1664** British take New Amsterdam (now known as New York) from the Dutch. Royal Marines formed

- **1665** War between England and the Netherlands (to 1667). Great Plague in London

Right: The Great Fire of London in 1666 destroyed the medieval city and made 100,000 people homeless. The diarist Samuel Pepys gives a harrowing report of London in flames: "All over the Thames, with one's face in the wind, you were almost burned with a shower of fire drops."

THE GREAT FIRE OF LONDON

The following year saw another disaster, the Great Fire of London. This began in a baker's house in Pudding Lane and quickly swept through the crowded wooden houses. It raged for several days, until houses were blown up to make gaps which the fire could not cross. King Charles himself directed the firefighters and even worked among them. The fire was not an unmixed disaster; filthy alleys were burned down, the plague was halted, and London was rebuilt with wider streets and improved water supplies.

After the fire, many new buildings were erected in stone and brick, instead of wood. Among them were 52 churches designed by the architect. Christopher Wren, including his most well-known building, St Paul's Cathedral, built in 1675-1710.

SAMUEL PEPYS'S DIARIES

We know a lot about both disasters in London thanks to the diaries of Samuel Pepys. He was a civil servant helping to improve the navy. He also had access to Charles II's Court and was a great gossip. He kept a diary for nine years but wrote it in secret and in code. The diaries were then lost, and not rediscovered until 1825. The diary has since became one of the most famous ever written in Britain. Its pages bring alive the London of Charles II with its theatres, coffee houses, horse-racing, gambling and beautiful women.

THE DUTCH WAR

The English and Dutch were rivals in fishing and trade, and when the Dutch started settlements on the Hudson River of North America among the English colonies, the merchants appealed to

Left: A sea battle fought between heavily armed galleons during the Dutch War of 1665-1667. Some ships carried more than one hundred guns. Here a Dutch ship has had its masts and sails blasted away by a barrage of English cannon fire. However, it was the Dutch who sailed up the River Medway in Kent, and captured the royal flagship *Royal Charles*.

Above: **James II (1685-1689) was the first Catholic monarch after Mary I. Arrogant, obstinate and a fervently religious, James failed to re-establish a Catholic dynasty. His reign ended in flight and exile.**

Parliament and war was declared. It began with an English victory in a naval battle of 300 ships off Lowestoft in 1665. In 1667, when the English fleet was unable to put to sea because of lack of supplies, the Dutch sailed up the Medway, raided the naval dockyard at Chatham, and captured the flagship *Royal Charles*, which they took back to Holland as a war trophy.

Other battles were fought during the two years that the war dragged on. One, in June 1666, in the North Sea, lasted for four days. The Dutch were led by their great admiral De Ruyter, and the English fought under George Monk, Duke of Albemarle. Both sides claimed victory.

James II

CHARLES II HAD NO CHILDREN with his wife Catherine of Braganza from Portugal, but he had many mistresses who gave him 14 illegitimate sons and daughters. The most popular of his sons was James, Duke of Monmouth, called the Protestant Duke. Monmouth was a capable soldier, who had commanded English troops during the Dutch War. When Charles II died, his brother James became king in 1685, Monmouth thought he could rally the Protestant cause against the Catholic James and win the throne for himself. But he picked his time badly: James had not been king long enough to make himself unpopular, and the motley army Monmouth was able to raise was defeated at the battle of Sedgemoor, in Somerset. Monmouth was executed for treason, and so were nearly 300 of his followers. A further 800 were sold as slaves to Barbados.

JAMES II AND CATHOLIC PLOTS

James's succession was also threatened by fears of a Catholic plot. The Exclusion movement, led by the Whigs – the first political party in English history – believed the new king would try to restore the Roman Catholic religion. They wanted to exclude him from the throne. From 1688 James tried to introduce pro-Catholic measures including a Declaration of Indulgence which cancelled all laws against Nonconformists (chiefly Catholics). Seven bishops were arrested because they would not read out the Declaration in church, but were found not guilty. The arrests were very unpopular.

● **1666** French declare war on England. English privateers take Tobago in the West Indies. Great Fire of London started from Pudding Lane: 180 hectares of the city destroyed

● **1667** Dutch burn the English fleet in the River Medway. Peace of Breda between Dutch, French and English

● **1668** Charles II's brother James, Duke of York, becomes a Roman Catholic

● **1670** First British settlement in South Carolina, America. Secret Treaty of Dover between Charles II and Louis XIV of France. Hudson's Bay Company formed to trade in Canada

● **1672** England goes to war against the Dutch

● **1673** Test Act excludes Catholics and Nonconformists from holding public office

● **1674** Peace declared with the Dutch. Ex-pirate Henry Morgan becomes Governor of Jamaica

● **1675** Greenwich Observatory founded. Work begins on St Paul's Cathedral, London

● **1677** William of Orange marries Mary, daughter of James II

● **1678** John Bunyan publishes the first part of *Pilgrim's Progress*

● **1679** Disabling Act bars any Roman Catholics from entering Parliament

● **1680** William Dockwra sets up penny post in London

● **1681** Charles grants the right to settle Pennsylvania, America, to Quaker William Penn. Parliament meets in Oxford, but is dissolved

● **1685** Charles dies; succeeded by his brother James II. Monmouth lands to claim the throne: defeated at Sedgemoor. The Bloody Assize: hundreds of rebels hanged or sold as slaves

- **1686** James II introduces pro-Catholic measures

- **1689** Son born to James. Seven English lords invite William of Orange to England. William lands at Torbay: James flees. Convention Parliament elected: declares James to have abdicated, offers throne to William III and Mary II jointly. Window tax (to 1851)

- **1690** William defeats James at the battle of the Boyne in Ireland: James flees to France

- **1692** Massacre of Glencoe, Scotland

- **1694** Bank of England founded. Death of Mary II

- **1697** Treaty of Ryswick ends French war

- **1701** Act of Settlement establishes Protestant succession. James II dies: France recognizes his son as James III (the Old Pretender). War of the Spanish Succession begins

- **1702** William III dies; succeeded by sister-in-law Anne. First English daily newspaper, the *Daily Courant* published

- **1703** Work begins on Buckingham Palace, London

- **1704** English capture Gibraltar from Spain as a naval base. English win battle of Blenheim

- **1707** Union of England and Scotland as Great Britain

- **1708** Robert Walpole becomes Parliamentary Secretary for War

- **1710** St Paul's Cathedral finished. Duke of Marlborough falls from favour

- **1711** South Sea Company formed

- **1713** Treaty of Utrecht ends War of the Spanish Succession

- **1714** Death of Queen Anne

WHIG AND TORY

The terms Whig and Tory came into use at this time as terms of abuse for political opponents. Whig was originally a name for Scottish cattle thieves, but it was applied to those people who wanted to exclude James II from the throne because of his Catholic sympathies. James made a promise to uphold the Church of England (despite being a Catholic) to quieten the protesters. Tory was originally the name given to Irishmen whose land had been taken away and who had become outlaws. But the term Tory was given to those people who supported James II and the claims of the Crown. How the terms came to be applied to English political groups is obscure. But the name became thoroughly established in British politics.

Left: **William of Orange landing in Britain on November 5, 1688. He led a powerful fleet as a precaution but met with no resistance. William's peaceful invasion is known as the "Glorious Revolution," and Parliament willingly offered William and Mary the Crown. They reigned for 14 years.**

Above: **William and Mary (1689-1702) ruled as joint monarchs. They were both Protestants and during their reign a number of Acts were passed which limited royal power. The Protestant succession was also secured by the Act of Settlement of 1701 which barred Catholics from the British throne and also prevented any British monarch from marrying a Catholic.**

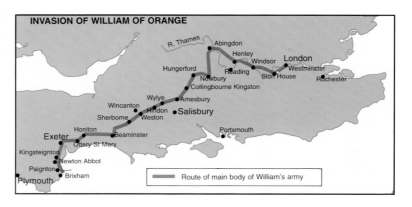

INVASION OF WILLIAM OF ORANGE

Route of main body of William's army

Left: **By the time William of Orange reached London, James II had fled the country to seek more support across the Channel in France.**

William and Mary

JAMES II'S OBVIOUS ATTEMPTS to favour Catholics so angered the Protestants that Parliament invited the Dutch Protestant prince, William of Orange to come and deliver the country from its unpopular ruler. Parliament was prompted to this action by the birth of a son to James by his second wife. This pushed the claim of the Protestant Princess Mary, James's daughter and William's wife, into second place.

William's invasion consisted of some 250 ships which anchored at Torbay in Devon in November 1688. William with his Protestant army landed to press his wife's claim to the throne. Mary had refused to accept the Crown unless Parliament also offered it to her husband. When William arrived in London James fled to France. As a result Parliament agreed that James had vacated his throne and offered the Crown to William and Mary.

IRISH PROTESTANT RULE

After he was deposed by William of Orange, Irish Catholics sided with James, while the Protestants of Ulster supported William. James went to Ireland where he raised an army. In 1689 he laid siege to Londonderry where thousands of Irish Protestants sought refuge. He failed to take the city and William finally defeated James at the battle of the Boyne in 1690. This battle is still celebrated annually by the Protestant Orangemen of Ulster. James fled back to France, where he died in 1701.

Left: Anne (1702-1714) was a shy, plain woman. She had 17 children, all of whom died in infancy or childhood. During her reign science, art and literature flourished.

QUEEN ANNE

The Treaty of Ryswick made in 1697 between England, France, Holland and Spain had acknowledged William III as the rightful King of England, and Anne, James II's Protestant daughter, as his successor. She became Queen Anne I in 1702, aged 37, and was the last Stuart monarch. Her life was full of great personal sadness and bad health. She had 17 children but all of them died in infancy or childhood. Her reign was dominated by the War of the Spanish Succession abroad and by rivalry between Whigs and Tories at home.

By the terms of the Act of Succession of 1701 the throne was to pass to the nearest Protestant heir, in the House of Hanover. Anne hated her German cousins and refused to allow them to come to England. But as her reign drew to an end she sent an envoy to the future George I, assuring him of her friendship. By so doing she played a vital role in ensuring that there was a peaceful change of dynasty.

Right: This tapestry at Blenheim Palace shows John Churchill, Duke of Marlborough at the battle of Blenheim in 1704 where he crushed Louis XIV's army. Other notable English victories in the War of the Spanish Succession included Ramillies (1706), Oudenarde (1708), and Malplaquet (1709). After his victory at Blenheim the magnificent Blenheim Palace was built near Woodstock in Oxfordshire. It was based on designs by the architect Sir John Vanbrugh and the gardens were landscaped by Capability Brown.

ACT OF UNION

The political union of England and Scotland, which James I had tried to bring about when he became King of England in 1603, was finally accomplished in 1707. The Scots did not accept the English Act of Settlement, which in 1701 had settled the Crown on the descendants of the Protestant Sophia of Hanover (grand-daughter of James I and mother of the future George I). There was an unspoken threat that Scotland might, when Queen Anne died, bring back the Catholic Stuarts by making James II's son, James Francis Edward the Old Pretender, King of Scotland.

This threat brought the English Parliament to support the move towards union. The Scots had come to realize that their country could no longer prosper as an independent nation. Under the Act of Union, their Parliament gained free trade with England, and cash to pay off huge debts acquired in a disastrous colonising venture in Darien in Central America. The Scots also kept their own legal system and Presbyterian church.

BIRTH OF GREAT BRITAIN

The resulting kingdom of England and Scotland was called Great Britain. For some years after the union the people of Scotland, felt they were at a disadvantage in an unequal partnership. The

Right: The Act of Union was passed in 1707, legally uniting the kingdoms of England and Scotland. The English flag, the red cross of St George on white (*top left*), and the white cross of St Andrew of Scotland on a blue background (*top right*), were joined to form the first Union flag, soon called the Union Jack. The diagonal red cross of Ireland's St Patrick was added in 1801.

English majority in the combined Parliament meant that measures which favoured England at Scotland's expense were passed. One example was a special tax on linen, which was unimportant in the south but a major industry north of the border. However, the union was in Scotland's favour as it was now able to trade with England's various colonies. After decades of conflict the two countries combined in an uneasy but peaceful alliance.

FOCUS ON THE COFFEE HOUSES

During the 1600s coffee was brought to England from the Middle East. In 1652 the first coffee house was opened in London. Coffee houses quickly spread to become popular places where people went to gossip, do business deals and discuss politics. In 1688 Edward Lloyd opened a coffee house in Tower Street, a rendezvous for people who would insure ships and their cargoes, and read a publication called *Lloyd's News*, which gave important shipping details. From this original 17th-century coffee house sprang the modern Lloyds, the world's foremost shipping insurers. From about 1704 single news-sheets – the first form of newspapers – could also be bought and read at coffee houses.

THE HANOVERIANS
(1714 – 1837)

THE HANOVERIAN KINGS ruled Britain for 123 years, presiding over the growth and loss of one empire (America) and, through exploration and trade around the world, the beginning of another. They ruled through two revolutions in America and France, which shook the established order and laid the foundations of the modern world. Britain itself underwent two other revolutions. The first was the Agricultural Revolution, which saw improved methods of growing crops, better livestock by selective breeding, and the invention of new farm equipment. Next came the Industrial Revolution, which saw the invention of machines to do work that had once been done by hand, and the harnessing of the power of steam to drive these machines.

Brighton Pavilion was rebuilt for George IV from 1815 to 1822 to look like an oriental palace.

George I

Above: George I (1714-1727) was 55 years old when he became King of England. He arrived from Hanover in Germany speaking no English, with two mistresses, two Turkish servants and several German advisers. A shy man, he proved to be a shrewd ruler.

Above: Robert Walpole, Britain's first prime minister, who advised both George I and George II from 1721 to 1742.

THE HANOVERIAN kings were descended from James I's daughter Elizabeth. She married the Elector Palatine Frederick V, who was chosen as King of Bohemia in 1619, defeated in battle the next year and exiled. His brief reign brought Elizabeth the nickname the Winter Queen. Their daughter, Sophia, married the Elector of Hanover. She was recognized as Queen Anne's heir when Anne outlived all of her 17 children, but Sophia died a few months before her, so the throne passed to Sophia's son, George.

George I was the great-grandson of James I. He was also, through his father, Elector of Hanover. This title meant that he was not only the King of Hanover, one of the states of the Holy Roman Empire, but also one of the nine German princes who had the right to elect the emperor whenever the imperial throne fell vacant.

GEORGE: THE GERMAN KING

George came to the English throne with very little knowledge about his new kingdom. He spoke no English: he and his ministers conversed in French. At first George relied on his Hanoverian advisers. He never became accustomed to England and remained isolated as he surrounded himself for most of his reign with fellow Germans.

Only in his later years did George begin to rely increasingly on the First Lord of the Treasury, Robert Walpole, who is regarded as Britain's first prime minister. Walpole was prime minister from 1721 to 1742, and later served George II.

THE AGRICULTURAL REVOLUTION

Farming methods had not improved since the Middle Ages. This changed dramatically in 1701 when a Berkshire gentleman farmer, Jethro Tull, invented the first farm machine which drilled holes in the soil and put a seed in each (until then sowing had always been done by hand). Tull also wrote about sowing crops in rows, or drills, with a gap between every two or three rows wide enough to allow his horse-drawn machine to be pulled.

In 1730 Viscount Townshend retired from government to his estates at Raynham in Norfolk. He improved on Tull's sowing methods by planting in rotation certain crops that in turn absorbed or put back different nutrients in the soil. Previously farmers would leave each field fallow (unused)

TIME CHART

● **1714** Queen Anne dies; succeeded by Hanoverian, George I (to 1727)

● **1715** Impeachment of Earls of Bolingbroke and Oxford, and Duke of Ormonde, for Jacobitism. The 'Fifteen' Jacobite rising. The Old Pretender James Edward Stuart lands in Scotland but leaves at once. Whig Robert Walpole becomes First Lord of the Treasury (effectively prime minister)

● **1716** Septennial Act: duration of Parliaments prolonged to seven years. Treaty of Westminster between Britain and Holy Roman Empire

● **1717** Triple Alliance between Britain, France and the Netherlands. Walpole resigns

● **1718** The empire joins to form the Quadruple Alliance. Britain at war with Spain

● **1719** Declaratory Act affirms the right of British Parliament to legislate for Ireland. Irish Parliament passes Toleration Act to help dissenters. James Figg becomes first boxing champion of England

● **1720** Heavy speculation in South Sea and other companies; South Sea Bubble bursts: many investors ruined

● **1721** John Aislabie, Chancellor of the Exchequer, sent to Tower for fraud. Walpole is prime minister again

● **1722** Bookseller Thomas Guy founds Guy's Hospital, London

● **1723** Treaty between Britain and Prussia, secured by royal marriages

● **1724** Lord Carteret becomes Lord Lieutenant of Ireland

● **1725** Treaty of Hanover between Britain and Prussia. George I revives Order of the Bath

every third year. One crop used by Townshend was turnips, from which came his nickname of Turnip Townshend. The turnips were used to feed cattle in the winter months, so not only was the soil improved by introducing turnips to the crop rotation cycle, but a better supply of meat was also ensured. A Leicestershire farmer, Robert Bakewell, improved the breeds of sheep, and paved the way for modern methods of stock breeding. Bakewell introduced the well-known breed of Leicester sheep, and England continued to dominate the supply of wool overseas. Such changes in farming methods in the 1700s became known as the Agricultural Revolution.

THE SOUTH SEA BUBBLE

In the 1700s many nobles and merchants made money by investing in British overseas trade in slaves, wool and other goods. The South Sea Company was a trading venture formed in 1711 promising profits from taking over all the trade in the Pacific Ocean. Shares were bought and sold for ten times their real value. Eventually the promises were found to be lies and in 1720 the South Sea Bubble – as the financial boom was called – burst. The company's shares dropped in value and thousands lost their savings.

Below: **Thomas Coke, Earl of Leicester, with some of his Southdown sheep. He increased his income almost ten times by introducing scientific methods of agriculture, and turned his estate at Holkham in Norfolk into an efficient model farm.**

- **1726** John Harrison invents "gridiron" (temperature proof) pendulum

- **1727** Death of George I: succeeded by George II (to 1760)

- **1729** Treaty of Seville, between Spain, France, Britain: Britain keeps Gibraltar. Scientist Stephen Gray discovers principle of electrical conduction. John and Charles Wesley start sect, later called Methodists

- **1730** Viscount Townshend begins experiments in agriculture. Edinburgh Royal Infirmary founded

- **1731** Treaty with Holy Roman Empire ends. Dutch set up rival East India Company. Spanish coastguards seize British ship *Rebecca*: her captain, Robert Jenkins has an ear cut off

- **1732** Walpole is offered No.10 Downing Street, London, as official residence; he is regarded as prime minister

- **1733** Walpole plans to introduce tax on wines and tobacco. National campaign against new taxes: Walpole withdraws them. John Kay patents his flying shuttle. George II's wife, Caroline, has Serpentine lake made in London's Hyde Park

- **1734** Jack Broughton, inventor of boxing gloves, wins championship of England from James Figg

- **1736** John and Charles Wesley organize groups of Methodists

- **1737** Licensing Act for London theatres: all plays to be censored by the Lord Chamberlain

- **1739** War of Jenkins' Ear with Spain (to 1748)

- **1740** War of the Austrian Succession (to 1748): Britain on Austrian side. Admiral Edward Vernon (Old Grog) makes first navy issue of rum diluted with water (called grog after him)

Jacobite Rebellions

THE CATHOLIC STUART KING James II had been overthrown in the Glorious Revolution of 1688. But many people still sympathized with the Stuart cause. They were known as Jacobites, from the Latin name *Jacobus* for James. In 1715 Scottish Jacobites rebelled, supported by a small revolt in the north of England. The 'Fifteen', as it was later known, was fairly easily suppressed, and James Edward Stuart, son of James II and called the Old Pretender, arrived from France to find the rising all but over. He soon went away again.

BONNIE PRINCE CHARLIE

George I was determined never to trust a Tory government, for he looked upon all Tories, who supported hereditary kingship, as being Jacobites.

In 1745, during the reign of George II, the Jabobites tried again. The Old Pretender's son, Charles Edward Stuart, the Young Pretender or Bonnie Prince Charlie, arrived in Scotland to raise his standard on his father's behalf. Only a few of the clans rose to join him.

At first Charles Edward and his men were successful. They captured Edinburgh and then marched south into England as far as Derby. The news of his arrival there caused a financial panic in London, but it was needless: Charles, finding no support for his cause in England, was already retreating.

Above: Charles Edward Stuart (1720-1788) was the last serious Stuart contender for the British throne. He was a handsome young prince and known as Bonnie Prince Charlie. He was also called the Young Pretender, to distinguish him from his father who was known as the Old Pretender. But when Charles Edward died, aged 67, he had not fulfilled the promise of his earlier years.

Right: In 1715 at the battle of Sheriffmuir, 10,000 Jacobite troops led by the Earl of Mar fought against 4,000 English troops led by the Duke of Argyll. Both sides claimed it as a victory. Later that year the English Jacobites surrendered at Preston in Lancashire.

THE BATTLE OF CULLODEN

On April 15, 1746, Jacobite clansmen supporting the Young Pretender were severely beaten at the battle of Culloden, a fight which lasted only half an hour. William, Duke of Cumberland, George II's son, pursued the Scottish troops without mercy. Charles escaped to France and stern action was taken against the Highlanders. Many chiefs were executed and the clans were banned from wearing tartan or playing bagpipes.

FLORA MACDONALD

After the disaster of Culloden Moor, Charles Edward was a wanted man, hunted throughout the Highlands. But although the government put a price of £30,000 on his head, a great fortune in those days, none of the clansmen of the western Highlands betrayed him. Charles remained a fugitive for five months before a French ship picked him up and took him to safety.

During this time Charles was aided by many people, including Flora Macdonald, who became a Scottish heroine. She helped him to travel to the island of Skye disguised as her Irish maid. Flora was later arrested and jailed in the Tower of London, but was later freed by an Act of Indemnity in 1747. She married, and emigrated to North Carolina in America. Flora Macdonald eventually returned to Scotland in 1779.

Left: Jacobite surrender at Preston marked the end of the 'Fifteen' rebellion.

Below left: In the 'Fifteen' rebellion, battles were fought at Sheriffmuir and Preston. The 'Forty-five' rebellion saw battles at Prestonpans, Falkirk and Culloden.

Below right: At the battle of Culloden in 1746, the Jacobites were defeated by English troops led by the Duke of Cumberland.

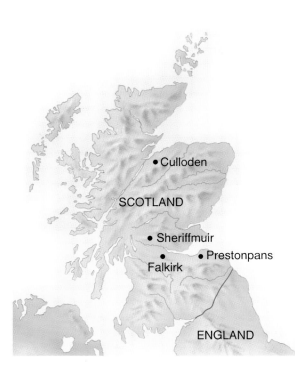

FOCUS ON THE BANK OF ENGLAND

Originally established to help finance the wars against the French in 1694, the Bank of England became a stable source of money for the government. Until George II's reign it was located in the Grocer's Hall, east London. It moved to its current site at Threadneedle Street in the City of London in 1734.

Above: George II (1727-1760) was advised by prime minister Robert Walpole (who had also served George I), and later by William Pitt, the Elder, whose skills he came to appreciate, especially with victory in the Seven Years War.

George II

GEORGE II SUCCEEDED his father in 1727 but, unlike his father, George could speak English. He was well advised by Robert Walpole, the first British prime minister, for the first 15 years of his reign. He was also influenced by his wife, Queen Caroline.

George had been a soldier all his life, serving under the Duke of Marlborough at the battle of Oudenarde in 1708 when Britain was dragged into a series of European wars. At the age of 60 he commanded the English and Hanoverian forces that won the battle of Dettingen in 1743, in the War of the Austrian Succession. George II was the last English monarch to appear on a battlefield.

George II's reign also saw the end of the Jacobite Rebellions and the start of the Seven Years War.

THE SEVEN YEARS WAR

The Seven Years War (1756-1763) was a conflict fought worldwide. It was fought between Britain and France for colonial possessions in America and India; and between Prussia, supported by Britain and Hanover, against an alliance of Austria, France, Russia and Sweden in Europe. Spain became involved as an ally of France.

The British conduct of the war was masterminded by the prime minister, William Pitt. He was known as Pitt the Elder to distinguish him from his son, William Pitt the Younger (also a prime minister).

Above: **Joseph Brant (1742-1807) was a Mohawk. When he was 12 years old he fought with the British against the French in North America in the war of 1754 over disputed boundaries. His Mohawk name was Thayendanega, but when he became friends with an English official he was given an English name and education.**

- **1750** First local cricket club formed at Hambledon, Hampshire. Jockey Club founded. Westminster Bridge completed

- **1751** Calendar change: January 1 declared to be New Year's Day in England (it was previously March 25), as in Scotland and the rest of Europe. Frederick, Prince of Wales, dies. Robert Clive leads British troops to victory against French at Arcot in India

- **1752** Britain adopts Gregorian Calendar: 11 days are dropped

- **1753** Surveyor George Washington is posted to drive the French out of Ohio, America. Newmarket races established

- **1754** French and British at war over boundaries in North America. Washington surrenders to French at Fort Necessity

- **1755** Royal and Ancient Golf Club, St Andrews, founded. French defeat British at Fort Duquesne (now Pittsburgh). Samuel Johnson publishes his great *Dictionary*

- **1756** Black Hole of Calcutta: many Britons are imprisoned in tiny room; 123 die. Seven Years War against France begins

- **1757** Robert Clive defeats ruler of Bengal at Plassey, and retakes Calcutta. Sankey Navigation canal built, linking St Helens coalfield to Mersey

- **1758** George Washington takes Fort Duquesne (Pittsburgh). Robert Clive becomes Governor of Bengal

- **1759** Battle of Quebec: British conquer Canada. British Museum opens

- **1759-64** Bridgewater Canal built

- **1760** Death of George II: succeeded by grandson, George III (to 1820). Clive leaves India; becomes Member of Parliament

Left: An English official in India is transported by elephant, and accompanied by an armed Indian escort. The British extended their influence in India after the East India Company's army fought the French with their Indian allies. In 1757 Robert Clive, an employee of the company, led the army to victory at Plassey against the Indian ruler of Bengal which was one of the richest areas of India. Clive later became Governor of Bengal and helped to establish British rule in India.

Pitt the Elder was rewarded for his successes in the war with the title Earl of Chatham.

The Seven Years War spilled over into North America with border disputes between British and French colonies. These conflicts are often called the French and Indian Wars. The French had early successes, but were decisively beaten when a British force under General James Wolfe captured the French city of Quebec in a night assault in 1759. The battle lasted less than 15 minutes – Wolfe and the French commander, the Marquis de Montcalm, were both killed – but victory against the French helped to secure Canada for the British empire.

CLIVE AND INDIA

The Seven Years War extended to India where the British East India Company had much influence. The company had been formed originally in 1600 to compete with the Dutch East India company for the spice trade. But it was later given the right to govern over British subjects in its overseas posts and make treaties with non-Christian powers, such as the various Indian rulers called Moguls. The East India Company's soldiers, commanded by one of its clerks, Robert Clive, fought against the French in India, capturing and holding the city of Arcot in 1751.

At Arcot Clive and his English army, with the added help of some Indian soldiers, resisted a siege for 53 days before the French finally gave up. This marked a turning point in the struggle between the French and English in India.

THE BLACK HOLE OF CALCUTTA

During the Seven Years War, Siraj-ud Daulah, the Nawab (ruler) of Bengal, tried to oust the French and the British from India. He began by capturing Calcutta from the British. In 1756 he took 146 prisoners, who were herded into a room about 4.5 by 5.5 metres. It was extremely hot and badly ventilated and only 23 of the prisoners came out alive. Clive, with an army of 3,000 men, defeated the Nawab at the battle of Plassey in 1757. Bengal passed into British rule.

THE PEACE OF PARIS

The Peace of Paris, signed on February 3, 1763, finally ended the Seven Years War between England and France for overseas territories, and restored various islands and coastal forts to their former owners. France lost all but a few small bases in India and, in North America, all of Canada and possessions east of the River Mississippi. From Spain, Britain gained Florida.

The Industrial Revolution

Left: The first steam engines were invented to drive pumps which could prevent flooding in mine pits. One of the most successful was invented by Thomas Newcomen in 1712. His engine was slow and noisy but the miners were thankful for it, and improvements were made to make the engines pump more quickly.

FROM THE 1730s manufacturing in England went through many changes. Before then most people worked on the land or at home, producing goods by hand or using simple machines worked by human or animal strength. All this changed dramatically with the invention of larger machines driven by water wheels and windmills and later by steam power.

The first steam engines were developed in the early 1700s and were used mainly for pumping water out of mines. In 1782 James Watt invented a steam engine which could drive the new machines being used mainly to help produce cotton and other textiles. Factories were built to help increase production. This change was called the Industrial Revolution, a process which continued well into the 20th century until the arrival of new technologies.

Left: During the Industrial Revolution many factories were built very quickly in the developing industrial centres. The ever-increasing drive to manufacture goods created appalling working conditions. In the textile mills, for example, women and children often worked 12 hours every day for a pitiful wage.

THE NEW FACTORIES

When people made hand-crafted goods, such as weaving cloth on hand looms, they did so mostly from home with simple machinery worked by hand or foot. Often the whole family would be involved. Now, in the new factories, people had to work to the orders of those who employed them. Factory conditions were noisy, dirty and dangerous. Women and children as young as 5 or 6 might work from 5 o'clock in the morning to 8 o'clock at night, 6 days a week.

POPULATION EXPLOSION

Between 1780 and 1851 the population of Britain increased from 13 million to 27 million, so there were a lot more people looking for work. Many flocked to the new mines, workshops and industrial cities, such as Manchester and Liverpool.

Before the growth of industry, people had lived in country towns and villages. There were only a few big cities, such as London and Bristol. But by 1851 more than half the population lived in cities, most in miserable conditions. Overcrowding became a problem with houses crammed together in streets with no running water or proper drains.

CANALS

A combination of things made the Industrial Revolution possible. Money for trade and investment was readily available from a well-run banking system. Above all, it was the improvement in transport for carrying goods across the country that really spurred development. James Brindley was one of the early canal builders. His first canal took coal from mines at Worsley into Manchester. It helped reduce the cost of coal and in the 1790s other towns also built canals. By 1800 there was a network of linked canals across the country.

On the seas, wooden and later iron steamships began to replace sailing ships for overseas trade. Roads, bridges and tunnels were greatly improved, while later the invention of long-distance railways gave Britain another vital transport network.

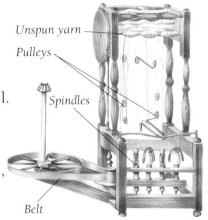

Unspun yarn
Pulleys
Spindles
Belt

Above: **James Hargreaves' spinning jenny of 1764 which allowed a worker to spin with several spindles at once. It was one of many ingenious and complicated machines invented during the Industrial Revolution. It altered work methods that had not changed for hundreds of years.**

Below: **Early 18th century weaving shuttles. On the right is a flying shuttle, invented by John Kay in 1733. Instead of being passed to and fro by hand, it flew on wheels. It greatly speeded up weaving.**

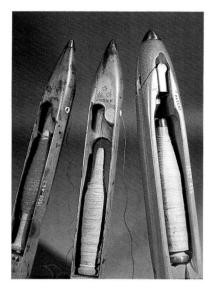

Left: **Canals were built throughout Europe so barges could carry heavy goods cheaply and easily. A single horse could pull a barge containing the same amount of coal that it would take over 60 pack-horses to carry. Canals were also better than bumpy roads for transporting delicate goods such as pottery. Pottery owner Josiah Wedgewood paid engineer James Brindley to build a canal from Stoke-on-Trent to the port of Liverpool.**

DISCOVERIES IN SCIENCE

Modern scientific ideas had been greatly boosted by the formation of the Royal Society in 1662, in Charles II's reign, to promote scientific research and discovery. British scientist Robert Boyle experimented with gases and founded the ideas for modern chemistry, while Sir Isaac Newton made the first mirror telescope and explained for the first time how the force of gravity kept the sun and the planets in orbit.

HADLEY'S SEXTANT

Isaac Newton died in 1727, but before his death he had also suggested adding a telescope to an existing navigational aid called the quadrant. This was to become the sextant invented by John Hadley in 1731. Hadley produced an instrument with which navigators could fix their position by the position of the stars and the sun. The sextant measures the height of a star above the horizon against a scale using mirrors and lenses. Knowing the height of the star above the horizon and the time of day, the navigator could plot his position.

HARRISON'S CHRONOMETER

Many great scientific discoveries and voyages of discovery would not have been possible without accurately made instruments such as the sextant. One of the great instrument makers was John Harrison who succeeded in 1759 in designing a watch – called the chronometer – which lost only five seconds during a two-month voyage to Jamaica.

Left: **John Harrison invented the marine chronometer in 1735. The bottom dials read days, the left-hand dial minutes, the right-hand dial hours and the top dial seconds. For the first time sailors could measure their precise position at sea.**

This was a vital invention because a captain had to know the exact time in order to work out his position at sea. Son of a Yorkshire carpenter, Harrison was self-taught and went on to build four chronometers which are now housed at the Royal Observatory in Greenwich. A prize of £20,000 had been offered for such an invention but the commissioners in charge of the fund would not release the money. George III decided to intervene personally to ensure that the prize money was paid in full to Harrison. Three years before his death in 1776, Parliament voted to pay 'Longitude' Harrison his just reward. His chronometer enabled a captain for the first time to pinpoint exactly where his ship was in the ocean even if there was no land in sight. The first captain to benefit from this invention was James Cook, who called it "our trusty guide".

JAMES COOK

James Cook was the son of a farm labourer from Yorkshire. In 1755, during the French and Indian Wars, he joined the British navy and piloted Wolfe's boats to Quebec. Cook was quickly promoted because he showed great courage and skill as a navigator. Cook's navigational skills were so good that in 1768 he was chosen to sail the ship *Endeavour* to Tahiti with a group of astronomers on board. They wanted to study the planet Venus from the southern hemisphere.

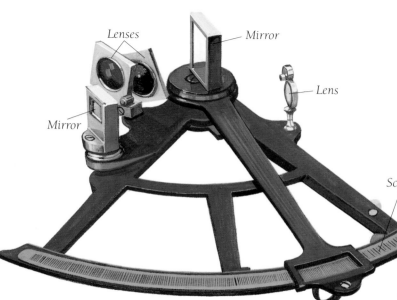

Lenses
Mirror
Lens
Mirror
Scale

Left: **The sextant was first thought of by the great British scientist Isaac Newton but was first made by John Hadley in 1730. It is an instrument used as an aid to navigation. A sailor can determine his latitude (position relative to the equator) at sea by measuring the angle between a star or planet and the horizon, but the weather has to be clear.**

BOTANY BAY

On his way back from Tahiti, Cook sailed right round New Zealand, charting its coasts, and landed eventually at Botany Bay in southeast Australia. Naturalists on board picked 1,300 flowers in Botany Bay that Europeans had never seen before, and carefully sketched them as a record to bring back to Britain. The natural harbour on which Sydney is situated, Cook named Port Jackson, after Sir George Jackson, Secretary of the Admiralty.

FURTHER VOYAGES

On a second voyage from 1772 to 1775, Cook discovered Antarctica as well as returning to New Zealand and the New Hebrides for further exploration. Cook died during his third voyage in 1779. He was killed by angry Hawaiian islanders. Cook is famous for having been the first seaman to introduce fresh fruit and vegetables to the crew's diet to prevent outbreaks of the disease scurvy, caused by lack of vitamin C. His aim in life was "not only to go farther than anyone had done before but as far as possible for man to go".

Above: **George III (1760-1820) was very interested in farming, and he particularly liked his nickname, Farmer George. He also took an interest in science and championed John Harrison's invention of the chronometer, which in turn enabled Captain Cook to make his voyages from 1768 to 1779.**

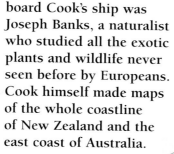

Below: **Captain Cook arrives in Tahiti in the Pacific Ocean. His voyages were those of scientific discovery. With him was a group of astronomers who wanted to observe the stars from the southern hemisphere. Another scientist on board Cook's ship was Joseph Banks, a naturalist who studied all the exotic plants and wildlife never seen before by Europeans. Cook himself made maps of the whole coastline of New Zealand and the east coast of Australia.**

- **1760** Botanical Gardens at Kew open

- **1762** War against Spain declared. Tory Earl of Bute becomes prime minister

- **1763** Peace of Paris ends the Seven Years War: British proclamation provides government for Florida, Grenada and Quebec. Tory ministry falls: Whigs take office under George Grenville. John Wilkes attacks King's Speech and is arrested

- **1764** Wilkes expelled from Commons. James Hargreaves invents the spinning jenny. Clive returns to India to govern Bengal

- **1765** Stamp Act imposes further taxes on American colonies; challenged in Virginia. Clockmaker John Harrison perfects his chronometer which enables navigators to pinpoint exactly where they are. Captain Cook later uses it on his famous voyage to Australia

- **1766** Stamp Act repealed. Pitt the Elder, now Earl of Chatham, forms new government. John Byron takes the Falkland Islands for Britain. Theatre Royal, Bristol opens (oldest in Britain still in use)

- **1767** Tea, glass, paper and dyestuffs taxed in American colonies

- **1768** James Cook begins first voyage of discovery to the Pacific Ocean. Royal Academy founded

- **1769** Richard Arkwright invents the spinning frame. Wilkes expelled from Commons

- **1770** Parliament repeals all but tea tax in American colonies. Cook discovers Botany Bay

- **1771** Spain agrees to cede Falklands to Britain after near war. First edition of *Encyclopedia Britannica*

American Colonies

THE BRITISH COLONIES in North America largely looked after their own affairs and made their own laws. But Britain controlled their overseas trade, and limited what they could manufacture. In practice, however, the restrictions on manufacturing were often quietly ignored.

Trouble began when the British conquered the French colonies in North America, and decided they had to keep a British army on the continent to ensure the safety of the colonies against a possible French rebellion.

HATED TAXES

The British government also decided to tax the colonists to pay for this army. Successive attempts to tax sugar and imports of lead, paint, paper and tea to America met with fierce opposition, as did a stamp tax on all legal documents and newspapers. The colonists stated that they should not be taxed by a parliament where they were not represented.

All taxes except the one on tea were lifted, but an attempt by the British to make sure that only British-imported tea was drunk led to the Boston Tea Party in 1773, in which a group of colonists, disguised as Native Americans, threw a cargo of tea from three British ships into Boston Harbor.

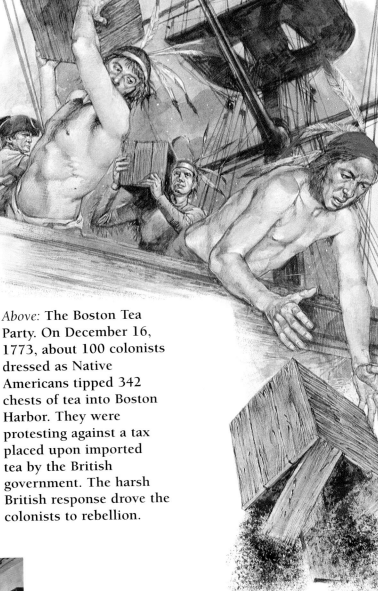

Above: **The Boston Tea Party. On December 16, 1773, about 100 colonists dressed as Native Americans tipped 342 chests of tea into Boston Harbor. They were protesting against a tax placed upon imported tea by the British government. The harsh British response drove the colonists to rebellion.**

Left: **A detail from the painting *The Declaration of Independence* by John Trumbull. On July 4, 1776, representatives of the 13 American colonies met in Philadelphia. The five Americans standing at the table are John Adams, Roger Sherman, Robert Livingstone, Thomas Jefferson and Benjamin Franklin.**

- **1772** Warren Hastings appointed Governor of Bengal. Lord Chief Justice, Lord Mansfield decides a slave is free on landing in England. Daniel Rutherford discovers nitrogen. James Watt improves steam engine to drive factory machines

- **1773** Boston Tea Party; cargo of tea dumped in Boston Harbor

- **1774** Britain passes Coercive Acts to control colonies, and closes port of Boston. John Wilkes becomes Lord Mayor of London.

AMERICAN WAR OF INDEPENDENCE

This was one of the many incidents that led to the Revolutionary War in America from 1776 to 1783. The situation deteriorated rapidly, until the night when British troops, called redcoats, marched to Concord, Massachusetts, to seize a colonial supply of arms. Silversmith Paul Revere sped on horseback that night to warn fellow American colonists of the redcoats' advance. Armed colonists and British soldiers faced each other in the cold dawn light at Lexington, on the road to Concord. A shot was fired – described by the great American poet Ralph Waldo Emerson as "the shot heard round the world". No one knows who fired it, but the war, which lasted for eight long years, had begun.

DECLARATION OF INDEPENDENCE

On July 4, 1776 American patriots including Thomas Jefferson, Benjamin Franklin and John Adams, issued their world-famous Declaration of Independence in which they listed their grievances against George III. They began by stating that "All men are created equal, that they are endowed by the Creator with certain inalienable rights; that among them are Life, Liberty, and the pursuit of Happiness". It was read out publicly and copies were given to most of the colonists.

Britain tried to crush the rebellion. In New York a British army advanced against American troops which were led by George Washington. Washington and his troops retreated. France then recognized the independence of the United States and entered the war, followed by Spain and Holland. Britain now faced many enemies and was forced to make peace at the Treaty of Versailles in 1783.

Above: **General George Washington (far right) led the rebellious American armies to victory over the British in the American War of Independence. He eventually became the first President of the United States in 1789.**

Below: **The battle of Yorktown, Virginia. On October 17, 1781, the British army, led by General Cornwallis, surrendered to the American forces backed by the French. Britain had lost the war and the American colonies.**

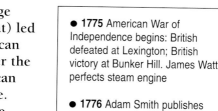

- **1775** American War of Independence begins: British defeated at Lexington; British victory at Bunker Hill. James Watt perfects steam engine

- **1776** Adam Smith publishes *The Wealth of Nations*. British forces driven from Boston, but capture New York. 13 American colonies declare independence

- **1777** British victory at Brandywine. American victory at Saratoga. John Howard begins prison reform

- **1778** Britain declares war on France

- **1779** First steam-driven spinning loom. Spain declares war on Britain. James Cook killed in Hawaii. First cast-iron bridge completed at Coalbrookdale

- **1780** Henry Grattan demands Home Rule for Ireland. Gordon Riots (anti-Catholic) in London. Britain declares war on Holland. The Derby horse race founded

- **1781** William Herschel discovers the planet Uranus. British surrender at Yorktown

- **1782** Spain captures Minorca from Britain. Wilkes wins support of House of Commons

- **1783** Britain grants Ireland the right to pass her own laws. Treaty of Versailles ends the American War of Independence

Slavery

SLAVES were people who were bought, sold and owned by someone else, just like property. The Romans used slaves, and even the serfs of feudal times, who worked for nobles in return for a little land, really had no more freedom than slaves, even if they could not be bought or sold.

Left: **Slaves worked at cutting and refining the sugar on plantations in many parts of the Caribbean. Some slave owners were prepared to work their slaves to death (which took six years on average) and then replace them, rather than feed and care for them properly. Many slaves tried to run away to freedom.**

THE SLAVE TRADE

The trade of capturing and transporting slaves from Africa to work in the new American colonies began in the 1500s with the Spanish and Portuguese. In 1562, John Hawkins became the first English slave trader. By the middle of the 1700s more than 100,000 slaves were being transported in appalling conditions to North America or the Caribbean, to work on the cotton or sugar plantations. At least half of these slaves were carried in British ships which sailed from Bristol and Liverpool. The slave trade through these ports was one of the richest ever seen.

THE TRIANGULAR ROUTE

The route of the slave trade resembles a triangle: ships from Bristol or Liverpool sailed to West Africa with cargoes of iron goods such as guns; these goods were exchanged for slaves who had been captured by local slave traders. Packed with slaves,

the ships then set sail across the Atlantic to the Americas where the survivors were sold at auctions. The now empty ships completed the triangle back to the British ports carrying sugar, cotton and tobacco from the colonies. British traders made vast profits while some twenty million slaves suffered life without freedom.

MOVES AGAINST THE SLAVE TRADE

Until the late 1700s most people had regarded the treatment of slaves with indifference. In fact many wealthy traders and colonists would bring back slaves with them as personal attendants. However, some believed that any slaves brought back to Britain were automatically emancipated (made free). By the end of the 1700s people, especially those who followed simple Christian beliefs, saw how cruel the slave trade was and denounced it.

WILLIAM WILBERFORCE

A society to suppress slavery was formed by William Wilberforce in 1787. Wilberforce was the Member of Parliament for Hull, a slave trade port, and a friend of William Pitt, the prime minister. Wilberforce persuaded Pitt to appoint a committee to look into conditions on board the slave ships. The results of the inquiry opened people's eyes to the horrors of slavery.

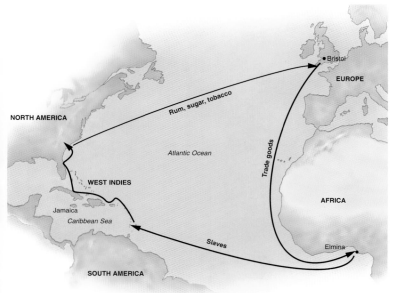

Left: **The slave trade triangle. British goods were traded for African slaves. Slaves transported to America produced raw materials, such as cotton, tobacco and sugar-cane for use by British factories.**

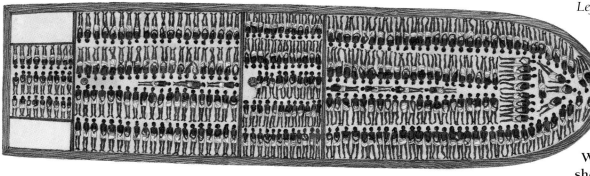

Left and below: Plans of the cruelly cramped conditions in which slaves were stowed on ships for the Atlantic run. The slaves could hardly move and were manacled in irons. William Wilberforce showed such plans to convince Parliament of the need to end the slave trade.

Above: **William Wilberforce (1759-1833) fought for the abolition of slavery as a Member of Parliament. The slave trade was finally banned in 1807 in the British empire.**

● **1783** Portland's coalition government is defeated: William Pitt the Younger forms a ministry. First paddle steamer crosses the English Channel

● **1784** General Election: Pitt wins a large majority in the House of Commons. India Act controls the East India Company

● **1785** Warren Hastings is recalled from India for bad administration. First balloon crossing of the English Channel. *Daily Universal Register* (now called *The Times*) is launched

● **1787** Sierra Leone founded as settlement for freed slaves. Edmund Burke impeaches Warren Hastings (trial 1788-1795)

THE CASE OF JAMES SOMERSET

Another turning point in people's attitudes to slavery came when Granville Sharp fought in the courts to maintain that "as soon as any slave sets his foot on English ground, he becomes free". He selected the case of James Somerset, a slave from Virginia, to contest. The case was decided in favour of Somerset. At a stroke 14,000 people who were held as slaves in England were set free.

ABOLITION OF THE SLAVE TRADE

In Parliament, Wilberforce continued his campaign to halt the slave trade. Members of Parliament Charles James Fox and Lord Grenville passed a resolution in favour of abolishing the slave trade. The abolition of slavery became law in 1807. But employers and traders in the West Indies still wanted slaves and the trade continued secretly.

FREEDOM FROM SLAVERY

Wilberforce and his supporters formed the Anti-Slavery Society in 1823 to continue trying to ban slavery altogether. He began another long campaign to ban people from owning slaves, which would help ensure the end of any trading in slaves. While Wilberforce was ill and close to death, the Emancipation Act of 1833 was passed which ensured that slaves in the colonies would be freed. But it was not fully effective until the end of the 1830s. Former slave-owners in the British empire were paid £20,000,000 compensation. France and Holland passed similar acts. But slavery was not abolished in America until 1863.

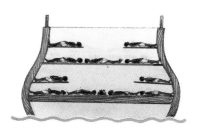

Below: **Slaves working the treadmill in a Caribbean sugar plantation in the 1700s. They did this day in and day out and were whipped if they did not work hard enough. It is not surprising that many died from ill-treatment.**

Revolutionary Years

GEORGE II'S GRANDSON became George III in 1760. He was the first Hanoverian king to be born and educated in England. He was to reign for 60 years, but from 1811 to 1820 he suffered such poor mental health that his son ruled as Prince Regent. George's reign witnessed great political and social upheavals.

WILKES AND LIBERTY

George's first prime minister, Lord Bute, was unpopular and faced the challenge of John Wilkes, a Member of Parliament, calling for freedom of speech. Wilkes attacked Bute and the king in his newspaper, *The North Briton*. For this Wilkes was sent to the Tower. A court judged that his privileges as a Member of Parliament exempted him from imprisonment except for treason or felony, and he was freed.

Wilkes's enemies had him expelled from the House of Commons, and he was tried in his absence for libel and outlawed. With the watchword of "Wilkes and Liberty!" he was twice more elected and expelled. Wilkes was also a keen supporter of the American colonists, again attacking the king and his ministers at every opportunity. Wilkes then turned to local government, and became alderman, sheriff and later Lord Mayor of London. In 1774 he was yet again elected to Parliament, and this time held his seat for 16 years. He died in 1797.

Below: **On July 14, 1789, the people of Paris attacked the Bastille, a fortified prison. The British government feared that revolutionary fervour would sweep into Britain.**

THE RIGHTS OF MAN

One of the leading revolutionaries of the 18th century was the agitator and pamphleteer, Thomas Paine. He was a friend of Benjamin Franklin, and went to America. There he wrote many pamphlets, including *Common Sense*.

Above: **The guillotine, used during the French Revolution was nicknamed the national razor. It was invented by Dr Guillotin, a physician, in 1789. In Paris alone, 2,690 victims were guillotined in 1793 during the time called the Reign of Terror, while across France 40,000 died.**

This pamphlet recommended the separation of the American colonies from Britain. Paine also served in the revolutionary forces. In 1787 he went to France, returning to England in 1791 to write *The Rights of Man*, a defence of the French Revolution which had begun in 1789.

Paine was promptly accused of treason, but before he could be tried he escaped to France. There he was made a French citizen, and served in the Convention. His outspokenness landed him in jail. He later returned to America in 1802, where he died in 1809 aged 72.

REVOLUTIONARY WARS

The French Revolution of 1789 was regarded with fear by many British politicians, because they thought the revolutionary movement might spread to Britain. The execution of the French monarch, Louis XVI, and his queen Marie Antoinette, in 1793, led Britain to became part of a coalition with Austria, Prussia, Spain, Portugal, Sardinia and the Netherlands against France. From 1793 to 1802 the French armies had many victories on land.

THE PRESS GANG

Although Britain depended on the navy for its safety, the sailors who served in its ships were treated very badly. This was the era of the cat-o'-nine-tails and ship's biscuits (which were often infested with beetles called weevils). Few men were willing to volunteer to join, so naval captains were allowed to send out groups of sailors called press gangs to drag any men between the ages of 18 to 55 on board their ships against their will. They were then forced to serve in the king's navy. This was known as impressment. Most sailors were conscripted by the press gangs. Once trained, their pay was only a few pence a day for ordinary seamen.

THE NAVAL MUTINIES

In 1797 the sailors serving in the fleet which was anchored at Spithead mutinied. They had asked for better pay and food, and the dismissal of about a hundred officers whom they considered too severe. After some negotiation their demands were met. The fleet at the Nore, near Sheerness on the River Thames, also mutinied, but their demands were more extreme. They did not get their way, and several of the ringleaders were hanged.

Above: **Sailors haul down the red flag on the *Royal George* during the Spithead Mutiny of 1797. They refused to set sail again unless they were given one shilling (5p) a day more and better conditions. Agreement was finally reached.**

MUTINY ON *THE BOUNTY*

Another very famous mutiny took place in 1789 on board the British ship HMS *Bounty* far away in the Pacific Ocean. The ship was captained by William Bligh to collect a cargo of breadfruit plants from Tahiti in the south Pacific. The crew enjoyed their stay at Tahiti and hated Bligh who was extremely harsh. Led by Fletcher Christian, they rebelled against Bligh rather than sail on.

Bligh and 18 loyal crew were set adrift on an open boat with no map and very little water. Bligh survived a journey of 7,000 kilometres. Several of the mutineers were executed but the rest eventually settled on the remote Pitcairn Island where some descendants still live today.

The Napoleonic Wars

THE BRITISH FLEET under Horatio Nelson finally destroyed the French navy at the battle of the Nile in 1798. At the battle of Copenhagen in 1801, Nelson was in desperate danger and was ordered to withdraw by his commander, but he put the telescope to his blind eye (which he had lost in a sea battle off Corsica) saying: "I really do not see the signal". He went on to destroy the Danish fleet, who were allied with the French.

During the French Wars from 1793 to 1802, one of the world's most famous generals had emerged from France, the Corsica-born Napoleon Bonaparte. Napoleon became Consul, then Emperor of France, and from 1803 to 1815 the wars between France and Britain and allied countries became known as the Napoleonic Wars.

Right: **Admiral Horatio Nelson (1758-1805) lost the sight in one eye in 1794 and his right arm in 1797 in naval battles. He was killed at Trafalgar in 1805 and buried in St Paul's Cathedral.**

Below: **Nelson's signal to his fleet before the battle of Trafalgar was "England expects that every man will do his duty", and this decisive encounter stopped Napoleon's forces from advancing to invade Britain. They had been gathered at Boulogne on the French coast, waiting to cross over in barges. Nelson knew that if he could destroy the French fleet at Trafalgar there would be no invasion.**

NELSON AND TRAFALGAR

In 1805 Napoleon, now Emperor of France, made great preparations for invading England. At the port of Boulogne, a flotilla of gunboats was ready to carry 150,000 soldiers over to England. Nelson returned from the West Indies to lead the British navy. In 1805 he won the memorable battle of Trafalgar, but was shot in the moment of victory.

Nelson died a few hours later, after saying the immortal words, "Thank God, I have done my duty". It is possible to see where he was shot and taken below deck on board HMS *Victory*, at Portsmouth Harbour in Hampshire. The life of a wartime sailor in the low-ceiling decks with the ear-splitting din of cannon-fire is brought to life vividly at this museum.

Left: **The Duke of Wellington defended Britain successfully against Napoleon. After his victory at Waterloo he was given a hero's welcome and later became prime minister. He also gave his name to a type of boot and a style of cooking beef.**

THE PENINSULAR WAR

The Peninsular War, so called because it took place in the Iberian Peninsula (which contains Spain and Portugal), was Britain's main contribution to the land war against Napoleon in Europe.

Spain was ruled by Napoleon's brother, Joseph, but its people, and the Portuguese, asked for Britain's help. Napoleon lost the Peninsular War, which he called the "Spanish ulcer" because it drained away armies and money he needed for his conquests elsewhere.

THE DUKE OF WELLINGTON

The hero of the Peninsular War was Arthur Wellesley, who became, as his victories mounted up, a viscount, a marquis, and finally Duke of Wellington. Napoleon's invasion of Russia was a failure, and defeat in Europe forced him into exile. In 1814 Wellington played a leading part at the Congress of Vienna, which tried to settle the future of Europe after Napoleon's exile. Representatives of all the major European powers wished to see their monarchies strengthened after years of revolution and war.

THE BATTLE OF WATERLOO

When Napoleon escaped from the island of Elba off the west coast of Italy and made himself emperor again in 1815, it was Wellington, aided by the Prussian field marshal, von Blücher, who defeated him at the battle of Waterloo in Belgium. Wellington held out with a smaller army against Napoleon by forming his infantry into squares which fired rapid volleys against French cavalry charges until the Prussian troops arrived. The British exiled Napoleon to the island of St Helena in the South Atlantic, where he died in 1821.

Above: **A scene from the the battle of Waterloo fought in Belgium on June 18, 1815, when 45,000 died or were wounded.**

Below: **On June 22, 1815, Napoleon Bonaparte signed his second and final abdication, and was banished to St Helena where he died.**

- **1793** France declares war on Britain. Britain seizes Corsica and French settlements in India

- **1794** Lord Howe defeats French fleet in the English Channel. Britain takes Seychelles, Martinique, St Lucia and Guadeloupe from France

- **1795** Lord Fitzwilliam, Lord Lieutenant, fails to carry through Catholic emancipation in Ireland. Dutch surrender Ceylon (Sri Lanka) to Britain. Hastings cleared of treason. Methodists separate from the Church of England

- **1796** Spain declares war on Britain. Ireland put under martial law. Edward Jenner vaccinates against smallpox

- **1797** Rebellion in Ulster quelled. Naval mutinies at the Nore and Spithead

- **1798** Wolfe Tone's Irish rebellion quelled. Horatio Nelson wins naval battle of the Nile. Lord Wellesley becomes Governor-General of India. Thomas Malthus writes *Essay on the Principle of Population.* Wordsworth and Coleridge's *Lyrical Ballads* appear: beginning of the Romantic Movement

- **1799** Britain becomes first nation to introduce a national Income Tax

- **1800** Britain captures Malta. Combination Act forbids trades unions. Attempted assassination of George III. Royal College of Surgeons founded

- **1801** Act of Union: Ireland becomes part of United Kingdom; Union Jack adopted as official flag. Nelson wins naval victory off Copenhagen. British occupy Cairo. General Enclosure Act passed. Elgin Marbles acquired for Britain. Richard Trevithick builds a steam road carriage

- **1802** Peace between Britain and France. Thomas Telford builds roads through Highlands

- **1802** John Dalton produces his atomic theory and tables of atomic weights. Madame Tussaud arrives in Britain from France

- **1803** Britain declares war on France, beginning the Napoleonic Wars. Irish patriot Robert Emmet rebels: is captured and executed. Caledonian Canal begun. British penal colony in Van Diemen's Land (Tasmania) set up

- **1804** Spain declares war on Britain. Richard Trevithick makes first successful steam train. British use shrapnel against the Dutch in battle (first use ever)

- **1805** Battle of Trafalgar: Nelson dies defeating the French. Napoleon decides not to invade Britain

- **1806** British forces occupy the Cape of Good Hope in South Africa. Pitt the Younger dies. Sir Francis Beaufort designs his scale to measure wind force

- **1808** British army sent to Portugal: start of Peninsular War. British commander Sir John Moore killed at Corunna: succeeded by Arthur Wellesley, later the Duke of Wellington

WILLIAM PITT THE YOUNGER

William Pitt the Younger was the son of William Pitt the Elder and in 1783 became England's youngest prime minister. He was a brilliant speaker and favoured moderate parliamentary reform. But he fell out with the king on the issue of Catholic emancipation in 1801. He came back to power from 1804 to 1806. As prime minister he reduced Britain's debt by raising new taxes, including the country's first income tax. He also played a vital role in organizing Britain and the other European allies against Napoleon.

WARREN HASTINGS AND INDIAN RULE

In 1773 Warren Hastings became the first British Governor General of India. Many Indian princes fought among themselves, and Hastings had to quell the civil wars and make alliances with friendly Indian rulers to defend the East India Company's territories. With little help from home, Hastings was sometimes ruthless, especially in raising money to pay for protecting Indian allies. Corruption was rife in India, but Hastings' actions were singled out by his political enemies, led by Edmund Burke. On his return to England in 1785, Hastings was impeached for corruption, but cleared after a famous seven-year trial.

Below: **This working model, called "Tipu's Tiger", shows a tiger devouring a European. It was made for Tipu, Sahib of Mysore. Between 1767 and 1799 Tipu tried to resist British control of his lands in India with the support of the French.**

FOCUS ON THE BRITISH MUSEUM

One man's collection of treasures from around the world formed the basis of the British Museum – that of Sir Hans Sloane, an Irish-born physician of Scottish ancestry. Besides being a well-known doctor and naturalist, he was a man with wide-ranging interests. In 1753 Sloane left his collection to the nation on condition that the government pay his heirs £20,000. It was a generous offer – Sloane's

collection included 50,000 books and manuscripts, 23,000 coins and medals and 20,000 natural history specimens. Other collections already in public hands were added to Sloane's. The British Museum was rebuilt in the 1800s to make room for the vast collection of treasures now on display.

UNION WITH IRELAND

In 1801 the union of Britain with Ireland, a dream of English kings for hundreds of years, was finally brought about. The British Parliament was all for the union. The Irish Parliament hesitated, but it was a corrupt body, and when some of its Members were offered pensions, peerages and other inducements, a majority was persuaded to vote for union. Only a few Irish Members, headed by Henry Grattan, fought to the last against it.

EMMET: THE IRISH REBEL

Despairing of Ireland's future, many Irishmen looked to France for help. Among them was Robert Emmet. After visiting Napoleon in Paris, Emmet believed the French would soon invade England. He decided to start a rebellion to help the French and so liberate Ireland from British political control. However, the rebellion in 1803 was badly organized, and ended in complete chaos. Emmet was arrested, tried and hanged for treason outside the Church of St Mary's, in Dublin. Despite his failure, Emmet has been regarded as a young hero by Irishmen ever since.

THE CATHOLIC QUESTION

As prime minister, Pitt had also hoped to see a law passed to lift the ban on Roman Catholics holding public office, including membership of Parliament. But here he was opposed by George III. This obstinate monarch, hovering on the edge of insanity, believed that if he were to agree to such a step he would be breaking his coronation oath to uphold the Church of England. To avoid driving the king over the brink into madness by opposing him on the Catholic question, Pitt gave way. Catholic emancipation was delayed for almost 30 years.

As a result, Ireland was at first represented in the Union Parliament only by its Protestant minority, which tended to be of either English or Scottish descent. As Protestants and Catholics were fiercely opposed to one other, the situation in Ireland remained very troubled.

JOHN WESLEY AND THE METHODISTS

During the Hanoverian period, more and more people moved into the new industrial and mining towns, but often lost their churches and beliefs.

Above: **William Pitt the Younger, Britain's youngest ever prime minister, led the Tory government in 1783-1801 and again in 1804-1806.**

Below: **John Wesley (1703-1791), founder of the Methodist Church.**

- **1810** Duke of Wellington forces the French army to withdraw from Portugal. Durham miners strike

- **1811** America bans trade with Britain. George III becomes permanently insane: his son George is appointed Prince Regent

- **1812** Wellington storms Ciudad Rodrigo. British capture Badajoz. Prime Minister Spencer Perceval is assassinated at the Commons. America declares war on Britain. Napoleon invades Russia but most of his army dies in bitter winter. Wellington enters Madrid. Henry Bell's steamship *Comet* sails on the River Clyder. Main streets of London lit by gas

- **1813** American troops force Britain to abandon entire Niagara frontier. The American warship *Chesapeake* is captured. Wellington routs French at Vittoria: King Joseph Bonaparte of Spain flees to France. American naval victory on Lake Erie. British take Fort Niagara. Elizabeth Fry begins prison visits

- **1814** Allies enter Paris. British burn city of Washington. Statute of Apprentices repealed. Treaty of Ghent ends war with America. Treaty of Paris ends war with France: Britain retains Mediterranean island of Malta. MCC first play cricket at Lord's

John Wesley, who had once been a clergyman in the Church of England, changed this. He decided to take religion to these working people. From 1738, he travelled round the country on horseback, preaching over 40,000 sermons in the open air to the vast crowds which came to see him. Wesley believed the Church had become lazy and remote. His followers became known as Methodists because they followed a stricter method of prayer and study. In 1804, the Methodists split away from the Church of England.

Arts and Architecture

Theatre had thrived under Charles II with witty and satirical plays known as comedies of manners. During George III's reign, Oliver Goldsmith's comedy *She Stoops to Conquer* (1773), Richard Sheridan's *School for Scandal* (1777) and *The Rivals* (1775) continued the tradition – all three plays are still performed today.

SAMUEL JOHNSON

Dr Samuel Johnson established himself as the most famous literary figure of this period with his *Dictionary of the English Language* (1755). Johnson was also the subject of one of the greatest English biographies, *The Life of Samuel Johnson* (1791), written by his friend James Boswell. Among Johnson's friends were David Garrick, a great Shakespearean actor of his day (the Garrick Theatre in London is named after him), and Sir Joshua Reynolds, the painter, and first President of the Royal Academy. Johnson's loathing for the journalist and Member of Parliament John Wilkes was well known though the two men did meet and exchange views.

ROBINSON CRUSOE AND GULLIVER

Novels became very popular in the 18th century. *Robinson Crusoe* by Daniel Defoe was published in 1719, and many people regard it as the first successful English novel. It tells the story of a man who is being shipwrecked on a desert island, and is based partly on the true-life adventures of a traveller called Alexander Selkirk. Other famous novels of the period include Jonathan Swift's

Above: **The Elgin Marbles after their installation in the British Museum. They were brought by the Earl of Elgin from Greece to England between 1803 and 1812. They were claimed back by Greece in the 1990s, but Britain disputed the claim and they remain in the British Museum.**

Gulliver's Travels, which is a satire, or biting comic criticism of the way human beings live. Written in 1726, it describes four imaginary journeys by a ship's doctor named Gulliver: first to Lilliput where everyone is tiny, then to Brobdingnag where the people are giants, and finally to a country ruled by talking horses far more gentle and intelligent than humans. In 1760 Laurence Sterne wrote *Tristram Shandy,* a comic novel which expressed the author's own views on life using the technique of flashbacks and with less concentration on the plot.

The writer Jane Austen carried the novel's popularity into the 1800s.

Left: The Haywain **by John Constable (1776-1837), one of Britain's finest landscape painters. Many of his paintings showed scenes of Suffolk and Hampshire country life. His style was to record real places under different lighting and weather conditions.** *The Haywain* **shows a wagon crossing the River Stour near Flatford Mill in Suffolk.**

Above: **Jane Austen wrote romantic stories about attractive heroines and observed English society with a wry humour and insight. Her novels include** *Pride and Prejudice* **and** *Sense and Sensibility.*

THE HANOVERIANS (1714– 1837)

The seventh child of a Hampshire clergyman, Jane Austen wrote witty novels with attractive heroines searching for ideal husbands. Today her novels such as *Pride and Prejudice* and *Sense and Sensibility* have been turned into highly successful films and television series. Her house at Chawton is a now a museum containing many of her personal effects.

Poetry also enjoyed something of a golden age with William Wordsworth, George Byron, John Keats and Robert Burns, the national poet of Scotland, among the leading poets in what was called the Romantic movement. Poets took British people, places and nature as a source rather than looking to classical Greece and Rome for inspiration. They also wrote using a simpler style of language that many more people could understand and enjoy.

ENGLISH PAINTING

In the 1700s a type of painting known as the English School emerged. Thomas Gainsborough became a fashionable society portrait painter who painted famous personalities of the time and was commissioned by wealthy businessmen to paint family portraits.

Right: German-born George Frederick Handel worked for George I and George II. His most famous works were oratorios, a type of opera with choral singing and stories taken from the Bible, such as *Messiah* (1741). Other works include *Music for the Royal Fireworks* which accompanied a great firework display in London's Hyde Park to celebrate peace with France in 1748. English classical music developed dramatically in what is known as the Baroque period (1600s-1750s).

In 1689, Henry Purcell produced *Dido and Aeneas*, often considered as the first English opera. Purcell wrote music for the Church, Court and the theatre.

Two of the greatest landscape painters to emerge at this time were John Constable and JMW Turner, while George Stubbs studied and painted superb horses. William Hogarth depicted startling and often cruel scenes of London street life, and Thomas Rowlandson made fun of society with his caricatures (cartoons).

Left: St Paul's Cathedral, London, was completed by Christopher Wren in 1710. He had introduced the new style of Baroque architecture from Italy, and it would continue under the Hanoverians. Sir John Vanbrugh's Blenheim Palace in Oxfordshire (1705-1724) is another great example of English Baroque architecture.

The Age of Transport

THE IMPROVEMENT OF ROADS and the building of bridges and tunnels in the 1700s and 1800s made the transport of goods and people much easier then ever before. Nobles and businessmen alike invested their wealth from slavery and other overseas trade into general improvements and inventions.

IMPROVEMENT TO ROADS

Most of the Roman roads had been allowed to fall into disrepair and many other roads had become dirt tracks again. From the mid 1700s, however, these roads were mended and new ones built. One of the most remarkable road builders was John Metcalfe, who was blind. He would feel the surface of the road to make sure it met his requirements.

A Scotsman, John Macadam, introduced the tarmac road surface which is still used today. Prisoners and people from workhouses would break the stones into thousands of small chipped pieces of the same shape and size. These would then be flattened with a heavy iron roller and sprayed with tar.

The results were dramatic for regular road users and travellers: a stagecoach journey between London and Edinburgh that took two weeks in 1745, took only 2½ days by 1796. Road repairs and improvements were paid for by Turnpike Trusts, which raised tolls on everyone travelling on their new roads.

THOMAS TELFORD

The most famous road engineer, who also designed canals, bridges, lighthouses and tunnels, was Thomas Telford, another Scotsman. Telford believed that roads must be well-drained and built on a solid base of stone blocks – like the Roman roads. He built the famous road from London to Holyhead at the tip of Anglesey. In 1826 he completed the famous Menai Straits Bridge linking the north of Wales to the island of Anglesey, to carry his road. He was buried in Westminster Cathedral. Telford in Shropshire was named after him.

Right: **The world's first cast-iron bridge (1779) is located at Coalbrookdale. The 30 metre single iron arch spans the River Severn.**

Below: The heyday of horse transport was from the late 1600s to the mid-1800s. Stagecoaches took passengers, luggage and mail over long distances. With improvements to the roads, such journeys were now quicker and safer.

Right: In 1804 Trevithick bet that his steam engine could haul nine tonnes of iron over 15 kilometres of mine railway in Wales. He won his bet.

THE RAIL REVOLUTION

Railways became the main transport in the 1800s thanks to the invention of the steam locomotive by Richard Trevithick in 1804. This engine could move on rails under its own steam, pulling a train of wagons. Trevithick's locomotive proved that steam power could replace horses for freight and passenger transport. George Stephenson pioneered successful rail travel with his steam engine *Locomotion* in 1825. It was chosen to pull 12 wagons loaded with coal and 21 coaches with passengers along some 40 kilometres of track at the new Stockton and Darlington Railway – the first public steam railway in the world. On September 27th, crowds flocked to see the first trial run. A man on horseback rode in front with a red flag to make sure everyone kept well clear. But the loud hiss of steam scared the crowds and made the horse rear in panic! Nevertheless, this episode signalled the start of the railway age and at Darlington, in Durham, Stephenson's early engine can be seen standing on two original rails. In 1830 Stephenson supplied his locomotive *Rocket* for the new Liverpool and Manchester Railway. By 1841 there were more than 2,300 kilometres of track laid down in Britain.

Below: George Stephenson's *Rocket* won the 1829 trials to find the fastest locomotive for the Liverpool-Manchester Railway, the world's first all-steam public railroad. It reached a top speed of 58km/h.

THE WAR OF 1812

The War of 1812 between Britain and the United States broke out when the Americans objected to British ships blockading Europe during the Napoleonic Wars, and also stopping and searching American ships to look for British deserters. Britain announced it would lift the blockade for American ships.

But two days later, before word of this decision reached them, the Americans declared war. The war included the burning of the capital, Washington DC, by British soldiers. It was from this that the White House, the president's official home, got its name. It was blackened by fire and was painted white to conceal the damage, and its name and colour stuck. This inconclusive conflict ended with the Treaty of Ghent in 1814.

THE PETERLOO MASSACRE

Two of the major issues of the early years of the 19th century were the repeal of the corn laws, which kept corn and bread prices high, and parliamentary reform. On August 16, 1819 a crowd of 80,000 gathered in St Peter's Fields, Manchester, to hear a well-known radical speaker, Henry Hunt, demanding an end to the high price of bread and the reform of Parliament.

The local magistrates decided to arrest Hunt and other leaders of the demonstration, but instead of doing so before the crowd gathered, they waited until the people were listening to Hunt, in an orderly manner, and then sent in soldiers and cavalry with drawn swords. In the confusion that followed 11 people were killed and 400 seriously injured. The incident became known as the Peterloo Massacre, a belittling reference by the government's enemies to the battle of Waterloo. The name stuck and the government eventually changed a number of its policies – among them reducing public hangings and reforming the prisons.

PRINCE REGENT

Before George IV was crowned in 1820, he had already been ruler for nine years as Prince Regent on behalf of his father, George III, who had been declared insane. The period 1811 to 1820 is called the Regency period and it witnessed a dashing style in architecture, interior design and fashion.

Above: **A scene from the Peterloo Massacre. The mounted Yeoman officer, *(left)* is shouting "Chop 'em down, my brave boys… the more you kill the less poor rates you'll have to pay …"**

Below: **When George IV was Prince Regent he was a leader of fashion. The style of architecture, furniture and clothes at this time is labelled Regency.**

- **1815** Apothecaries' Act stops unqualified doctors practising. Humphry Davy invents the miner's safety lamp. Battle of New Orleans: British defeated by Americans. Corn law prohibits corn imports. Battle of Waterloo: Napoleon defeated and sent to St Helena. Income Tax ends

- **1816** Poverty in England causes emigration to America

- **1817** March of the Blanketeers: Manchester protesters, each carrying a blanket, demand political reform. *The Scotsman* newspaper founded

- **1818** Canadian-US border fixed at the 49th parallel. *Vulcan:* first all-iron sailing ship is built

- **1819** Britain gains Singapore. Peterloo Massacre: 11 killed when troops dispel mob in St Peter's Fields, Manchester. Working day for children cut to 12 hours in England

- **1820** George III dies: succeeded by Prince Regent as George IV (to 1830). First iron steamship launched

- **1821** *Manchester Guardian* founded

- **1822** Bottle Riots: Viceroy of Ireland attacked by Orangemen in Dublin. Royal Academy of Music founded

George IV

Left: **George IV (1820-1830) was secretly married to a Catholic widow, Mrs Fitzherbert, but this was not recognized officially and in 1795 he formally married Princess Caroline of Brunswick to help him pay off his debts.**

GEORGE IV WAS A COMPLETE contrast to his father. George III had been a simple, kindly man, known to his subjects as Farmer George because he took such an interest in agriculture and in his farm. He had also provided a moral example to his subjects through his virtuous way of life.

George IV was clever, generous, a patron of the arts and a good linguist. But he was also vain, a drunkard, a gambler and lazy, and faithless to his friends and his many mistresses. His conduct disgusted even his close friend, George Brummel, known as Beau Brummel because of the elegance of his dress and his excellent taste.

PEEL AND THE FIRST POLICE FORCE
It was the new home secretary, Robert Peel who helped bring about changes in capital punishment, prisons and law and order in the streets. After the Peterloo Massacre, Parliament realized it was wrong to send the army in to control crowds so they agreed to Peel's proposal in 1829, to set up a police force at first in London – providing it stayed unarmed. Within 30 years the "peelers" or policemen were on patrol in every town in the country.

FREEDOM FOR ROMAN CATHOLICS
The Catholic Relief Bill of 1829 lifted the ban that prevented Roman Catholics from sitting in Parliament or holding public office. The only posts barred to them after this were those of Lord High Chancellor or Lord Lieutenant of Ireland, and no Roman Catholic could succeed to the throne – a restriction which still applies today.

SMUGGLERS AND HIGHWAYMEN
In the Hanoverian period passengers on stage-coaches were at risk from attack by highwaymen such as Dick Turpin (who was caught and hanged in 1739). The law was also broken by smugglers who brought wine, tobacco, spirits, silk and sugar by boat to secret coves along the south coast to avoid customs duties. If they were caught, smugglers could face severe punishments, including hanging or being transported to Australia. Robert Peel introduced laws which helped to stop smuggling.

Above: **Smugglers brought valuable goods into creeks and coves by boat at night and avoided paying customs duties at ports.**

Right: **Until the police force became established around the country it was difficult to catch highwaymen who robbed on horseback with guns.**

Rich and Poor

IN THE 1700S AND 1800S, as people moved away from the countryside into the expanding industrial towns and pit villages, there was a widening gulf between the rich and the poor.

THE NEW INDUSTRIAL RICH

Prosperous traders and business-people lived in new elegant terraced houses like those that can still be seen in the fashionable Georgian spa town of Bath. George IV's Royal Pavilion was an exotic palace with extravagant interiors. It began life as a simple farmhouse and ended up looking like an Indian palace. George's palace helped transform a village called Brighthelmstone into the fashionable seaside resort of Brighton.

The rich enjoyed the new restaurants, theatres and meeting places such as the Pump Room and Tea Rooms in Bath. They ate rich foods such as partridge and swan and drank fine claret wine. Country landowners built grand stately homes set in magnificent parks, such as Harewood House in Yorkshire, decorated by Robert Adam in 1759 and landscaped by Capability Brown who was much in demand at this time. Castletown House, Celbridge, was completed in 1760 and is considered the finest Georgian house in Ireland.

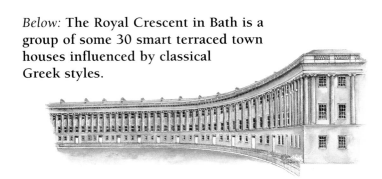

Below: **The Royal Crescent in Bath is a group of some 30 smart terraced town houses influenced by classical Greek styles.**

THE NEW INDUSTRIAL POOR

The poor workers lived in tiny houses, often built by the factory owners and close to the factories so the workers could start work there early. These houses were built back-to-back with outside earth toilets and one street pump to serve the whole row. Children could only play on the street, as there were no gardens or parks for them to play in. A family of three or four would be crowded into one room and slept in one bed.

Parts of the north-west such as Teeside, and South Wales, Birmingham and Glasgow saw the greatest growth in urban housing. The new factory chimneys belched out smoke which created the beginnings of industrial pollution.

Poorer people's food was nothing like the delicious fare consumed by the rich. They ate bread made from rye or barley, with cheese or butter.

Left: **Wealthy Georgian society in the Pump Room at Bath. The well-to-do liked to "take the waters" of this fashionable spa town with its hot springs. This scene is based on a famous cartoon by Thomas Rowlandson which poked fun at the upper classes.**

HOW THE POOR SURVIVED

The poor could only afford the cheapest meat and usually put it into a broth. There were vegetables such as carrots, parsnips and cauliflowers to help give them some vitamins. To help ease their hard life, some people took to drinking an alcoholic spirit called gin which became popular in this period. It was very strong and people became very drunk. They also became violent and mob riots in London forced Parliament to try to limit sales of the drink. Beer and ales were also consumed in vast quantities by the poor.

For entertainment there was the blood sport of cock-fighting or boxing with boxing gloves or bare-knuckled. The rich preferred the sport of cricket.

CHILD LABOUR

Most boys and girls did not go to school but worked in the factories from the age of six. Small children were used to crawl into or under machines to mend broken threads or collect fluff, to prevent the machines from jamming – the work was hard and dangerous. Under the Poor Law, if a child did not have a mother or father or other relatives, they had to be brought up in the local poor-house. Factory owners bought many of these children for a small fee paid to the owner of the poor-house.

Under the Poor Law Act of 1834, workhouses were built to house homeless families and encourage them to pay their way through hard work. These were grim buildings run on very harsh rules.

Above: **The evils of gin as drawn by the famous painter and engraver William Hogarth. He produced *Gin Lane* in 1751 and later painted a series of famous social scenes including the drunkenness and rioting of elections, which were very corrupt affairs.**

Right: **Any family who wanted help from public funds had to enter a workhouse to receive it. In these grim buildings, husbands and wives were separated, food was scarce and people had to sleep in dormitories. Work included having to break stones for the new roads.**

- **1823** Death penalty abolished for more than 100 crimes. Game of rugby football first played at Rugby School. Charles Babbage begins building the first forerunner of the computer

- **1824** Combination Acts of 1799-1800, banning trade unions, repealed

- **1825** Stockton and Darlington Railway opens: the first passenger-paying railway in the world

- **1827** Robert Peel reforms the criminal law code

- **1829** Corn law eases imports of corn. Roman Catholic Relief Act frees Catholics from discrimination

- **1829** Metropolitan Police established by Sir Robert Peel. British ban *suttee* (suicide by widows) in Hindu India. Rainhill locomotive trials: George Stephenson's *Rocket* wins. First horse-drawn omnibus in London provides cheap public transport. First Oxford-Cambridge Boat Race

- **1830** George IV dies: succeeded by brother William IV (to 1837). King's College, London, founded. Royal Geographical Society founded

- **1831** Reform battle begins: Lords reject Reform Bill. Electromagnetic induction discovered. Charles Darwin begins his voyage in HMS *Beagle*. James Clark Ross reaches North Magnetic Pole

- **1832** First Reform Act passed; it gives the vote to more middle-class men. Geological Survey begins. Durham University founded

- **1833** Britain reaffirms sovereignty over Falkland Islands. Factory Acts: no child under 9 to work in factories, 8-hour day for 9- to 13-year-olds. Slavery ends in British empire. First State grant for education

William IV

Left: William IV (1830-1837) was a sailor from the age of 13. He was blunt, tactless and nicknamed Silly Billy. But as king he worked hard and his common sense ultimately led him to support the Great Reform Bill of 1832.

AS THE THIRD SON OF GEORGE III, William was not expected to become king and was not trained for the monarchy. Instead he began an early career in the navy as a midshipman at the age of 13, and later became a Rear Admiral and because of this he was known as the Sailor King.

THE DEMAND FOR REFORM

When William IV succeeded his brother George IV, who died in 1830, he was already 64. William's reign saw a period of great social, political and constitutional reform. The sufferings of the poor and their appalling working conditions, and the neglect of the lower and middle classes from proper representation in Parliament, had created an explosive situation. A second revolution in France, against the despotic King Charles X, led to the overthrow of the French monarchy for a second time. The demand for reform at home was strengthened by this event.

POLITICAL PARTIES

The main political parties were called Whigs and Tories: these terms had come into use in Charles II's reign as terms of abuse for political opponents. Whig was originally a name for Scottish cattle thieves; it was applied to those people who wanted to exclude James Stuart from the throne because of his Catholic sympathies. Tory was the name for a group of Irish bandits, and it was applied to those people who opposed James's exclusion from power.

Both the Whig and Tory parties realized that something must be done to meet the rising resentment about rotten boroughs and the limits on who had the right to vote. But both parties were reluctant to surrender power enjoyed by the governing classes to which they both belonged.

The Whig party favoured some reform as a matter of justice and to prevent possible riots. The small Tory party led by the Duke of Wellington, and supported by the king, was opposed to sweeping reform simply to pacify the people. By about 1835 the Whigs had become known as the Liberals, and the small Tory party took on the name of Conservatives.

ROTTEN BOROUGHS

Despite the upheavals in agriculture and industry, which affected the way people lived and worked, and the warnings to the ruling classes of the French and American revolutions, Britain remained governed by the same sort of people who had governed the country since the 1700s.

FOCUS ON FARADAY

Michael Faraday (who lived from 1791 to 1867) was a scientist who is most famous for his research into the relationship between electricity and magnetism. He was offered a job by Sir Humphry Davy, the brilliant chemist who invented the miner's safety lamp. Faraday worked at the Royal Institution in London.

He discovered the dynamo (*left*) and his findings led to the invention of electric motors and generators. The farad, a unit to measure electrical capacity, is named after him. Faraday was also noted for giving talks which made scientific subjects easy to understand for ordinary people.

Members of Parliament represented the interests of the factory owners, not the interests of workers. There were no Members of Parliament from the new towns that had developed during the Industrial Revolution. Many Members belonged to ancient seats based on only a handful of electors. These rotten boroughs, as they were known, included Old Sarum in Wiltshire, which had no houses, and Old Dunwich, in Suffolk, which was mostly submerged by the sea. Pocket boroughs were those owned by weathy landowners who could evict tenants if they did not vote to their wishes.

Left: In 1833 the first of several Factory Acts was passed which safeguarded against child labour in textile mills. The Mines Act of 1842 stopped the employment of women and children altogether in coal mines. Christian men and women, such as Richard Oastler and Elizabeth Fry, helped to change the government's attitude to poor people.

REFORM OF PARLIAMENT

The Whigs came to power in 1830, after almost 50 years in the political wilderness, and at once set about the long overdue issue of parliamentary reform. Lord John Russell was a Whig who had supported Catholic emancipation and now led the movement for the Great Reform Bill of 1832. The First Reform Act of 1832 sorted out most of the redundant rotten borough seats, and local landowners lost their right to nominate, or suggest, Members of Parliament. The Act also created 455,000 new voters, by giving the vote to town's people occupying property worth at least £10 a year.

REFORMS IN WORKING CONDITIONS

In 1833 the new Parliament passed additional reform acts including the first Factory Act, by which children under 12 were not allowed to work in the factories for more than 8 hours a day, and women not more than 12 hours.

Left: English artist and engraver William Hogarth's cruel and vivid view of the corruption that went on during voting for a Member of Parliament. There was no secret ballot, voters had to declare their choice in public and so they were open to bribes and threats. In pocket boroughs, for example, which were voting areas owned by one wealthy person, voters could be evicted from their homes if they did not vote as the owner wanted them to. The First Reform Act of 1832 attempted to stop such practices.

The Factory Act further stated that children under nine were not to be employed at all. Later factory acts were to stop child labour altogether in all factories. They were also to stop the use of women and children in coal mines where they were employed dragging trucks along underground railway lines for up to 12 hours a day in the dark. Another important reform act in 1833 was the Abolition of Slavery in all the British Dominions.

THE TOLPUDDLE MARTYRS

Another issue that caused resentment among working people against the government and the ruling classes was the right to belong to a trade union. These were the new associations of workmen formed to protect their rights and wages in the new agricultural and industrial work places. The Combination Laws had made it unlawful to take an oath of allegiance to a union. In 1824 these laws were overturned by Parliament and trade unions were at last allowed. But a group of farmers and landowners found a loophole in the law and used it against the Tolpuddle Martyrs.

The Tolpuddle Martyrs were six labourers from Tolpuddle in Dorset who formed a trade union. They were tried for this, found guilty, and sentenced to seven years' transportation to Botany Bay in Australia. But there was such an outcry that

Left: **A Luddite protestor disguised in female clothes. The Luddites were craftworkers who opposed the new industrial machinery which they saw as a threat to their traditional jobs. Between 1811 and 1816 they smashed new machinery in factories in Lancashire. Six years later, a group of workers called the Blanketeers (because they wrapped themselves in the woollen cloth they wove), marched from Manchester to London to ask George, the Prince Regent, for help.**

they were pardoned and brought back in 1836. Five of them emigrated to Canada.

A year later William IV died, having reigned over a turbulent decade when many social evils were abolished and serious political reform began.

Right: **There were many protests against the sentence given to the Tolpuddle Martyrs in 1834. Such protests led to their pardon in 1836.**

- **1834** Tolpuddle Martyrs deported to Australia. Fire destroys Houses of Parliament

- *c.* **1835** Terms Liberal and Conservative begin to replace Whig and Tory

- **1836** Civil marriages allowed for the first time. London University founded

- **1837** William IV dies. Succeeded by his niece, Victoria (to 1901)

IMPERIAL BRITAIN
(1837 – 1913)

THE PERIOD FROM THE ACCESSION of Queen Victoria to the outbreak of World War I has been called the Age of Empire. The British empire reached its greatest extent, covering one fifth of the world's land area, and containing one quarter of the world's population. During this period there were two reigns and the beginning of a third: Queen Victoria (1837 to 1901) was the last of the Hanoverian line which had started with George I. After her came Edward VII of Saxe-Coburg (1901 to 1910); this period is called the Edwardian era. George V was the last of the Saxe-Coburgs and the first of the House of Windsor.

The Victorian era witnessed great progress in medicine and public health, which helped to improve the lives of working people in the industrial cities. Social evils such as child labour in mines and factories were also abolished. More adults had the right to vote, though women were still excluded. The coming of the railways heralded a new age of travel for everyone.

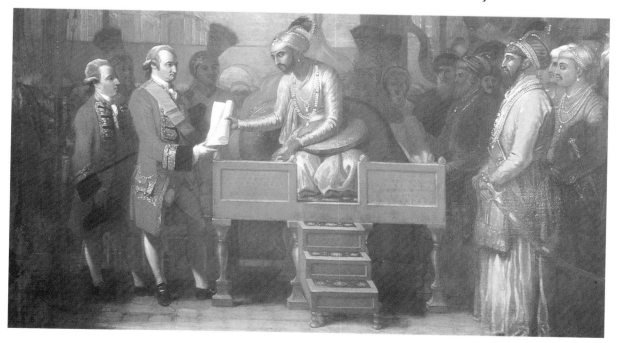

Robert Clive receives documents from the Mughal emperor which grant Britain the right to collect revenues in the 1750s. Direct rule followed in 1858 and Victoria was crowned Empress of India in 1877.

Queen Victoria

VICTORIA'S REIGN saw no conflicts on the scale of the Napoleonic wars or the later world wars, but plenty of small wars broke out in this period, many of them as Britain gradually expanded its empire. Britain was not the only country to build an empire in the 19th century. France, Germany and Italy all gained territories, and Austria and Hungary had united to form the Habsburg empire. The German Reich, which means empire, was formed in 1871 when the German states of Europe, except Austria, were united. The Russian empire expanded eastwards to the Pacific Ocean; at one time it even included Alaska, which the Russians sold to America for five cents per hectare. In the Near and Middle East the Turkish Ottoman empire declined.

Above: **Victoria (1837-1901) was only 18 when she came to the throne and needed guidance from her first prime minister, Lord Melbourne. She went on to be the longest reigning monarch in British history.**

Below and below left: **Victorian men of property were influenced by the fashions worn by Prince Albert, Victoria's husband. He introduced checked and tartan trousers and black frock coats. In the 1870s women wore bustle gowns. The bustle made the back of the skirt stick out.**

FAR EAST WARS

There were three Afghan wars, caused by Russian infiltration of Afghanistan; the British fought because they were anxious to stop the Russians advancing into India.

There were two Opium wars in this period fought by the British against the Chinese. The first in 1839 arose when the Chinese seized opium belonging to British merchants at Canton, in an effort to stop them trading in it. The British declared that the Chinese had no right to do this. The war ended with the Treaty of Nanking in which China gave Hong Kong to the British, who had taken it in the war. (From 1997, Hong Kong is returned to China.)

In India small wars frequently broke out as British forces defended the East India Company's possessions there. Over the years these had come more and more under the control of the British government. After the particularly bloody Indian Mutiny of 1857, all the British lands in India passed finally into government control.

THE CHARTISTS

Despite the Reform Act of 1832, the vast majority of people still had no vote – and because of this no say in the running of the country. Only men of property had the vote. Chartism was a movement calling for political reform. Its name was based on the People's Charter of 1838. Its leaders included William Lovett, Feargus O'Connor and Francis Place.

The six points of the Charter were: votes for all adult males (it would be a while before women got the vote); voting by secret ballot (voting was still done in public); elections for Parliament every year; Members of Parliament (MPs) should be paid a salary and should not have to own property; and finally all constituencies (places that sent an MP to the House of Commons) should be the same size.

CHARTIST DEMONSTRATIONS

There were many Chartist demonstrations including the riots in 1839 when 24 people were killed at Newport and Birmingham. In 1848 the greatest Chartist demonstration of all assembled on Kennington Common to march across the Thames towards the Houses of Parliament. However, the bridges were sealed off by special police. Three taxi-cabs were allowed through to deliver the Chartists' petition.

Despite the peition having two million signatures of support, the movement faded because of weak leadership. But most Chartist demands were eventually met and these helped to form the parliamentary system in place today.

Below: **Planning began in the late 1840s for the Crystal Palace, a huge glasshouse built in London's Hyde Park to hold the Great Exhibition of Arts and Industry of 1851. It was organized by Prince Albert to encourage trade and progress in manufacturing techniques. The aim of the exhibition was to prove that Britain was the "workshop of the world", but foreign exhibits such as American farm machines and sewing machines, and German industrial diamonds, showed that Britain was about to be challenged in that role. The Crystal Palace was three times the size of St Paul's Cathedral. Every part of its structure was made in Birmingham.**

TIME CHART

● **1837** Eighteen-year-old Queen Victoria succeeds her uncle and reigns until 1901. Last use in England of the pillory

● **1838** Manchester merchants form the Anti-Corn Law League. First Afghan War, to check Russian infiltration (to 1842). Lord Durham sent to Canada to report after rebellion there. Working Men's Association sets up People's Charter, seeking reforms. National Gallery opened

● **1839** Parliament rejects Chartist petition: weeks of rioting follow. Anglo-Chinese Opium War begins, and lasts until 1842. W.H. Fox-Talbot invents light-sensitive photographic paper to produce photographs. Grand National first run at Aintree. Treadle bicycle invented. Turner paints *Fighting Temeraire*

● **1840** Victoria marries Prince Albert of Saxe-Coburg-Gotha. Universal penny post introduced: first adhesive postage stamps. Treaty of Waitingi with Maoris gives Britain New Zealand

● **1841** The satirical magazine *Punch* begins publication

● **1842** Mines Act bans women and children under the age of 10 from working underground. Disputed American-Canadian boundary is defined

● **1843** British forces conquer Sind, in India. Maori War: revolt against British. Thames Tunnel is opened. 474 clergy leave the Scottish General Assembly to form United Free Church of Scotland. Steamship *Great Britain* launched. William Wordsworth is appointed Poet Laureate. *News of the World* first published

● **1844** Factory Act: female workers limited to 12-hour day; 8- to 13-year olds to a 6½-hour day. Ragged School Union forms to co-ordinate schools for poor children. Rochdale Pioneers found the first Cooperative Society

THE FACTORY ACTS

Beginning in 1833, a series of 40 Factory Acts was passed by Parliament to improve conditions in the factories where most people were now working. One of the most important Acts was that of 1847, which cut working hours for women and children to 10 hours a day. This, and many other similar measures, were inspired by the seventh Earl of Shaftesbury. He is commemorated by a statue in Piccadilly Circus, London, popularly called Eros, intended to symbolize Christian charity.

Shaftesbury was also a patron of the Ragged Schools, an early attempt to provide education for poor children. It was estimated that over half the children in England and Wales could not read, though Scottish children were better educated.

THE IRISH FAMINE

Although Ireland grew large quantities of wheat and other crops, most of this food was exported to enrich absentee landlords, many of whom were living in England. About half of Ireland's eight million people survived almost entirely on potatoes.

Blight (disease) ruined the potato crop in 1845 and again in 1846, causing terrible suffering. Repeal of the Corn Laws, to allow the import of cheap corn from America, came too late to save people. The Great Famine killed almost one million Irish people, while one million more emigrated to America. The famine, and Britain's slowness to act, added to bitter Irish hatred for the British.

THE CRIMEAN WAR

The Crimean War of 1854 to 1856 was originally a conflict between Russia and Turkey. The Russians felt that the Muslim Turks had failed to deal fairly with Christians in their Balkan territories, or in the question of access to the Holy Places in Palestine. The Russians also wanted access for their warships through the Black Sea via the Bosporus and Dardanelles. Negotiations between Turkey and Russia broke down, and the two countries went to war.

Above: **The potato was the main food for most Irish people. The attack of potato blight lasted three years, during which time many starved to death or were forced to emigrate, especially to America. Many travelled in converted slave ships from Liverpool, in appalling conditions.**

Above: **Many Irish people had to choose between starving or leaving the country during the Irish potato famine in 1846 and 1847. About one million starved to death and another million emigrated over the next five years, mainly to America.**

- **1844** First public baths and wash houses opened in Liverpool. YMCA founded. Cheap train fares introduced. Irish Statesman Daniel O'Connell sentenced for sedition but House of Lords reverses verdict

- **1845** Maoris again rebel against the British in New Zealand. Blight wrecks Irish potato crop. Robert Thomson invents a pneumatic tyre

- **1846** Robert Peel repeals the Corn Laws. Potato failure leads to severe famine in Ireland. *Daily News* founded, with Charles Dickens as editor

- **1847** Factory Act: 10-hour day for children aged 13 to 18 and for women. Sir James Simpson uses chloroform as an anaesthetic. United Presbyterian Church of Scotland formed

- **1848** "Year of Revolutions" in Europe stimulates renewed Chartist demonstrations and petition to Parliament. Irish group led by Smith O'Brien rebel in Tipperary. Irish famine ends, but thousands emigrate to America. Public Health Act improves sanitation

- **1850** Tenant Right League founded in Ireland. Britain buys Gold Coast forts from Denmark. Local authorities empowered to start public libraries

- **1851** Window Tax abolished. The Great Exhibition is held

- **1852** British annex part of Burma. Britain gives New Zealand a new constitution

- **1853** Queen Victoria has chloroform for birth of eighth child. Smallpox vaccination compulsory. Crimean War: Britain, France, Turkey, Piedmont-Sardinia against Russia

- **1854** Siege of Sevastopol; Florence Nightingale pioneers modern nursing

- **1855** Fall of Sevastopol. *Daily Telegraph* first published

Britain and France feared Russia expanding her territory, and sent their fleets into the Black Sea to protect Turkish coasts, and were quickly allied on Turkey's side. The kingdom of Piedmont-Sardinia later joined the conflict against Russia.

SIEGE OF SEVASTOPOL

Forces from Britain, France and Piedmont-Sardinia landed in the Crimea and besieged the Russian fortress of Sevastopol (also known as Sebastopol) in 1854. The allies were badly supplied and managed but they won three battles against the Russians, at the Alma River, Balaclava, and Inkerman. The Russians were held back because a lack of railways prevented supplies and reinforcements from getting through. Disease and bad weather took a fearful toll of both sides. Eventually the besieged city of Sevastopol fell to the allied troops, and soon afterwards peace was made. The Turks guaranteed the rights of Christian subjects, and Russia was forced to give up some small amounts of territory.

Above: **The charge of the Light Brigade in 1854, during the battle of Balaclava in the Crimean War where the French and British fought the Russians. The battle was won by the British. But owing to the confusion of their officers, nearly 250 of 673 men in the Light Brigade were killed or wounded during this misjudged charge.**

Left: **The Victoria Cross is the highest decoration in Britain. It was instituted by Queen Victoria in 1856 and first awarded during the Crimean War. It is awarded to members of the British and the Commonwealth armed forces for exceptional gallantry in the presence of the enemy. It consists of a bronze Maltese cross on a crimson ribbon with an inscription saying *For Valour*.**

Medicine

The cholera epidemic of 1854 killed 52,293 people, while one in 1848-1849 killed 72,000. These outbreaks spurred people to fight the disease by improving sanitation, especially in the bigger cities. The creation of modern sanitation was supported by a network of associations in which politicians, medical men and social scientists worked together to bring about reforms.

It was during the Crimean War that Florence Nightingale made a name for herself as the nurse who developed methods of sanitation and cleanliness in military hospitals. The British, lacking any other heroes in the Crimean War, acclaimed Florence Nightingale as a national heroine.

THE FIRST MODERN SEWERS

In London the work improving sanitation was entrusted to the engineer Sir Joseph Bazalgette. His task was to provide a system of sewers which would not only drain off surface rainwater, but also take household sewage: at that time

Above: **The accident ward in Guy's Hospital, London on a visiting day in 1887. The work of Florence** **Nightingale and Joseph Lister made people realize that by killing germs they were killing disease.**

householders were forbidden to discharge their waste into the sewers, and had to use cess pits, which were emptied perhaps once every year. Bazalgette constructed five major sewers, into which a network of smaller ones flowed. One of the main sewers runs under the Embankment. The Embankment was specially built to disguise the sewers. Bazalgette's sewers have remained in use for over a century.

PUBLIC HEALTH

Edwin Chadwick helped to create a Board of Health in London with the power to set up local boards in areas where death rates were exceptionally high. The boards organized street cleaning, the building of pavements and the development of proper sewers. Slowly, decent sanitation, public water supplies and street lighting (first gas then electric) were to be found even in the poorest areas of Victorian cities.

HOSPITALS

In the 19th century, life expectancy increased more from public health improvements than from medical discoveries. Throughout the 1800s the death rate in the cities far exceeded that in rural areas. The building of modern hospitals was important: Great Ormond Street Children's Hospital opened in 1852, and Broadmoor was built for the criminally insane in 1862.

FOCUS ON FLORENCE NIGHTINGALE

Florence Nightingale (1820-1910) founder of modern nursing, was born of wealthy parents in Florence, Italy. She trained as a nurse against their wishes. In 1860, Florence Nightingale founded the first training school for nurses in London after the terrible sights she and her 38 nurses saw during the Crimean War (1854-1856). There the wards were filthy, with unwashed, blood-stained beds. Medical supplies, food and bedding consistently failed to arrive. Florence Nightingale took charge and by the end of the war had saved many lives. She died in 1910 aged 90.

In 1899 the School of Tropical Medicine was started. Medical pioneers Manson and Ross identified the mosquito that carried malaria, which was of significant benefit to people in the British colonies.

VACCINATION

Edward Jenner (1749-1823) was an English doctor who helped to make people immune to smallpox. At this time the disease killed one in ten people, mostly children. Jenner noticed that dairy maids never seemed to catch smallpox. But they did catch a milder form of the disease called cowpox from the cows.

In 1796 Jenner took cowpox from the infected finger of a dairy maid and injected a volunteer 8-year-old boy with tiny amounts of the virus. This caused the disease to stimulate the body's natural defences. The word vaccine comes from the Latin *vacca*, meaning cow. When Jenner injected the boy with the smallpox virus later, no disease developed. Free vaccination was made available in 1840. By the 1880s smallpox had been virtually wiped out in England.

Left: **The British surgeon Joseph Lister (1827-1912) radically reduced the risk of infection during operations by using antiseptics. He used a solution of carbolic acid to clean wounds and to scrub surgeons' hands. He also pioneered the practice of sterilizing instruments.**

PAINKILLERS

Another important step for modern medicine was the use of anaesthetics (painkillers). In the 1840s, a Scottish doctor, Sir James Simpson (1811-1870) put patients under chloroform vapour to ease childbirth pains. Queen Victoria was given it during the birth of her eighth child.

ANTISEPTICS

In the 1860s Joseph Lister (1827-1912) worked to combat the dangers of wound infections. From reading Louis Pasteur's work on how infections came from germs, Lister developed chemical disinfectants to make everything that came into contact with a wound antiseptic (or germ free). Lister began to practice antiseptic surgery in Glasgow in 1865.

Such advances in science and medicine laid the foundations for modern medical practises; for example, vaccination was later used to fight cholera, typhoid fever, tetanus and polio.

Microscope

Thermometer

Early syringe

Stethoscope

Syringe

Artificial hand

Lister's carbolic acid

Left: **Some of the medical appliances and instruments used today date from earlier eras: the microscope was invented in 1590, thermometers in the 1600s. Lister's carbolic spray disinfected the air during operations thus reducing death after surgery.**

CHARLES DARWIN

Charles Darwin, born in England in 1809, became one of the world's most famous naturalists. He developed his theory of evolution, largely from observations of nature made during a five-year voyage on HMS *Beagle*. Darwin set off in 1831 to Tahiti, New Zealand Australia and South America. The Galapagos Islands lie about 1,610 kilometres off the coast of South America and home to animals found nowhere else. Here he observed that these animals had adapted and evolved to survive.

In 1859, Darwin finally published his theory in his book *On the Origin of Species*. At first his theory met with great opposition, especially from the Church, and he was ridiculed by cartoonists. Today much of his thesis is widely accepted. Darwin died in 1882 and was buried in Westminster Abbey in London.

THE INDIAN MUTINY

By 1850, 200 million people of India remained under the rule of the East India Company that Robert Clive had help to secure in the 1750s. The Company had started as a trading concern but had turned into a government, ruling a huge area with people who had different religions and languages.

Above: **A newspaper cartoon making fun of Darwin's misunderstood proposal that all people are descended from apes. His theory of evolution upset many people.**

● **1855** Chemist Alexander Parkes invents xylonite (early form of celluloid). Dried milk powder invented. London sewers modernized. YWCA founded. Missionary David Livingstone discovers the Victoria Falls in Africa

● **1856** Victoria Cross instituted. Treaty of Paris ends Crimean War. William H. Perkins makes first aniline dye (mauve). Big Ben cast at Whitechapel. War with Persia (to 1857)

● **1857** Anglo-Chinese War (to 1858). Indian Mutiny begins: Massacre of Cawnpore (Kanpur), relief of Lucknow. Matrimonial Causes Act: divorce courts set up in England and Wales. Albert created Prince Consort. National Portrait Gallery opens. Charles Halle founds Halle Orchestra in Manchester

● **1858** Indian Mutiny ends. Government takes over control of India from East India Company. Jews allowed to sit in Parliament and hold office. Charles Darwin and Alfred Russel Wallace announce theory of evolution of species

● **1859** Charles Darwin publishes *On the Origin of Species*; John Stuart Mill publishes *On Liberty*; Samuel Smith publishes *Self Help* – manual on how to succeed. Scottish National Gallery opened

● **1860** Second Maori War in New Zealand. Last bare-knuckle boxing match in England: 42-round draw. First modern Welsh Eisteddfod. British Open Golf Championship begins

Left: **During the Indian Mutiny bitter fighting took place in the cities of Delhi, Cawnpore and Lucknow. The rebellion ended in 1858 because the rebels were not united.**

There were a number of causes for the Indian Mutiny in 1857. Among them was the belief among the sepoys (Indian soldiers) that the British could not have much real power because the army of Bengal comprised five native soldiers to every British one. Also several British reforms imposed upon Indians interfered with their traditional customs, such as banning *suttee*. In this Indian custom, widows would lie on their husbands' funeral pyres to die with them. British authorities also objected to the custom of the throwing of babies into the River Ganges.

The flashpoint for the mutiny was the issue of new Enfield rifles with cartridges greased with animal fat. The sepoys had to bite the ends off the cartridges, and so taste the fat: this went against both Hindu and Muslim religions. The Indian government gave orders that no cow or pig fat was to be used, but the sepoys were not reassured. On May 10, 1857, sepoys at Meerut, 65 kilometres north of Delhi, shot their British officers and moved up the river until they captured Delhi. The mutiny spread quickly throughout the Bengal army.

BRITAIN TAKES DIRECT CONTROL

The mutiny continued with the massacre of British prisoners by mutineers, and the bloody revenge taken by the British, as well as the Sikhs who supported them, when suppressing the revolt. As a result of the mutiny, the British government took control of India from the commercially-minded directors of the East India Company, and thoroughly reorganized the Indian army.

Right: **Big Ben is the name given to the bell in the clock tower of the Houses of Parliament. The bell was cast in 1858 and nicknamed after Sir Benjamin Hall who was responsible for supervising the building. The tower was completed two years later.**

CONVICTS SENT TO AUSTRALIA

In 1868, the punishment of transportation, which began in the reign of Elizabeth I, ended. It was an extension of the older punishment of banishment or exile. The British had established penal, or punishment, settlements in North America to which convicts could be sent. After the American War of Independence, North America could no longer be used for transportation, so Australia was opened up as a new place for penal colonies. More than 174,000 convicts were shipped over mainly to Sydney to spend their sentence in work gangs, for periods varying from a few years to life. Many convicts settled there after their release. Settlers and Aborigines fought over the land and many Aborgines were killed.

Left: **A chain-gang of prisoners in 1831 returning from their hard labour in Hobart, Tasmania, an island off the south coast of Australia. Transportation to new colonies, often for life, was punishment for many criminals until 1868.**

Feats of Engineering

MANY OF THE DEVELOPMENTS in factory production methods, transport, and communications and the growth of urban areas, which we call the Industrial Revolution, took part before the Victorian era, from the 1750s onwards. But these developments gathered pace in the mid-1800s.

The roads at the time of the Industrial Revolution could not cope with the heavy loads of coal and iron urgently needed by the new industries. The easiest way to move such loads was by water. The solution was to dig canals, which were known as "navigations" at the time. Britain's new canal network began in 1757 with the Sankey Navigation, which linked St Helen's coalfield to the Mersey River, and ended in 1847 with the Caledonian Canal in Scotland.

COMMUNICATIONS SPEED UP

Roads and railroads had also become more efficient. Not long before Victoria's accession to the throne, Thomas Telford and John Macadam made well-surfaced, level roads that were inexpensive. A journey by stagecoach from London to Edinburgh might have taken two weeks in 1745, but took only two and a half days by the early 1800s.

During the 1840s trains became the chief form of transport for passengers, freight, post and newspapers – which helped to speed up a revolution in communications. By 1879, trains could average 96.5 kilometres per hour, and cut travelling time even further. A journey which would have taken 20 hours by stagecoach took under seven hours by train.

TRANSATLANTIC TRAVEL

Sea transport was revolutionized by steamships. During the late 1800s, shipbuilders began to use steel rather than iron mainly because steel ships were stronger and lighter than ships constructed of iron. Isambard Kingdom Brunel was an early and major contributor to iron and steam transport. As a highly gifted and imaginative engineer he also built many tunnels and bridges, for example, the Clifton

Above: **The Victorian engineer, Isambard Kingdom Brunel, designed the Clifton Suspension Bridge which spans the Avon Gorge near Bristol. It is 75 metres high and was erected in 1864.**

Below: **Brunel completed the *Great Eastern* in 1858. It was an enormous passenger ship for its time with berths for 4,000 passengers. This ship measured 211 metres long and 26 metres wide.**

Suspension Bridge at Bristol. Brunel built the largest iron ship of its time in 1843, the *Great Britain*. In 1970 it was rescued as a rusting hulk from the Falkland Islands and towed back to Bristol Docks where it was fully restored. Brunel also introduced the broad gauge railway (with tracks about two metres apart). This was later abandoned for a narrower standard gauge.

The effects of the travel revolution by steamer and steam train during the 19th century can be compared to the way the telephone, television and transport by air changed the way we lived from the 1960s.

In just 40 years since the opening of the first public railway from Stockton to Darlington in 1826, a rail network linked all the major towns in Britain. Many cities showed off impressive public stations, such as St Pancras in London, which was combined with a hotel and was designed by Gilbert Scott. The first *Railway Time Tables* were also completed in the 1860s.

THE POST ARRIVES

It was not only passengers who benefitted from this new cheap and quick way to travel. In 1840 the first adhesive postage stamp was introduced – the Penny Black – and in 1855 came the first letter boxes, called pillar boxes, in London. The post was at first carried by stagecoach but the new postal service soon came to rely on the quicker and cheaper transport of the railways.

Above: **Many Victorian railway stations were grand buildings with elaborate ironwork and delicately carved wood.**

Above: **Isambard Kingdom Brunel (who lived from 1806 to 1859) was not only the engineer behind the Great Western Railway but was also responsible for three steamships and several dockyards.**

VICTORIAN BOOKS

Victorian novelists, poets and other writers reflected much more on the social changes and problems of their day than the earlier Romantic novelists like Sir Walter Scott or the poet William Wordsworth. The wretched life of the poor was described with great skill by Charles Dickens in books such as *Oliver Twist*. William Thackeray evoked an image of country and town living among the middle and upper classes in *Vanity Fair*, and Elizabeth Gaskell depicted life in the new manufacturing cities of the north in such books as *North and South*.

The strong and sometimes strict religious faith of the time was the subject of many lesser writers, especially those aiming at young readers. A typical such author was ALOE (A Lady of England, the penname of Charlotte Maria Tucker). Her highly moral tales were often given as Sunday School prizes. Anna Sewell's one book, *Black Beauty*, did much to awaken people to the cruel treatment often suffered by horses.

Above: **William Wordsworth (1770-1850). His poetry was called "romantic" because it described the joys and beauties of nature.**

Above: Victorian author Charles Dickens. His first stories appeared in weekly or monthly periodicals.

Left: An illustration from *Oliver Twist*, a novel written by Charles Dickens in which he portrayed the harsh conditions suffered by orphans at the time. Dickens was a keen observer of Victorian life and fiercely dedicated to social reform.

THE BRONTË SISTERS

Some of the most remarkable novels in the English language were written in this period by three sisters who lived in isolation on the Yorkshire moors. Charlotte, Emily and Anne Brontë, probably wrote to escape their oppressive surroundings, and produced thousands of poems and romantic stories involving handsome heroes and passionate women. Emily Brontë's great novel *Wuthering Heights* is still widely read today. The main character in Charlotte Brontë's *Jane Eyre*, an instant best-seller at the time and still popular, reflected women's growing spirit of independence.

THE CLIMBING BOYS

Charles Kingsley's book *The Water Babies*, described as a fairy tale, exposed a cruel 19th-century practice. Sweeps used to send little boys up chimneys to clean them. Because of the soot, the boys often suffered from breathing disorders. The book appeared in 1863, and the next year Parliament passed the Chimney Sweeps Act against this ill treatment. The practice was finally stamped out by a further, stiffer Act in 1875.

TRADE UNIONS RECOGNIZED IN LAW

The first trade unions, or combinations, came into existence early in the 1700s as the Agricultural and later the Industrial Revolution completely changed the way labourers worked. Unions ran into trouble in 1799 when they were officially banned because it was feared they might encourage the workers to revolt. This was at a time when the violent excesses of the French Revolution were still very much on people's minds. This ban was lifted in 1824, and after that unions grew rapidly, as did strikes against the payment of poor wages and bad working conditions which were common at that time.

Some unions were ruthless in their methods: Sheffield cutlery workers were known to drop a keg of gunpowder down the chimney of a fellow worker who did not follow the union line. However, most unions were just and responsible. The Trade Union Act of 1871 finally made the unions legal, and gave them certain rights and protection for their funds. This law was passed by Parliament – the result of pressure from the newly formed Trades Union Congress.

Above: **A Victorian dustman talks to a chimney sweep and his child assistant.**

The Water Babies **changed attitudes about sweeps using small boys to climb up sooty chimneys.**

Below: **This is the membership certificate of the National Union of Gas Workers and General**

Labourers, one of the trade unions formed in the 1880s following their legalization.

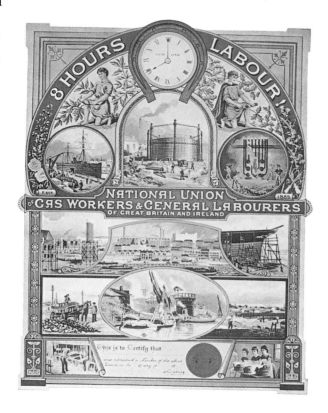

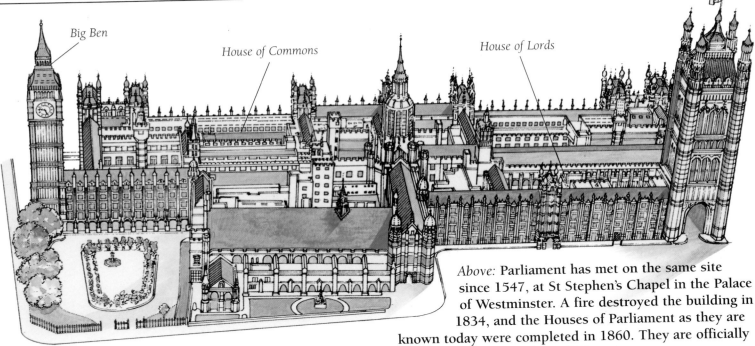

Big Ben

House of Commons

House of Lords

Above: **Parliament has met on the same site since 1547, at St Stephen's Chapel in the Palace of Westminster. A fire destroyed the building in 1834, and the Houses of Parliament as they are known today were completed in 1860. They are officially known as the New Palace of Westminster.**

● **1869** Irish Church disestablished. Debtors' prisons abolished. Slum clearance begins. Clipper *Cutty Sark* launched

● **1870** Married Women's Property Act gives women greater control of their own property. Education Act sets up school boards

● **1871** Local Government Boards set up in England. Trade unions formally legalized. Army reorganized: purchase of commissions abolished. Henry Stanley meets David Livingstone at Lake Tanganyika. Bank holidays introduced in England and Wales. FA Cup competition established. *Oceanic:* first large luxury liner.

● **1872** Secret ballot for elections introduced by the Ballot Act. *HMS Challenger* begins mapping the ocean bed (to 1876). First international football match, England v Scotland

● **1873** Supreme Court and Court of Appeal established. W.C. Wingfield invents game of Spharistiké (now lawn tennis)

Above: **Benjamin Disraeli (1804-1881) Conservative prime minister and outstanding political leader. He introduced several reforms and was keen to expand the empire. A witty and cultivated man, he was especially adept at dealing with Queen Victoria who could be difficult.**

THE SUEZ CANAL

When France and the Turkish rulers of Egypt undertook the construction of the Suez Canal in 1859, which opened ten years later, British traders welcomed it. However, the government opposed the canal as a threat to British trade and other links with India because it created the shortest route to India and was not controlled by Britain. Sixteen years later the spendthrift Khedive (viceroy) of Egypt was short of money, and offered his shares in the Suez Canal Company to Britain.

DISRAELI'S VISION

The prime minister, Benjamin Disraeli, wanted to expand the empire, while his political opponent and leader of the Liberal Party, William Gladstone, favoured limiting it. Disraeli was more far-seeing than his predecessors and the Foreign Office, and overruled the foreign secretary, Lord Derby, by promptly buying the Suez shares for £4 million. He borrowed the money from the international bankers, the Rothschilds, until Parliament could vote the necessary funds. The British government now owned 176,602 out of the total of 400,000 shares of the Suez Canal Company.

By this action Disraeli secured British control of the most vital trade waterway to the East. Queen Victoria gave him support for this shrewd purchase.

Left **The Temperate House at the Royal Botanic Gardens, Kew, built in 1848. This structure is used to cultivate and then exchange plants with other countries. For example, tea from China was introduced as a crop to India through the work of botanists at Kew. The Palm House was built to house the exotic tropical plants that were discovered in Britain's new colonies.**

KEW GARDENS

The Royal Botanical Gardens at Kew, in the London borough of Richmond, began in the 1600s with a plant collection by Lord Capel. In 1759 Princess Augusta, the mother of George III, set aside part of the gardens of Kew Palace for plant experiments, including the cultivation of rubber plants. This garden covered 3.6 hectares.

Kew Gardens continued to expand until they covered more than 117 hectares. They are dominated by a decorative pagoda designed by Sir William Chambers, which is nearly 50 metres tall, that was completed in 1762. In 1841 the gardens were handed over to the nation.

Today Kew Gardens are officially called the Royal Botanic Gardens. They are world famous as a centre of botancial studies and have the largest collection of living and preserved plants in the world. They are also important as a quarantine station for plants newly introduced to Britain and as a centre for botanical analysis.

The Princess of Wales Conservatory, opened in 1987, houses the Victorian waterlily which was introduced from South America in honour of the queen in 1837. Its leaves can be as much as two metres across.

THE RUBBER INDUSTRY

The demand for rubber grew rapidly in the 19th century, but the only source of supplies was South America. The British government decided to cultivate rubber in its newly acquired lands in the Far East. Rubber seeds were collected in Brazil and shipped to Kew Gardens, where they were raised. In 1877, 2,000 young plants were shipped to Ceylon (Sri Lanka) in special containers, and from there distributed to other countries such as Malaysia and Indonesia where the plants flourished. Today southeast Asia produces 90 percent of the world's natural rubber.

Below: **The first bicycles were uncomfortable and dangerous. This Matchless bicycle made in 1883 was nicknamed the "Penny Farthing" because of its shape. It had solid rubber tyres and no brakes.**

Expansion Into Africa

THE INTERIOR OF AFRICA was largely unexplored by Europeans until the 19th century. Africa was opened up by a series of British, French and German explorers. In 1788 the Association for Promoting the Discovery of the Interior Parts of Africa was set up in London, which began to send expeditions to explore the continent. Among the explorers were David Livingstone, Henry Morton Stanley, Samuel White Baker, Richard Burton and John Speke.

LIVINGSTONE THE EXPLORER

David Livingstone was born in Scotland and travelled to South Africa in 1841 to do missionary work. He made many journeys, at first with his wife and children. In 1853 he walked from the middle of Africa to the Atlantic coast. He then returned across the continent to the Indian Ocean. On his way he became the first European to see the Victoria Falls (named in honour of Queen Victoria). His second expedition was by steamboat up the Zambezi River , but it was a disaster and his wife died on the journey. He also explored the Congo River and discovered Lake Nyasa in southern Africa.

"DR LIVINGSTONE, I PRESUME"

On an expedition to find the source of the River Nile, Livingstone disappeared and was feared lost and possibly dead. In 1871, an American journalist named Henry Morton Stanley found Livingstone alive at Ujiji on the shores of Lake Tanganyika. Stanley approached Livingstone with the immortal words: "Dr Livingstone, I presume". Livingstone died in 1873 and is buried in Westminster Cathedral.

THE ZULU WAR

Britain was involved in two wars in southern Africa in three years. The Zulu War began when a large Zulu army of 40,000 men under King Cetewayo threatened the Transvaal. The Boers (farmers) of the Transvaal sought British protection. In the middle of January 1879, the local commander sent a force into Zululand, only to have it massacred by the Zulus. Reinforcements from Britain had to be brought in to subdue the Zulus.

Above: **The missionary Dr Livingstone explores the Zambezi River. In the mid-1800s he made a number of expeditions into the African interior.**

Below: **Until 1880 most of Africa was independent. But by 1914 European nations had divided it up between them and claimed areas as their colonies.**

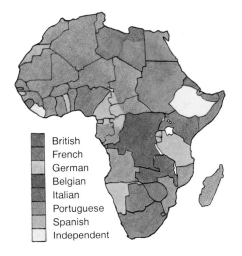

British
French
German
Belgian
Italian
Portuguese
Spanish
Independent

THE FIRST BOER WAR

In April 1880, Gladstone's Liberal government took power. The First Boer War broke out when the Boers (descendants of Dutch settlers) of the Transvaal formed the idea that they might persuade the new British Ministry to give them back their independence, which they had surrendered when they sought British aid against the Zulus. On December 16, 1880, the Boers, under the leadership of Paul Kruger, proclaimed their independence. After they defeated the British at Majuba Hill in 1881, the independence of the Transvaal was again recognized by Gladstone's government, though the British kept control of its foreign policy.

THE SCRAMBLE FOR AFRICA

After 1870 more and more colonies were established by Britain. British governments were especially concerned to take over large parts of Africa before their rivals. Britain and France were first in what became called the "scramble for Africa" – a race to acquire colonies. Other colonial powers included Italy, Germany, Spain, Belgium and Portugal.

The European powers held a conference in 1884 and 1885 to divide Africa between them. The British gained colonies on the coasts of both west and east Africa. On the west coast they colonized Gambia, Sierra Leone, the Gold Coast and Nigeria. On the east coast they took control of Uganda and Kenya. By 1902, there were only two independent African countries left, Ethiopia and Liberia.

Above: **The Zulus are a tribe of South Africa. They defeated British troops at the battle of Isandhlwana in the Zulu War of 1879. They lost the battle of Rorke's Drift and the British won the war.**

Right: **European heads of state attended a conference in Berlin in 1884 to decide who controlled the various parts of the African continent. They drew lines across a map of Africa to stake their claims. Native Africans were not consulted or given any say in what happened to their countries.**

- **1874** Conservatives win election: first clear majority since 1841. Britain annexes Fiji

- **1875** Public Health Act: rules for sanitation for all house-owners. Britain buys shares in Suez Canal. Plimsoll Line introduced to stop overloading of ships: it consists of a line drawn on the outside of a ship, which is not allowed to go below the water line. Artisans' Dwellings Act: local councils empowered to clear slums. Food and Drugs Act controls the substances added to food. Matthew Webb becomes first man to swim the English Channel. Gilbert and Sullivan produce their first opera: *Trial by Jury*

- **1876** Benjamin Disraeli becomes Earl of Beaconsfield. Grey squirrel introduced from US. Queen Victoria is proclaimed Empress of India.

- **1877** Britain annexes Walvis Bay and the Transvaal in South Africa. First Wimbledon championships

- **1878** The formation of the Irish National Land League. Electric street lighting in London. First British telephone company. William Booth names his mission the Salvation Army. Red Flag Act: steam road vehicles limited to 6.4 km/h, and required to be preceded by a man with a red flag as a warning

- **1879** Zulu War. Afghans murder British legation: Britain invades Afghanistan. Worst crop failure of the century. London's first telephone exchange. First railway dining-car in Britain. Tay Bridge collapses in gale. William Crookes develops the cathode ray tube (essential part of early televisions)

- **1880** Flogging abolished in Royal Navy

VICTORIA WITHOUT ALBERT

The young Victoria, aged 21, was married to her German cousin Albert in 1840, having proposed to him in 1839. On her marriage to Albert, Victoria stopped calling herself a Hanoverian and became a Saxe-Coburg after her husband's family.

Prince Albert died from typhoid fever in 1861 and Queen Victoria went into a deep and apparently permanent mourning. Every night Albert's clothes were laid out on his bed at Windsor, and every morning fresh water was placed in the basin in his room. The queen kept a photograph of Albert above her bed. Although she dealt with ministers and state papers as dutifully as before, she made few public appearances, refusing even to open Parliament each year. She was nicknamed "the Widow of Windsor". In the late 1870s the prime minister Benjamin Disraeli persuaded Victoria to return to public life. After her Golden Jubilee in 1887, when she celebrated 50 years on the throne, she was seen in public more often. Victoria died in 1901.

THE BRADLAUGH CASE

In English law, an oath is an appeal to God to witness the truth of a statement. To help people whose religion forbids them to take oaths, the law allows affirmation – a solemn declaration of truth. But when the free thinker Charles Bradlaugh was elected a Member of Parliament it was found that the rules of the House of Commons did not allow affirmation, and he was excluded.

Bradlaugh offered to take the oath, but was again excluded on the grounds that as he was a free thinker the oath would not be binding. His constituents re-elected him three times, and each time he was ejected from the House, on one occasion by ten policemen. Finally, in 1886, the Speaker of the House of Commons ruled that he could take the oath. As a Member of Parliament, Bradlaugh persuaded the Commons to change the rules to allow affirmation to prevent other free thinkers from being excluded.

JACK THE RIPPER

Victorian London was rocked by the horror of the crimes committed by Jack the Ripper. He committed a series of at least seven

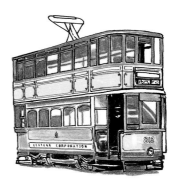

Right: **A double-decker electric tram which became a popular form of city transport during the late Victorian era. Public trams, and later buses, gave ordinary people the opportunity to travel cheaply and easily across towns for the first time.**

gruesome murders in the Whitechapel district in 1888. The ripper's victims were all prostitutes and were all killed in a similar way. Many attempts were made to catch the killer. At one stage a victim's eyes were photographed in the vain hope that the image of the killer would be seen on her retina. But the case remains one of Britain's most famous unsolved crimes.

KEIR HARDIE

Keir Hardie was one of the leading figures in the formation of the Labour Party. Hardie had a tough upbringing. He never went to school, but from the age of ten worked in the Lanarkshire mines. The only formal education he had was at night school. Hardie learned public speaking from temperance, or anti-alcohol meetings and became an active trade unionist and a journalist. In 1888 he founded the Scottish Parliamentary Labour Party. In 1892 he was elected Independent Socialist MP for West Ham, and a year later started the Independent Labour Party (ILP). A few years later he helped to establish the Labour Representation Committee, which became the modern Labour Party.

Above: **The first electric underground railway, or subway, was opened in London in 1890. Steam trains had been used on underground lines in London since 1863. This underground system soon became known as the "tube".**

Below: **In 1897 Queen Victoria celebrated her Diamond Jubilee – 60 years on the throne. She drove in an open carriage from Buckingham Palace to St Paul's Cathedral. Cheering crowds lined the streets.**

LONDON'S UNDERGROUND RAILWAY

London's underground system was the world's first. It was suggested by Charles Pearson, a city solicitor, as part of the improvement plans which followed the opening of the Thames Tunnel in 1843. It took Parliament a long time to accept the idea of a railway system under the streets of London.

However in 1853 and 1854 the Commons passed a bill approving the construction of the Metropolitan District Railway, an underground line which was to run between Farringdon Street and Bishop's Road, Paddington. It was to be just over six kilometres long.

Work began in 1860, and the line was opened to passengers on January 10, 1863. The trains were steam locomotives that burned coke as fuel, and getting rid of the smoke from under the ground proved to be a major problem. The first electric underground railway opened in 1890, charging 2d (two old pence) on any journey on the 4.8 kilometre City and Southwark Subway line.

- **1880** Relief of Distress Act for Ireland. Employers' Liability Act. Education up to age 13 becomes compulsory. Transvaal declares independence

- **1881** Transvaal Boers defeat the British at Majuba Hill, who recognize their independence. Land Act attempts to give fairer deal to Irish tenants. Charles Stewart Parnell MP, and others jailed for opposing the Act. Flogging abolished in the army. Postal orders first issued. Benjamin Disraeli dies

- **1882** Phoenix Park murders: Fenians kill Lord Frederick Cavendish, chief secretary for Ireland, and Thomas Burke, permanent under-secretary. British troops crush revolt in Egypt. Preliminary work on Channel Tunnel begins

- **1883** Irish terrorists try to blow up *The Times* office in London. Royal Red Cross Order founded

- **1884** Third Reform Bill: electorate increased to 5,000,000. Fabian Society founded. Work starts on *New English Dictionary*, which takes until 1928 (now the *Oxford English Dictionary*). Charles Parsons makes first practical steam turbine generator

Rhodes in Africa

ONE OF THE MOST INFLUENTIAL men in the history of southern Africa was Cecil Rhodes. A parson's son, he went to Natal from England at the age of 17 because his health was poor. He made a fortune in the Kimberley diamond mines, while paying frequent visits to Oxford to study for a degree. When gold was discovered in the Transvaal, Rhodes made another fortune. He went into politics, and by 1890 was Premier of Cape Colony. He acquired the rights to develop Matabeleland and Mashonaland and formed them into the colony of Rhodesia (now Zimbabwe and Zambia).

THE JAMESON RAID

Rhodes was eventually brought down by his friend, Dr Leander Starr Jameson. Jameson led an armed raid, comprising police from the British South Africa Company, into the Transvaal to try to overthrow the Boer government, which was denying voting and other rights to the *Uitlanders,* or foreign workers, in the gold fields. Jameson's attack failed. Rhodes was blamed for the raid, and had to resign as Premier of the Cape. Jameson, after a jail sentence in Britain, returned to Cape Colony and became its Premier. Rhodes died in 1902 aged 49. He left his wealth to create Rhodes Scholarships to Oxford University, for Commonwealth, German and American students.

Above: **A** *Punch* **magazine cartoon of Cecil Rhodes showing him straddling the African continent like a giant, just as the Colossus of Rhodes had straddled the harbour of Rhodes in Ancient Greece.**

Right: **Christ Church College, Oxford. The first Rhodes Scholars came to Oxford in 1904. About 90 scholarships are awarded each year. US President Bill Clinton was a former Rhodes Scholar.**

THE SECOND BOER WAR

The Second Boer War from 1899 to 1902 followed from the Jameson Raid of 1895, and had much the same cause. Britain supported the political rights of the *Uitlanders* (foreign workers), which the Boer rulers of the Transvaal refused to recognize. Thousands of the *Uitlanders* were British, and they sent a petition to Queen Victoria asking for help. Prolonged talks broke down, and the Boers declared war. They were supported by the Orange Free State, which was also Boer-governed.

THE RELIEF OF MAFEKING

The Boers, who greatly outnumbered the British, invaded Cape Colony and laid siege to the towns of Kimberley, Ladysmith and Mafeking. Mafeking was defended by Colonel Robert Baden-Powell, later renowned as the founder of the Boy Scout movement. In 1900, when the 200-day-long siege of Mafeking ended, rejoicing in London was so extreme that a new verb was coined: to *maffick,* or rejoice riotously.

Reinforcements were sent from England, and gradually the British conquered the country, though the Boers carried on a guerrilla campaign for another 18 months. Boer farms were burned and large groups of Boer women and children were sent to prison camps known as concentration camps, the first use of the term.

Above: **British troops attack a Boer stronghold. The Boers had commando units who were highly trained and armed and brilliant riders. Whole families fought vigorously to defend their freedom.**

Right: **Robert Baden-Powell (1857-1941) defended Mafeking in the Boer War. He became a national hero, and went on to found the Boy Scout movement in 1908.**

The peace treaty of Vereeniging in 1902 ended the war by annexing Transvaal and the Orange Free State, but promised them self-government, which they were given in 1907.

POPULAR REFORMS

Politics in the later part of Queen Victoria's reign were dominated by William Gladstone who served four terms as prime minister. Victoria did not get on as well with Gladstone as she had with Disraeli. Unlike Disraeli, Gladstone was not interested in expanding the British Empire. He was more concerned about making and passing laws which would help to bring about socal reform at home. In 1876 he helped to amend the Parliamentary Reform Bill and doubled the number of people able to vote. For the first time the vote was extended to almost all the working classes including two million agricultural labourers. Women, however, still had no vote.

● **1885** The Mahdi revolts in Sudan: British Governor General Charles Gordon slain at Khartoum. First Secretary of State for Scotland appointed. Francis Galton proves that each person's fingerprint is unique

● **1886** British annex Upper Burma. Irish Home Rule Bill defeated. Liberals split: some form Liberal Unionist Party. Severn Tunnel opened. Tilbury Docks, Essex, opened

● **1887** Queen Victoria's Golden Jubilee. Britain annexes Zululand. Bloody Sunday: Trafalgar Square protest over jailing of Irish nationalist William O'Brien. Coal Mines Act: no boys under 13 allowed to work underground

● **1888** County Councils established. John Boyd Dunlop re-invents the pneumatic tyre. *The Financial Times* first issued. Football League is founded. Jack the Ripper murders prostitutes in Whitechapel. London Miners' Federation founded

Above: **A cartoon in the magazine *Punch* of April 15, 1876. It shows Queen Victoria being offered the Imperial Crown of India, "the jewel in the crown", by the prime minister, Benjamin Disraeli.**

Below: **The Esplanade at Calcutta in the heyday of the British Empire. It was the capital of British India from 1773-1912 and many imposing buildings were built there in European style.**

Gladstone also supported improvements in the provision of education. More schools were built and education finally became free and compulsory for all children up to 13 years of age.

In 1886 Gladstone became prime minister for the third time and tried to persuade Parliament to give Home Rule to Ireland. But many members of his own Liberal Party were against the Bill and it was defeated.

THE MODERN NEWSPAPER

Many newspapers read today began life in the 1800s or even earlier – the most famous being *The Times*. This paper reported Nelson's victory and death at Trafalgar, the Battle of Waterloo, and an eyewitness account of the Peterloo Massacre. Above all it brought the blunders and horrors of the Crimean War to the public's attention. *The Times* was given the nickname "The Thunderer" and was highly critical of many politicians.

Modern popular journalism was begun by Alfred Harmsworth (who became Lord Northcliffe in 1905). Sensing there was a growing demand for newspapers among the wider public, Harmsworth launched the *Daily Mail* in 1896, described at the time as "a penny newspaper for one halfpenny". In only three years it had double the circulation of any other national newspaper, and by covering popular subjects of the time such as motoring and aviation, it increased its circulation by nearly one million by the end of the century.

- **1889** Major London dock strike. London County Council set up. Secondary Education for Wales established

- **1890** Charles Stuart Parnell sued for divorce: Liberal Party disowns him. London's first electric underground railway opened. Forth Bridge (rail) opened

- **1891** Liberals adopt programme dedicated to Home Rule for Ireland. Elementary education is made free. Leeds has Britain's first electric tramcar system

- **1892** Dam across river Vyrnwy, North Wales, to supply water to Liverpool. C.F. Cross develops viscose rayon

- **1893** Keir Hardie forms Independent Labour Party. Uganda becomes a British protectorate. Lords reject second Home Rule bill. University of Wales formed. Manchester Ship Canal completed. Liverpool overhead railway built

- **1894** Death Duties introduced. Parish councils established. James Dewar liquifies oxygen. Blackpool Tower opened

- **1895** Togoland annexed by Britain. Cecil Rhodes creates Rhodesia. London School of Economics founded. National Trust established. Westminster Cathedral begun. First Promenade Concert season. First London motor-car exhibition. Jameson Raid in Transvaal

- **1896** Fourth Ashanti War. Matabeles rebel in Rhodesia. Guglielmo Marconi patents wireless in England. Alfred Harmsworth (later Lord Northcliffe) starts the *Daily Mail*. Red Flag Act repealed: speed limit raised to 123 kph

- **1897** Victoria's Diamond Jubilee. Britain occupies Benin in protest at human sacrifices. Joseph Chamberlain's suggestion of Anglo-German alliance is poorly received

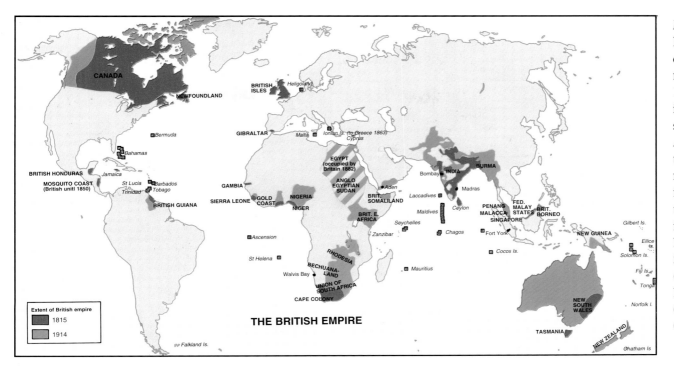

Left: **The British empire grew rapidly from 1870 to 1914 in Africa and southeast Asia. It also took hold of many key islands on trade routes including Hong Kong, Singapore, Cyprus, the Falklands, Ceylon and Gibraltar.**

THE BRITISH EMPIRE

Extent of British empire
1815
1914

Age of Empire

BY THE END OF QUEEN VICTORIA'S reign, Britain had gained more overseas lands and taken over more peoples than any other nation in history. Britain's empire included countries in every continent and islands in every ocean including colonies in the Caribbean, Africa, Asia, Australasia and the Pacific.

From the end of the Napoleonic Wars in 1815 to the start of World War I in 1914, Britain acquired so many new colonies that the empire stretched around the world. By the time Phileas Fogg made his story-book journey in *Around The World in Eighty Days* (published 1872) he could have travelled the world without having to visit an area that was not under some sort of British influence. Because the empire covered both hemispheres, it was known as "the empire on which the sun never sets".

IMPERIAL LOSS AND GAINS

Though Britain had lost the American colonies in 1783, a number of new overseas territories became part of the empire after the defeat of Napoleon in 1815. In addition, the Dutch, who had sided with the defeated French, were forced to give up lands to Britain. Britain already governed Australia as a penal colony, and had gained Canada from the French by capturing Quebec in 1759.

British naval strength was unbeatable and, for a time, "Britannia" did "rule the waves" – British boats constantly patrolled countries belonging to the British empire. The government made sure the British navy remained powerful. Britain's naval superiority was also used to maintain peace and to push forward further colonial enterprises. Strategic harbours such as Gibraltar, Hong Kong, Singapore and Aden came into British hands, and vital trading routes, such as the Cape Route (via the tip of South Africa) to India, or the Suez Canal (via Egypt) to the spice and rubber plantations of southeast Asia were also controlled by Britain.

EXPORTING BRITISH KNOW-HOW

By the 1880s, British engineers, surveyors and architects were helping to build railways, roads, bridges, factories and government buildings not only in the colonies, but also in places where Britain had influence. These people drew on the experience gained from the Industrial Revolution. Banking and investment were geared to financing the empire by trading raw materials from the colonies for home-made manufactured goods.

During the later 1800s, many people went to live and work in the colonies as traders, soldiers, engineers, diplomats and government administrators. These people took their industrial, educational and government systems with them.

India, for example, had originally been controlled by the East India Company to provided Britain with jute, tea and cotton. After British forces put down the Indian Mutiny of 1857, Parliament had to decide whether to govern India directly, or continue just to protect the trading interests of the East India Company that had been running the country. India became a colony administered by the government, as did Malaya and Burma shortly afterwards.

THE NEW DOMINIONS

By about 1900, about one-quarter of the world and its population were ruled from London and flew the Union Jack. British influence extended into mainland settlements in Central and South America and into China where it had outposts.

Queen Victoria, herself Empress of India since 1876, was a keen supporter of a foreign policy that pursued colonial expansion and upheld the empire, but not at any cost.

As more and more British and Irish people emigrated to countries within the Empire, so these lands were gradually given more freedom to govern themselves. Many colonies, notably Canada, Australia and South Africa, became known as dominions rather than colonies and allowed to govern themselves, but they still remained closely linked to Britain.

● **1897** Battle of Omdurman gives Anglo-Egyptian control of Sudan. Sale of Church livings ends. Waterloo-City Railway electrified. W. Ramsay and M.W. Travers discover neon, krypton and xenon gases

● **1899** Second Boer War begins (to 1902). London borough councils established. First motor-buses in London. First radio transmission from England to France

● **1900** Labour Representation Committee: to work for Labour group in Parliament. British relieve sieges of Ladysmith and Mafeking. Britain annexes Tonga, Orange Free State and Transvaal. Boxer Rising against foreigners in China: Britain helps suppress it. The Quaker, George Cadbury, founds Bourneville Village Trust. Arthur Evans begins excavations in Crete. *Daily Express* is founded

Above: **Canadian fur trappers developed a profitable trade around the Hudson Bay. Among the people who emigrated to Canada were many Scottish families from the Highlands.**

Below: **Winnipeg, a centre of the fur trade, was still a small town in 1870. In that year the province of Manitoba became part of the Dominion of Canada; Winnipeg became the province's capital.**

THE DOMINION OF CANADA

Canadians had become increasingly fearful that the United States might try to take them over. Canada was sparsely populated and full of natural resources. There was also the highly profitable fur trade which had been growing since the time of French explorers in the 1600s and the Hudson Bay Company in the reign of Charles II.

Several of the biggest colonies joined to form the Dominion of Canada in 1867. Each colony became a province: Quebec, Ontario, New Brunswick and Nova Scotia. The new country purchased the vast lands owned by the Hudson Bay Company. A trans-continental railway, the Canadian-Pacific, was also completed by 1885 and linked settlements across the vast area between the Atlantic and the Pacific coasts.

Left: **The expansion of the British Empire owed much to the daring and dangerous explorations of intrepid explorers all over the globe. Burke and Wills were the first white men to cross Australia. Their expedition set out in 1860 from Melbourne to the Gulf of Carpentaria but both died on their return journey. After such explorers came the settlers and later self-government. By 1890 all Australian colonies had self-government.**

THE AUSTRALIAN COMMONWEALTH

The success of the first independent dominion of Canada paved the way for the creation of a second. In 1855 the six separate Australian colonies of New South Wales, Queensland, Western Australia, Victoria, South Australia and Tasmania, had been granted self-government by Britain. They developed into democracies with elections (except for Aborigines).

The leaders of the colonies soon came to realize that some form of union was needed. None of the Australian colonies was willing to give up its individual independence, so in the end a federal form of government was agreed on. In a federal system a central government shares power with the independent regional or state governments, but is responsible for national concerns such as foreign policy. The Commonwealth of Australia finally came into being on the first day of 1901.

NEW ZEALAND

The third of the great dominions, which would eventually transform the British empire into the British Commonwealth of Nations, was New Zealand. The British government took possession of New Zealand in 1840, signing a treaty with some of the Maori chiefs and promising to protect their rights. The country had its own government from 1852, but Europeans took over Maori land and war broke out between Maoris and colonists in 1860. New Zealand troops fought bravely in the Boer War of 1899 to 1902 for Britain. Finally in 1907 New Zealand was proclaimed as a dominion, with full internal self-government. Britain retained control over defence and foreign affairs. Much of the country's progress to independence was the work of Richard Seddon, its prime minister from 1893 to his death in 1906. Seddon introduced votes for women in 1893, 25 years before Britain.

Social Change

THE INCREASE AND SUCCESS of industry meant that the middle classes grew in numbers and these people had more money to spend. People such as bank managers, factory owners and wealthy traders often built large elaborate houses to show off their wealth. We know a lot more about the people of this period because of the invention of photography from around the 1850s.

INSIDE A VICTORIAN HOME

Inside, a middle-class home the rooms would be full of over-stuffed velvet covered furniture, and heavily curtained windows often decorated with coloured glass panes. The rooms would be full of china and glass ornaments and paintings.

Below: **A big step forward in steel making was made by Henry Bessemer in 1856. In a Bessemer converter, hot air was blasted through melted iron to convert it into steel.**

Steel was stronger and more useful than iron. Before Bessemer's invention it had been very expensive to make.

Right: **Toys like teddy bears were hand-made but many other toys were now being made in factories.**

Middle class women were expected to manage the household, with servants, including a cook and possibly a butler and coachman. They would not have a job, apart from helping charities, because it was not considered "respectable".

VICTORIAN DRESS AND LEISURE

For the wealthy, fashions reflected increasing prosperity; women wore crinolines (hooped petticoats held out over a frame of cane or whalebone) which gave their dresses a bell shape. Later, women wore a bustle at the back. Men wore frock coats and winged collars. They also had tiepins, studs, watches and chains. In the 1860s walking-sticks with silver knobs also became popular, as did patent-leather shoes and shoes laced at the front.

As the new middle classes employed servants this gave more women leisure time to try the new sports, such as archery, tennis and croquet. Children from wealthy Victorian families saw little of their parents except at tea-time. They went straight from a nursery with a nurse or nanny to a schoolroom with a governess. Their life consisted of lessons at home, walks in the park and playing with other wealthy children. They also had the first teddy bears, metal toys to play with and children's books.

PUBLIC EDUCATION

Until 1870 most children did not go to school. Most of the schools at this time were run by local churches. The Education Act in 1870 set up elected School Boards which ensured that schools were provided for children up to the age of 13 in any district which did not have a church school. The government also gave money to fund church schools. It would be another 21 years before schools became free and education compulsory, up to the age of 13.

Left, right and below: **A selection of Victorian household appliances: sewing machine; ice box (forerunner of the refrigerator); and washing machine.**

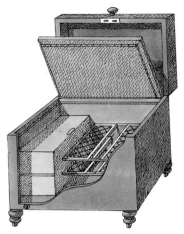

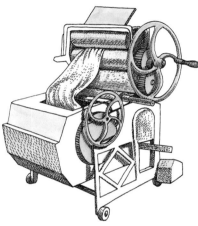

THE VICTORIAN POOR

For working class children life was very hard. Most poor children still did not go to school as they were expected to work. There was virtually no help for the unemployed, sick, old or poor at this time. People either starved, begged in the streets or were sent to the local workhouse. Here they would receive food and shelter in return for work such as breaking stones (for men) and doing laundry (for women and children).

The enormous difference between the wealthier Victorians and the poverty of the working classes stirred many social reformers to start voluntary organizations. For example Dr Barnardo founded the first of his famous homes for children in 1870. Reformers also persuaded Parliament to pass acts to improve schooling and healthcare in general and for children in particular.

In 1875 the Public Health Act attempted to make sure all houses were supplied with clean water and proper working drains. Local councils had to ensure that streets were regularly cleaned and that food sold in shops – whether cooked or raw – was clean and fit to eat.

Below: **The Salvation Army was formed by Catherine and William Booth in 1878, out of their Whitechapel Christian Mission. They offered practical help to poor people suffering from homelessness and alcoholism. It is now a worldwide organization helping those struck by poverty.**

● **1901** Queen Victoria dies; succeeded by son, Edward VII (to 1910). Anglo-Japanese Alliance signed. Balfour Education Act abolishes Board Schools. Australia becomes a Dominion. First petrol-driven motor-cycle. First British submarine launched. Marconi sends radio signal from Cornwall to Newfoundland

● **1902** Order of Merit established. Oliver Heaviside discovers ionosphere

● **1903** Britain conquers northern Nigeria. Car speed limit set at 32 km/h. Emmeline Pankhurst starts suffragette movement. First motor-taxis in London. Liverpool Cathedral begun. *Daily Mirror* founded. Universities of Liverpool and Manchester established

● **1904** *Entente Cordiale* signed. Workers' Educational Association begins. Frederick Kipping discovers silicones. J.A. Fleming invents thermionic valve. London Symphony Orchestra founded. Leeds University founded

● **1905** Automobile Association established. First public cinema shows in London. Sheffield University founded. British troops put down riot in Guyana

● **1906** Liberals win landslide election. Twenty-nine Labour MPs elected: Labour Representation Committee changes its name to Labour Party. Bakerloo and Piccadilly tube lines open in London. China and Britain agree to reduce opium production. F.G. Hopkins discovers vitamins

● **1907** New Zealand becomes a dominion. Motor-racing starts at Brooklands. Northern tube line opened. Triple Entente between Britain, France and Russia

● **1908** Herbert Henry Asquith becomes Liberal prime minister. Anglo-German tension grows. Port of London Authority set up

IMPROVED COMMUNICATIONS

Apart from the Penny Post, messages could be sent by electric telegraph and in 1858 the first transatlantic cable was laid on the bed of the Atlantic Ocean. Laying a cable on the ocean floor allowed telegraph messages to be sent between Britain and America. Scotsman Alexander Graham Bell perfected the first telephone in the late 1870s, in the United States. Britain's first telephone exchange was opened by the Telephone Company Limited. The exchange had 10 customers. By the 1890s Britain had over 45,000 telephones.

Below: **An early Marconi wireless set, with speakers and headphones. Before the wireless, sound waves were changed into electric current, sent along a wire and changed back into sound. But Guglielmo Marconi used electromagnetic waves, which travelled at the speed of light, without wires to carry sound.**

Right: **Edward VII visiting his nephew, the German Kaiser Wilhelm II. Edward's peace-seeking trips to European heads of state earned him the nickname "peacemaker".**

Edward VII

EDWARD, BORN IN 1841, remained Prince of Wales until he was 59. His mother, Queen Victoria, would not involve him in politics or give him any serious responsibilities. However, he did carry out many goodwill visits abroad. He became very fond of France even though Anglo-French relations were not that good. Thanks to Edward's efforts, several years of wrangling between Britain and France over overseas territories were ended by the signing of an *entente* (understanding), which became popularly known as the *entente cordiale* of 1903. The French, who had been quite hostile, were won over by the charm of Edward VII during his state visit to Paris in 1903.

THE EDWARDIAN ERA

Edward became king in 1901 and ruled for nine years. He was a popular king and continued to enjoy foreign travel and ceremonies, and took less interest in politics. On the surface, the Edwardian era, under a genial and pleasure-loving king, was a much brighter and more glamorous time than the closing years of Victoria's reign.

But beneath the apparent calm and settled order of things, there was growing unrest. Political strife was bitter, the Labour movement was growing in strength, women were battling for emancipation (including the right to vote) and over Europe the clouds of war were gathering.

Above: **Edward VII (1901-1910) influenced foreign affairs by making many visits to European capitals, in an attempt to calm international tensions and to prevent the outbreak of a European war.**

SCOTT OF THE ANTARCTIC

The British expedition of Robert Falcon Scott to the South Pole which took place from 1910 to 1912 ended in tragedy. On his way to Antarctica, at the age of 42, Scott heard that a Norwegian expedition led by Roald Amundsen, who was believed to be going to the Arctic, was also heading for the South Pole.

Amundsen used husky dogs to draw his sledges. Scott unwisely used ponies, which were not suited to the severe conditions and died. Snowstorms made his progress slow and difficult. Eventually Scott and four companions reached the Pole pulling their own sledges, to find that Amundsen had reached the Pole 34 days earlier.

On their way back Scott's party ran into unexpected blizzards, and died of cold and hunger only 18 kilometres from shelter and ample stores of food. Three bodies, as well as the records and diaries the men had kept, were found. Scott had written his diary up to the day of his death. News of the tragedy shook national pride.

● **1908** Robert Baden-Powell founds the Boy Scout movement. Old Age Pensions for over 70s. New universities: Belfast and University of Ulster. Start of Borstal system. First aeroplane flight in Britain (Farnborough). Election of Elizabeth Garrett Anderson as first British woman mayor (Aldeburgh). The IV Olympic Games are held in London

● **1909** House of Lords reject Chancellor of the Exchequer David Lloyd George's budget proposals spark off constitutional crisis. Girl Guides established in Britain. Selfridge's store opens. A.V. Roe begins building aeroplanes in Britain. Bristol University founded. Formal opening of Victoria and Albert Museum, London

● **1910** Union of South Africa becomes a Dominion. Two general elections over budget: Liberal majority cut. Parliament Bill to curb powers of Lords: Conservative peers resist it. Edward VII dies; succeeded by son, George V (to 1936). Dr Crippen poisons his wife (body discovered seven months later). First Labour Exchanges opened. Halley's Comet observed. Louis Paulhan wins prize for London to Manchester flight. George V gives secret pledge to create enough Liberal peers to force the Parliament Bill through. Dr Crippen hanged. Mining disaster (Hulton), 350 killed

Above: **Sheffield University, which opened in 1905, was of one of several new redbrick universities whose purpose was to broaden people's access to higher education.**

Left: **Roald Amundsen leads his huskies over the Antarctic. He reached the South Pole in December 1911, beating Robert Scott's expedition by 34 days.**

George V

George V's family name was Saxe-Coburg, which came from Prince Albert, his grandfather. For the first seven years of his reign George V kept this name. But with the outbreak of World War I against Germany, and with anti-German feeling running high, he changed his Germanic family name to Windsor. George was the second son of Edward VII (his elder brother died before him). He became king and Emperor of India at a time when Parliament was trying to limit the power of the House of Lords, and women were campaigning for the right to vote.

Left: George V (1910-1936) held old fashioned values and with his wife, Mary, kept the monarchy popular. But the power of British monarchs had declined so much in the 19th century that by the time of George V they were little more than figureheads.

Left: Suffragettes in 1908 celebrate the release of two of their members from Holloway prison. Faced with the government's continued resistance to votes for women, suffragettes resorted to violence such as smashing high street shop windows and even fire-raising. But their militant methods turned some people against them. At the Derby horse race in 1913, a suffragette named Emily Davison threw herself in front of the King's horse and died from her injuries.

VOTES FOR WOMEN

The campaign for the right of women to vote began in 1866. When an amendment to the Electoral Reform Act on female suffrage (the right to vote) was defeated, organizations were formed all over the country. In the cotton mills, women workers campaigned for the vote through trade unions and the Labour Party.

Most effective were the militant methods of the Women's Social and Political Union founded in 1903 by Emmeline Pankhurst. Its members became known as the suffragettes. These militant campaigners for votes for women tried to draw attention and support for their cause by interrupting political meetings, chaining themselves to railings and breaking windows.

SUFFRAGETTES' SUCCESS

Faced with continued resistance from the Commons who, in 1912, again rejected votes for women, the violence of the suffragette movement increased. The women resorted to arson, slashing

pictures, and destroying empty property on a huge scale. These acts led to arrests and the imprisonment of many suffragettes.

In prison many women went on hunger strike, which resulted in the "Cat and Mouse" Act of 1913. This allowed prisoners to be temporarily discharged for health reasons, while making them liable for re-arrest once they had recovered. The campaign halted with the start of World War I, but women over the age of 30 finally won the vote in 1918.

THE START OF STATE WELFARE

In the 1906 election the Liberals won a landslide victory. They were supported by members of the new Labour Party who were elected to help improve the lives of working people. Herbert Asquith was prime minister and David Lloyd George, Chancellor of the Exchequer, was the driving force behind many of the reforms.

Among the reforms was the establishment of the school meal service which gave free school meals to children of parents who could not afford them. Hundreds of thousands of children now had a good meal each day – some for the first time in their lives. A free school medical service was also started so many children also saw a doctor and dentist for the first time.

Also introduced for the first time in Britain were old age pensions, labour exchanges, National Insurance and similar measures which became the first steps towards the modern welfare state.

THE CRIPPEN CASE

The trial of Dr Harvey Hawley Crippen for the murder of his wife in 1910 gained an unusually high degree of publicity because of the unique manner of his arrest. When police inquiries became too close, Crippen fled to Canada by ship, taking with him his girlfriend, Ethel Le Neve, who was disguised as a boy. Aboard the ship the captain realized Le Neve was a girl, guessed who the couple were and radioed London. A Scotland Yard detective crossed the Atlantic in a faster ship, and Crippen was arrested before his ship reached Canada. This was the first time radio had been used to help catch a criminal. Crippen was brought back to England, tried and hanged for murder, but Le Neve was acquitted of a charge of helping him.

COMMONS AGAINST LORDS

The 1909 budget introduced a supertax on very high incomes and a tax on land ownership. These taxes were to raise money for old age pensions and for building new battleships called dreadnoughts which were needed to match the rising military might of Germany.

This started a severe battle between the Commons and the House of Lords, who rejected the budget. A bill aimed at depriving the Lords of the power of rejecting finance bills was resisted by Conservative peers. Edward VII had worked to reach a compromise, but died leaving the constitutional crisis to be solved. George V, however, finally agreed to create enough new Liberal peers to ensure the Bill would get through. In 1911, the Lords gave way and the budget was passed.

THE TITANIC DISASTER

The *Titanic* set out from Britain on her maiden, or first, voyage to New York City, on April 12, 1912. It was the biggest ship in the world, measuring 269 metres long, with a gross tonnage of 46,328.

The liner was described as "unsinkable" because she had a double-bottomed hull with 16 watertight compartments and could still float with any four flooded.

On the night of April 14-15, about 2,570 kilometres northeast of its destination, the liner hit an iceberg, which ripped open her hull. The *Titanic* sank two and a half hours later, with the loss of 1,513 lives. The other 711 people on board were picked up by the liner *Carpathia,* which arrived on the scene 20 minutes later. As a result, safety rules for ships were tightened: every ship must now carry enough lifeboats for everyone on board, whereas the *Titanic* had spaces for less than half its passengers; and ships must maintain a 24-hour radio watch.

Below: **The British luxury liner *Titanic* sank in 1912. A collision with an iceberg caused a 90-metre gash in its hull which led to flooding and eventual sinking. In 1985 the wreckage of the *Titanic* was found 800 kilometres southwest of Newfound and photographed.**

THE SHADOW OF WAR

Ever since the 1880s, there had been growing rivalry between the Germans and the British for territories in Africa. By the end of the century Germany was openly challenging Britain's once vastly superior navy and the British resented this. Both countries competed with each other in building bigger and better battleships. The Russians were also alarmed at Germany's growing military power and influence because it threatened their export route through the Black Sea.

At the same time, France also felt threatened by Germany's plans to expand its African empire, which led to a dispute between the two powers over Morocco. Meanwhile, relations between France and Britain slowly improved, so when Germany invaded Belgium in August 1914 there was much popular support for the belief that the Germans had to be stopped.

The war that followed from 1914 to 1918 was one of the greatest disasters in British history. In just four years nearly one million British men died and over two million were wounded.

FOCUS ON THE FIRST BRITISH MOVIES

The Lumiere brothers in France gave the first ever film show to a paying audience: in Paris over 100 years ago in 1895. But this was just the beginning. The invention of the movie camera and the development of the technique of story-telling on film was greatly helped by British pioneers. William Dickson, a Scottish assistant working for the American inventor Thomas Edison, produced the first reliable movie camera in 1891. Edison hoped it would be as successful as his phonogram (early record player) and light bulb.

Two Englishmen from Brighton started to move the camera to follow the action (previously cameras were static) and used the first close-up in cinema history – in *Grandma's Reading Glass* (1900).

In *Fire!* (1902) James Williamson, an early film-maker, was the first to combine outdoor location shots with indoor studio scenes.

Above: The *Dreadnought* was completed in 1906 in response to the growing fear of German military shipbuilding. At 20,000 tonnes, with a speed of 22 knots and ten mounted guns, this class of battleship helped Britain's Royal Navy to dominate the world's navies for 40 years.

- **1911** Ramsay MacDonald becomes leader of the Labour Party. Parliament Bill passed; Lords give way. Salaries for MPs. South Wales miners end ten month strike. Railwaymen strike. Shops Act: employees to have half a day off every week in addition to Sunday. First Official Secrets Act. William Morris (later Lord Nuffield) makes first Morris car. August 9th: 100°F in London. First women members of the Royal College of Surgeons. National Insurance Act gives help to those on low incomes

- **1912** Miners and London dockers strike. Commons reject votes for women; protests increase. National Health Insurance introduced. Scott dies reaching South Pole. *Titanic* sinks on maiden voyage, more than 1,500 passengers drown. First London-to-Paris flight. First London underground crash, 22 injured

MODERN BRITAIN
(1914 – 1990s)

WORLD WAR I is often seen as a dividing line between British prosperity and decline. But this is not an accurate view because, by 1914, Britain was already losing its pre-eminence in its navy and industry, and the monarchy and House of Lords had little authority. Workers were also becoming steadily better organized, and strikes were to become frequent.

After World War II (1939-1945), Britain quickly lost her empire; the countries belonging to it were almost all independent by 1970. They remained linked in the Commonwealth of Nations.

In the modern world, it has become apparent that a small country can no longer stand alone. So Britain has become a member of other organizations: the United Nations, the North Atlantic Treaty Organization and the European Union which provide support for trade and defence.

Elizabeth II is one of the longest reigning English monarchs.

World War I

BRITAIN HAD BEEN ENJOYING a period of isolation before 1900, but the build up of the German navy and the Kaiser's ambition to acquire more colonies worried Britain. Other European rivalry over trade, colonies and military power had also been growing, and the European powers had grouped in defensive alliances. In 1902, Britain's only ally was Japan.

World War I began when a Serb student assassinated Archduke Ferdinand, heir to the Austro-Hungarian throne, in Sarajevo on June 28, 1914. When Austria declared war on Serbia, Russia, a fellow Slav nation, went to Serbia's aid. Germany supported its ally, Austria, and France was allied with Russia.

Germany had always dreaded a war on two fronts (to the east and west of its borders), so it put the Schlieffen Plan into operation. Drawn up by General von Schlieffen, the plan aimed to beat France in six weeks so that Germany could concentrate its forces against Russia.

BRITAIN GETS DRAWN INTO WAR

The British Cabinet was divided on what steps to take. Some of its members still hoped that Britain would not have to take sides. But others feared that the Germans would take the Channel ports in France and Belgium. On August 3, 1914 the Germans invaded Belgium and started to march down towards Paris. The British then recalled their Treaty of London (1839) by which they had agreed to protect Belgian independence. It was on these grounds that Britain declared war against Germany on August 4, 1914. The BEF (British Expeditionary

Above: **A recruiting poster at the start of World War I with the message, "Your country needs you" from the War Minister, Lord Kitchener. Inspired by the call, volunteers crowded the recruiting offices, hoping to join up. Most people expected the war to be over by Christmas. But this soon changed when the horror of trench warfare became known.**

Above: **Armies faced one another across a narrow strip of ground known as "No Man's Land". Behind barbed wire defences, the soldiers dug trenches in which to shelter from the gunfire. Before an attack, heavy guns fired thousands of high explosive shells at enemy lines. Then the infantry charged out of the trenches. They wore steel helmets and carried hand grenades and rifles with bayonets.**

Right: **American, British and German infantrymen during World War I. Their uniforms were cut from khaki or green cloth. French soldiers wore pale blue uniforms. The opposing sides often faced each other in trenches only a few hundred metres apart.**

German soldier

British soldier

US soldier

Force) crossed swiftly to France and helped to hold up the German advance in Belgium (at Mons) and in France (at the battle of the Marne). The Germans could not reach Paris. Both sides then took up defensive positions and within three months a line of trenches was dug from the Channel coast to the Swiss frontier. The war had reached a stalemate.

TRENCH WARFARE

The British and French troops lined up against the German troops along a front which began in the west and extended eastwards. From 1914 to 1918 the western front did not move more than 32 kilometres in any direction. In a series of horrific battles, millions of lives were lost for the gain of only a few kilometres. The trenches were built to protect the troops from machine gun fire. Soldiers ate, slept and kept guard in the trenches. However, with severe rain, the trenches became muddy, water-logged and disease-ridden. Attacks involved the troops going over the top to face the barbed wire and machine guns of the enemy. The aim was to achieve a break-through, but the machine guns pinned men down in their trenches. The area of land between the opposing forces' front-line trenches was called No Man's Land. Generals on

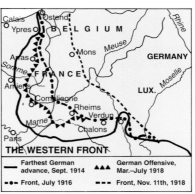

Above: **A map showing the western front – a line of trenches which ran from the border of neutral Switzerland to the English Channel. Neither side managed to advance for more than 32 kilometres and millions lost their lives in trench warfare.**

● **1914** Lords reject votes for women. Commons pass Irish Home Rule bill; Irish rebel in Dublin. Britain declares war on Germany. DORA (Defence of the Realm Act) passed. British troops land in France. Britain declares war on Austria-Hungary. Battle of Namur and Mons. Retreat from Mons. First battle of the Marne. Battle of the Aisne. Irish Home Rule suspended. Boers rebel. First battle of Ypres. Britain declares war on Turkey. British establish protectorate in Egypt. First Treasury notes: £1 and £10. Panama Canal opened

● **1915** HMS *Formidable* sunk. German airship bombs Britain. German blockade of Britain. Battle of Neuve Chapelle. Second battle of Ypres: Germans' first use poison gas. Allied fleets fail to force the Dardenelles. Allied troops land in Gallipoli. British liner *Lusitania* is sunk by U-boat; 124 Americans drowned. Herbert Asquith forms coalition government. Zeppelin airships over London. British take Mesopotamia. Boers surrender in South Africa. Allies withdraw from Gallipoli

● **1916** Conscription introduced. Clydeside munitions workers strike. Easter rebellion in Dublin. Battle of Jutland. HMS *Hampshire* sunk a week later: British war minister Lord Kitchener dies. National Savings begin. Daylight Saving (summer time) begins. Battle of the Somme: first tanks used. Germans shell English coast. David Lloyd George becomes PM

● **1917** British capture Baghdad. Imperial War Cabinet formed. US declares war on Germany. Battle of Arras: Canadians capture Vimy Ridge. Royal family stop using German family name: Saxe-Coburg-Gotha becomes Windsor; Battenberg becomes Mountbatten. Third battle of Ypres. Russian Revolutions: bolsheviks (communists) seize power

both sides of the western front (in France and Belgium) believed in frontal attacks. The tragic result was a series of huge battles in which heavy casualties were sustained to no real purpose. Britain lost 60,000 troops on the first day of the battle of the Somme in 1916. The technical problem was that attacks on properly entrenched positions almost always failed, at the cost of many lives on both sides.

PASSCHENDAELE

One of the worst battles was the third battle of Ypres in 1917, also called Passchendaele. This battle was planned on the basis of many incorrect assessments. It was fought in torrential rain, and the troops had to wade through mud up to their waists. Conditions were made even worse by the flat, low-lying terrain of Flanders and the fact that the Allied artillery had smashed the drainage pipes. In 102 days the British advanced just eight kilometres at a cost of 400,000 lives. They captured the site of Passchendaele, a village which was completely destroyed in the fighting. The introduction of tanks promised to end the deadlock of trench warfare, but they did not arrive in sufficient numbers to make a difference in World War I.

Above: **The first tanks were used in the battle of the Somme by the British in 1916. These machines** terrified the German soldiers but suffered too many mechanical failures to be fully effective.

THE WAR AT SEA

There were only two major sea battles in World War I. The first in 1914, was when a German fleet was destroyed off the Falkland Islands. Then, in 1916, the battle of Jutland took place in which both Britain and Germany claimed victory. The German fleet never left its port of Kiel again until the end of the war, when it surrendered to the Allies. Instead, the Germans concentrated on a relatively new weapon: the submarine.

The German submarines, called U-boats, attacked all shipping, even that of neutral countries, bound for Britain and France. From 1914 to mid-1915, and later from 1917, U-boats successfully sank all ships on sight and nearly brought Britain to defeat. This led to the introduction of convoys whereby fleets of merchant ships were accompanied by a ship-of-war for protection. When American ships were sunk in 1917, the USA entered the war.

Left: **Britain needed goods and food from overseas, so it had to ensure command of the seas. But German U-boats made sailing to and from Britain dangerous for merchant and passenger ships.**

At the same time, British battleships blockaded German ports, effectively sealing them off from getting food and supplies. By the end of the war, German food stocks were very low.

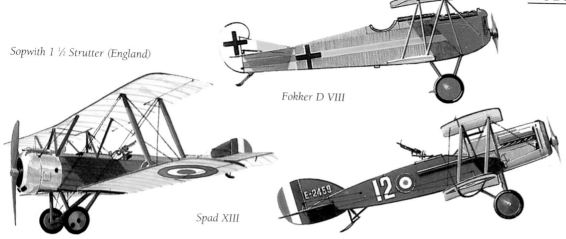

Sopwith 1 ½ Strutter (England)

Fokker D VIII

Spad XIII

THE HOME FRONT

A reforming Liberal government was in power, the last to hold office. It was headed by Herbert Asquith, who served as prime minister from 1906 to 1916. His conduct of the war drew criticism, largely that it was not dynamic enough. In 1915 a chronic shortage of shells prompted Asquith to create a Ministry of Munitions. This ministry was led by David Lloyd George.

The horrors of the Somme and the condemnation by *The Times* of Asquith's seeming inaction led to Lloyd George ousting Asquith as prime minister in December 1916.

CONSCRIPTION

Britain was the only country which did not have a huge reserve of trained men. The British Expeditionary Force contained less than 100,000 soldiers. But this professional army was wiped out in the costly battles of 1914. Volunteers flocked to join up, sometimes urged on by women who gave white feathers as a sign of cowardice to anyone of military age not in uniform. In January 1916 conscription (compulsory service) was introduced.

With so many men in the forces, women had to take over their jobs at home, gaining a big step towards the equality many of them sought. Women proved during the war that they could do "men's work".

Food was strictly rationed, largely to prevent people from hoarding supplies. National Savings were introduced to help finance the war. About 800,000 women worked in the new armaments factories to help the huge demand for weapons.

Above: **Three bi-planes from World War I. Only 12 years after the Wright brothers made their pioneering flight in North Carolina, American aircraft were being used in warfare. Although control of the air was not a deciding factor in World War I, the war led to many advances in flight technology.**

Below: **At the Versailles Peace Settlement of 1919, Germany gave back lands to France and Belgium and gave up its overseas**

colonies. **The Habsburg monarchy ended and Poland, Czechoslovakia, Hungary and Yugoslavia became new states.**

● **1917** Balfour Declaration: Britain promises Palestine home for Jews. T.E. Lawrence joins Arab revolt. Battle of Cambrai: British capture Jerusalem. Order of the British Empire and Companions of Honour founded. Chequers estate received by British nation as residence for prime minister

● **1918** Food rationing begins (to 1919). Major German spring offensive. Second battle of the Somme halts offensive. Royal Air Force (RAF) formed, replacing Royal Flying Corps of the army. British land at Vladivostok to fight the bolsheviks. British occupy Damascus. Influenza epidemic rages. Armistice with Austria-Hungary. Armistice with Germany (November 11th) ends the war. Labour Party quits coalition. "Khaki" Election: Liberal-Conservative coalition majority 262. Women over 30 get the vote; used for the first time in December general election. House of Commons rejects proportional representation. Stonehenge presented to the nation. First oil well in Britain (Hardstoft)

EUROPE IN 1918

Independent States created by war

THE EASTERN FRONT

In 1915 the Russian army faced German and Austrian troops on the eastern front, which ran from the Baltic to the Black Sea, with millions of Russian casualties. Britain and France tried to get supplies to Russia through the Dardanelles, the straits connecting the Mediterranean to the Black Sea, but the Turkish defences proved too strong. The ensuing Gallipolli campaign was also a failure for the Allies, including many ANZAC troops (from Australia and New Zealand).

THE END OF THE WAR

When a final German offensive failed in 1918, Germany's allies crumbled and German generals realized that they could not win the war. German delegates signed an armistice, and a ceasefire was ordered to take effect at 11 am on November 11, 1918, on all fronts. World War I had ended.

A DIVIDED IRELAND

When World War I broke out in August 1914, the "Irish Question" was put aside while politicians concentrated on the war. A Home Rule bill had been passed in 1914 – this would have allowed Ireland to remain as part of Great Britain, but granted it an Irish Parliament. However, the war prevented it from taking effect.

THE EASTER REBELLION

Irish frustration at Home Rule being granted and then delayed in World War I led to the Easter Rebellion on Good Friday 1916. The Fenian Irish Republican Brotherhood seized Dublin's public buildings. After four days of fighting, they surrendered. All but one of 15 leaders were executed. Eamon de Valera, the survivor, was spared execution only because he had been born in America. This harsh treatment made them heroes and gave support to a movement called *Sinn Fein* (Ourselves Alone). In the general election of 1918, the Sinn Fein Party won 73 seats at Westminster which it refused to take up. In an Act of 1920 Ireland was divided, with Parliaments at Belfast and Dublin. The IRA (Irish Republican Army), which demanded a united republican Ireland, started a war against this Act, killing government officials and policemen. The Black and Tans, British troops, sent to reinforce the RIC (Royal Irish Constabulary), led to more violence.

Below: **The Easter Rising of 1916 brought fierce fighting in Dublin. Civil war followed in 1922-1923 and an early victim of the conflict was Michael Collins. He was shot by republicans in 1922 for signing the treaty which created the Irish Free State but excluded the six northern counties.**

- **1919** War with Afghanistan. German East Africa handed over to Britain: renamed Tanganyika. German fleet scuttled at Scapa Flow. Lady Astor becomes first woman MP. First Atlantic aeroplane crossing by J.W. Alcock and A.W. Brown. First flight to Australia (Ross Smith), in 135 hours. League of Nations formed. Indian massacre at Amritsar. Lloyd George attends the Paris Peace Conference. British troops help anti-communists in Russian Civil War

- **1920** Former East African Protectorate becomes Kenya colony. Riots in Belfast against Irish independence. Admission of women degree students to Oxford for first time. Church of Wales disestablished. Unknown Soldier buried in Westminster Abbey. Palestine comes under British control

- **1921** Unemployment payments increased. British Legion founded. Irish Free State set up

- **1922** Fascists take power in Italy. Michael Collins murdered. Lloyd George coalition falls: Bonar Law (Conservative) becomes PM. British Broadcasting Company is founded. Geddes Axe cuts public spending. Gandhi imprisoned. IRA shoot British Field Marshal. Tutankhamen's tomb discovered

Right: **The traditional flag of Ireland was a blue flag with a golden harp.**

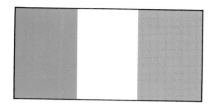

Left: **Today's Irish flag dates from 1919. Orange was adopted by the Protestants after William of Orange and the white stands for peace.**

Right: **The former flag of Northern Ireland, which today is only used as a loyalist emblem. The red upraised hand is an ancient symbol of Ulster.**

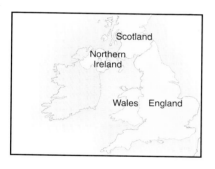

Left: **Great Britain is comprised of England, Scotland and Wales. With Northern Ireland, it becomes the United Kingdom.**

who agreed with the treaty like Collins, and those, including Eamon de Valera, who still wanted full independence for a united Ireland. The links between the Irish Free State and the United Kingdom were gradually broken during the 1930s. Following the abdication of Edward VIII, Ireland removed mention of the Crown from its constitution. In 1937 Ireland ended the Free State and proclaimed itself the Independent Republic of Ireland, or Eire. Many Roman Catholics in Northern Ireland refused to accept the division and relations between Catholics and Protestants became strained.

THE GENERAL STRIKE

The effects of World War I caused a huge strain on many nations' economies and employers wanted to cut wages. The General Strike of 1926 was called by most of Britain's major trade unions in support of miners who were fighting threatened wage cuts, but it failed because the government was able to organize volunteers to run essential services such public transport. The strike lasted nine days.

Below: **Crowds cheer as a bus is stopped during the General Strike of 1926. The original dispute was between miners and mine owners who wanted to cut wages by 25 percent. The owners shut the mines and other public workers – in steel, newspapers, electricity, transport and gas – all went on strike. Troops and volunteers with government support worked successfully to keep services running.**

ULSTER AND THE UNIONISTS

Six of the nine northern provinces of the country – together called Ulster – were determined to remain in union with England. The six were mainly Protestant, and wanted no part in an all-Irish, chiefly Catholic, Parliament. Despite having already agreed in principle to Home Rule for all Ireland, the English government gave in to unionist pressure. Lloyd George's treaty of 1921 gave the 26 southern counties of Ireland – called the Irish Free State – independence. It was signed with the Sinn Fein leaders, including Michael Collins who had led the IRA against the RIC. It was an attempt to end the violence and bloodshed, but the six northern counties were excluded from independence by their own wish to remain in the Union with Britain, and this led to a civil war in 1922-1923 between those

Left: **In October 1935, 200 unemployed men marched to London from Jarrow in northeast England. They were protesting about unemployment which had reached about 68 percent of the workers in their area. The closure of the ship-building yard on the River Tyne had sparked the march. The men carried a petition and gathered much support and attention to unemployment along the way. But despite a lot of publicity the government virtually ignored their protest and the men went home again. Nevertheless, their march became a landmark of the Great Depression.**

THE GREAT DEPRESSION

The world economic crisis known as the Great Depression started in the United States in 1929. Factories had been producing more goods than people could afford; workers had to work part-time and the reduced wages from reduced hours meant people could afford still less.

When the American stockmarket on Wall Street crashed in October 1929, it caused a collapse in world trade. When the United States and other countries stopped buying goods, British exporters saw their markets disappear.

Unemployment rose sharply, reaching almost three million by 1931. The worst unemployment was in the old industrial areas such as South Wales, Lancashire, Yorkshire and Clydeside. Unemployed workers queued up once a week to get their unemployment benefit (known as the dole) – money that was barely enough to live on. The government could not afford the high cost of the dole and faced a financial crisis. The economy recovered only slowly through the 1930s. As traditional industries of coal, iron and steel, textiles and shipbuilding declined, new industries such as manufacturing motorcars and electrical goods began to expand.

LEISURE

The 1930s saw an increase in leisure activities. People enjoyed a Sunday afternoon drive to the country in the new cheaper Morris, Austin and Ford cars. However, only about one family in ten owned a car, so motorbikes with side-cars and buses taking people on day trips and seaside holidays became popular. Visits to the cinema, to see the "Talkies" that had replaced silent films, became very popular. Odeon cinemas in the huge American style with restaurants and dance floors could be found in most large urban centres.

Below: **The 1930 Matchless Silver Hawk. Motorbikes were popular with people who could not afford a car.**

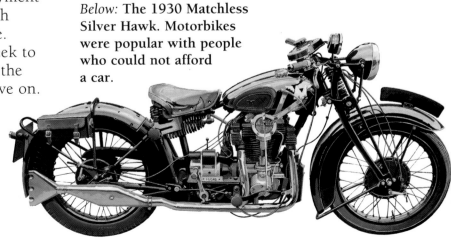

Left: Many young wealthy women in the 1920s scandalized their elders with their sophisticated evening clothes and their fast lifestyle. Many enjoyed jazz music and dancing.

HOUSING IN THE 1930s

There was a boom in the building of private houses, with some three million built in this decade. Many of these were built in so-called ribbon developments along roads into towns. People became interested in labour-saving devices, home comforts and entertainments such as gramophones, the wireless (radio), vacuum cleaners and refrigerators.

IMPERIAL TALKS

Imperial Conferences, the forerunners of today's Commonwealth Conferences, were held in 1926 and 1930. As a result of their discussions, the British Parliament passed the Statute of Westminster in 1931, which defined the laws concerning the independence of the dominions and their allegiance to the British monarchy more clearly.

The dominions were Canada, Australia, New Zealand, South Africa, the Irish Free State and Newfoundland. Allegiance to the Crown was, as now, the unifying factor. The statute also laid down that changes to royal titles and the succession to the throne had to be decided by the parliaments of all the dominions as well as that of the United Kingdom.

- **1923** Britain criticizes French and Belgian occupation of the Rhur. Benito Mussolini challenges the League of Nations over Corfu. Stanley Baldwin becomes PM (Conservative). General election produces hung Parliament

- **1924** First Labour government: Ramsay MacDonald PM. General election after only eight months returns Conservatives. British Empire exhibition opens. Britain's first national airline, Imperial Airways, is set up. Leigh Mallory and Irvine die below peak of Everest. Eric Liddell and Harold Abrahams win gold medals in Olympics. Indian campaigner for Indian independence Mahatma Gandhi goes on hunger strike in his efforts to persuade Britain to grant Home Rule. Winston Churchill becomes Chancellor of the Exchequer

- **1925** Cyprus becomes Crown colony. Unemployment Insurance Act passed. Britain builds Singapore naval base. First white lines on roads and first traffic lights introduced

- **1926** General Strike in Britain. Reading University founded. J.L. Baird demonstrates how television works. *Winnie the Pooh* is published

- **1927** IRA kill Kevin O'Higgins, Irish Minister of Justice. Trades Disputes Act: certain strikes and lockouts are declared illegal

- **1928** Women get the vote at 21. Alexander Fleming discovers penicillin mould in his laboratory. J.L. Baird demonstrates colour television

Right: In 1928 the British bacteriologist Alexander Fleming discovered the mould from which he developed the drug penicillin. This cured previously fatal diseases.

Left: Scottish engineer John Logie Baird (1888-1946) was the first to transmit a television picture by radio waves in 1926. His invention led to the first television sets and broadcasting companies.

EDWARD AND MRS SIMPSON

When George V died in 1936, his eldest son, Edward VIII, was 41 and unmarried. As Prince of Wales he had acquired great personal popularity, both at home and in the empire. Edward was aware of the social problems of the time, and had made public remarks about both slums and unemployment which earned widespread approval. However, the government saw this as political meddling and Edward spent much of his time living in France with his closest friend, Mrs Wallis Simpson. She was an American with one divorced husband and another whom she was divorcing.

Edward's infatuation with Mrs Simpson was the talk of the world's press, but by a voluntary agreement the British newspapers avoided all mention of it. The prime minister, Stanley Baldwin, spoke to the King about Mrs Simpson. Edward declared that he wanted to marry her, and proposed a morganatic marriage, a marriage in which Mrs Simpson would be his wife but not his queen. Baldwin consulted the dominions. They were against the King's proposal, and so were most of the people in Britain. Edward chose to abdicate (give up the throne) in 1936 and married Mrs Simpson in 1937.

Above: **Amy Johnson (1903-1941) an English pilot, was the first woman to fly solo, in 1930, from England to Australia.**

Below: **The Duke and Duchess of Windsor, formerly King Edward VIII and Mrs Wallis Simpson. After their marriage in 1937 they lived mainly in France.**

- **1931** National Government formed under Ramsay MacDonald; 3 million unemployed and dole cut by 10 percent. Whipsnade Zoo opened. First London trolley bus. Statute of Westminster drawn up

- **1932** Eamon de Valera elected President of Ireland. Former Labour MP Oswald Mosley starts British Union of Fascists. James Chadwick discovers neutrons. Jobless organize hunger marches

- **1933** Nazis take power in Germany. Gandhi released after hunger strike in jail. Oxford Union votes "not to fight for king and country". ICI company invents polythene

- **1934** Driving tests introduced. Liner *Queen Mary* launched with aid from government to help unemployment. First Mersey Tunnel opened. Manchester Central Library opens. Composer Edward Elgar dies

- **1935** Anti-Catholic riots in Belfast. Green Belt around London established to protect countryside from urban expansion. Robert Watson-Watt builds first practicable radar. Paperback revolution: Allen Lane founds Penguin Books. 48 km/h speed limit and crossing beacons introduced. Ramsay MacDonald retires: Stanley Baldwin (Conservative) heads National Government. Anglo-German Naval Pact allows German naval expansion. Lawrence of Arabia dies in motor bike accident. Clement Attlee becomes new Labour leader. Unemployed shipyard workers march from Jarrow to London

- **1936** George V dies: succeeded by son, Edward VIII. BBC starts regular TV service. Edward VIII abdicates: succeeded by brother, George VI (to 1952). British volunteers fight in Spanish Civil War. Hitler's remilitarization of the Rhineland goes unopposed. Pinewood film studios open. *Queen Mary* makes maiden voyage. Crystal Palace in destroyed in fire

GEORGE VI

Edward's successor was his brother Albert, Duke of York, who took the title of George VI in 1936. The new king was a quiet, shy man with a speech impediment. But he had the great advantage of a beautiful and popular wife, Elizabeth (later known as the Queen Mother), and together they gained the respect and affection of the people.

George VI had an extremely difficult reign, during which he took upon himself the task of maintaining the morale of the British people throughout World War II.

THE THREAT OF HITLER'S GERMANY

Like the new prime minister Neville Chamberlain, George VI had hoped that a peaceful solution could be found to Europe's growing insecurity. This was caused by German naval expansion and rebuilding its military might under Adolf Hitler who had become the Fuhrer, or leader, of the country in 1934. He wanted to avenge the humiliation brought to Germany by the Versailles Peace Settlement of 1919. Chamberlain pursued a policy of appeasement; that is, he sought to make concessions to Hitler in the hope that peace would be maintained.

Once it was evident that Hitler was set on the military domination of Europe, George VI did everything he could to encourage the countries which owed allegiance to him to play their part in the war. He took an active part in the war himself, and with his wife inspected the bomb damage of the Blitz and visited munitions factories. Through his efforts the royal family became an emotional rallying point in the struggle against Nazi Germany.

Above: George VI (1936-1952) the second son of George V, had not expected to be king. However, Edward VIII's sudden abdication meant that George VI became king without any chance to prepare for the role. George and his queen, Elizabeth, became a focus for all classes struggling through the turbulent years of World War II. Their devotion to duty in the war helped them to re-establish the reputation of the monarchy after the problems caused by the abdication crisis.

- **1937** Air raid precautions planned. Irish Free State becomes Eire. Frank Whittle builds first jet engine. Stanley Baldwin retires: Neville Chamberlain becomes PM

- **1938** National register for war service. Women's Voluntary Service founded. *Queen Elizabeth* (largest-ever liner) is launched. Britain allows Hitler's *Anschluss*, which is a union with Austria. Terrorist bombings in Palestine. *Mallard* sets locomotive speed record. Neville Chamberlain meets Adolf Hitler in attempt to resolve Sudeten crisis in which Hitler sought to reclaim the Sudetenland area of Czechoslovakia, which Germany was forced to give back after World War I. The Munich Agreement is signed, the height of appeasement, and Sudetenland is given to Germany. This fails to satisfy Hitler and German troops take over the whole of Czechoslovakia in March. Again many protests are made but no action is taken

- **1939** Morden-Finchley tube line constructed. Britain and France promise to support Poland, Greece and Romania against German aggression. Conscription introduced. George VI visits Canada and US. John Cobb sets land speed record of 594 km/h. Russo-German pact. First British transatlantic airmail service begins. Germans invade Poland. Britain and France declare war. Leaflet raids on Germany: the Phoney War period. Battle of the River Plate

- **1940** Food rationing starts. Women get old age pension at 60. Germans invade Norway and Denmark. Neville Chamberlain resigns: Winston Churchill forms coalition. Germans invade Netherlands, Belgium and France. Home Guard formed. Fire-watching compulsory. British forces evacuated from Dunkirk in northern France. Penicillin developed as antibiotic. French surrender. Battle of Britain. The Blitz: London the main target. The George Cross instituted

Right: On September 27, 1938 Queen Elizabeth launched the Cunard-White Star liner named for her, the *Queen Elizabeth*. It was the largest ship of its day.

World War II

BRITAIN HAD APPEASED GERMANY when the Nazi government of Adolf Hitler marched into Austria and then into Czechoslovakia. But Hitler's attack on Poland, a country which Britain had pledged to help, brought Britain and France into the war. On September 3, 1939 they declared war on Germany.

Britain's lack of military readiness meant that nothing could be done to help Poland. For the first seven months there was a "Phoney War", in which little happened that affected Britain directly, apart from a blackout against air-raids, food rationing and the evacuation of children from city areas to the relative safety of the country.

WINSTON CHURCHILL

The sudden unleashing of Hitler's war machine on Denmark and Norway led to a crisis of confidence in the government of Neville Chamberlain. An all-party coalition was called for, and by general consent the choice of leader fell on Winston Churchill. He had been in the political wilderness since 1929. Throughout the 1930s his had been a lone voice warning of the possibility of war and the need to prepare. Churchill had a lot of energy and a fertile mind, which gave him the qualities needed by a wartime leader.

THE BATTLE OF THE ATLANTIC

The battle which nearly defeated Britain was the battle of the Atlantic – a naval battle which lasted from 1941 throughout the war. German U-boats (submarines) sank hundreds of Allied ships that were bringing vital food and supplies to Britain. The use of convoys, and help from the United States even before it entered the war, gradually reduced the losses. The British navy managed to destroy three powerful German battleships: the *Graf Spey*, *Bismarck*, and *Tirpitz*.

Above: **Sir Winston Churchill (1874-1965) was a soldier, writer and statesman who led Britain through World War II. He became prime minister in May 1940.**

Below: **Adolf Hitler (1889-1945) was dictator of Germany from 1933 to 1945. He created the Nazi party, and his aggressive policies led to the outbreak of World War II.**

● **1941** Double Summer Time introduced. House of Commons bombed. Lend-Lease: US aid for Britain. Winston Churchill and US President Franklin Delano Roosevelt sign Atlantic Charter. Clothes rationing begins (to 1949). Conscription for women introduced. Russia invaded by Germany, and becomes an Ally. HMS *Ark Royal* is sunk. Japanese attack American naval base at Pearl Harbor, Hawaii: US brought into the war. British Eighth Army advances and retreats in Egypt and Libya

● **1942** Term United Nations first used. Japanese take Malaya, Singapore, Burma and Hong Kong. Baedeker raids: Germans bomb Bath and other cultural centres in Britain. British invade Madagascar. Mediterranean island of Malta resists continual attack: awarded the George Cross. India to get dominion status. Oxfam founded. Commando raid on Dieppe, France. Battle of El Alamein, Egypt: Allies begin final advance across Libya. Allies land in western north Africa. Economist Sir William Beveridge produces plan for social security

● **1943** Winston Churchill and President Roosevelt meet at Casablanca, Morocco. North Africa cleared of Germans and Italians. Allies land in Sicily. Allies invade mainland Italy. Italy surrenders, joins the Allies. Churchill, Roosevelt and Joseph Stalin of Russia meet at Teheran, Persia (now Iran)

THE WAR IN AFRICA

Italy, Germany's ally, joined the war in 1940, and tried to capture Egypt and the Suez Canal from its colony in Libya. The fighting raged to and fro in the Western Desert, until by July 1942 a combined Italian and German force had advanced to within 100 kilometres of Alexandria.

Three months later the British and Commonwealth armies, under new commanders (Generals Alexander and Montgomery), broke the German/Italian forces in the battle of El Alamein. By May 1943 North Africa was clear of the enemy, and two months later the Allies landed in Sicily. By October Italy had surrendered and changed sides to support the Allies.

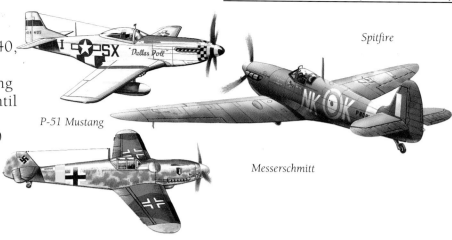

Spitfire

P-51 Mustang

Messerschmitt

THE D-DAY INVASION OF EUROPE

The invasion of Europe by Allied forces took 18 months to prepare. D-Day, the first assault, came on June 6, 1944, when an Allied force stormed ashore on the Normandy coast. A force of 3,000,000 men had assembled in Britain; and 11,000 aircraft, 5,000 large ships and 4,000 smaller landing craft took them across the Channel. The first wave of infantry and armoured troops waded ashore at 6.30 am under a cloudy sky. It was helped by Allied air superiority.

Above: **Hitler planned to invade Britain. He began with a series of daylight air-raids to cripple the coastal defences.**
In the desperate battle of Britain, German bombers and Messerschmitts were fought off by RAF (Royal Air Force) Spitfires. Foiled, Hitler cancelled his invasion plans. The Germans then switched to a series of intensive night-bombing raids, first on London and then on other industrial centres like Coventry. This became known as "the Blitz" – short for *Blitzkrieg* (the German word for lightning war). Air-raid sirens became a well-known sound. The Blitz eased in May 1941, when the Nazi bombers were switched to attack Russian targets.

Right: **Allied troops land on a Normandy beach on D-Day, June 6, 1944, to start the liberation of France. It was the greatest sea invasion in history.**

THE WAR IN THE EAST

The Japanese attack on Pearl Harbor, an American naval base in Hawaii, in December 1941 brought the US into the war against Japan and its ally, Germany. By May 1942 the Japanese had overrun British territories in the Far East and then threatened Australia and India. Much of the Allied counter-attack in the Far East was carried out by American and Australian forces. The British fought in Burma to protect India, aided by a commando force, the Chindits.

THE END OF THE WAR

The war in Europe dragged on until the beginning of May 1945. Then, with his armies retreating, and constant bombing knocking out his oil supplies and industries, Hitler committed suicide, and the Germans surrendered. Britain celebrated May 8th as VE-day (Victory in Europe).

The war with Japan threatened to be a much longer affair. But in August the Allies launched a new and terrifying weapon. They dropped two atomic bombs on Japan, and within days the Japanese surrendered. British and American scientists had been working on the bomb for several years, in the greatest secrecy. VJ-day was celebrated on September 2. Events to mark the 50th anniversary of both VE and VJ day took part across the country in 1995, amid much celebration and remembrance.

Valentine

Tiger 1E

M-26 Pershing

Left: The British *Valentine* tank first saw action in the Western Desert. Germany's *Tiger* tank was one of the most powerful with armour 10 cm thick. The American *Pershing* tank had a speed of 50 km/h.

Right: The first atomic bombs were dropped by the United States in World War II, on the Japanese cities of Hiroshima and Nagasaki. The destruction the bombs caused was horrific, 200,000 people were killed and about as many people, over a wide area, were injured.

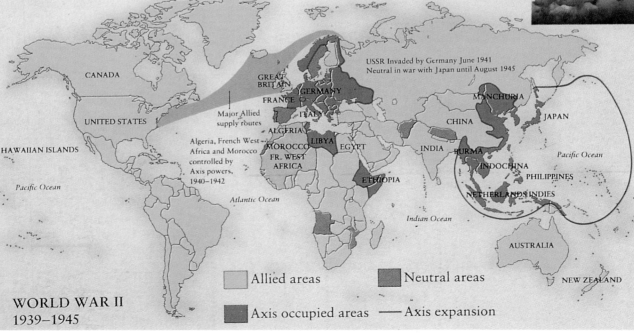

WORLD WAR II
1939–1945

Allied areas

Neutral areas

Axis occupied areas

Axis expansion

Left: By 1941 Germany had conquered most of Europe and entered North Africa. By 1942 the Japanese had overrun most of Southeast Asia and threatened Australia. Italy, Germany and Japan formed the Axis Powers; Britain, France, the US and Russia the Allied Powers.

Left: Excited crowds outside Buckingham Palace wait for the royal family to appear on VE (Victory in Europe) day, May 8, 1945. The royal family played a vital role during the war, helping to maintain morale. The king and queen refused to be evacuated from London and would frequently visit bombed areas to offer their support.

● **1944** Pay-As-You-Earn tax scheme introduced. New air-raids on London. National Health Service proposed. D-Day: Allied armies invade Normandy. Flying-bomb (V1) raids on London begin. Education Act plans to raise school-leaving age. Blackout restrictions lifted. Antwerp and Brussels liberated. British land on French Riviera. Battle of the Bulge (last major German offensive). First V2 rocket bombs launched. British paratroop attack on Arnhem (Netherlands) fails

● **1945** British 14th Army opens offensive in Burma. Churchill, Roosevelt and Stalin confer at Yalta, Crimea. Germans surrender (May 7). Coalition breaks up: Churchill forms Conservative caretaker government. General election: Labour landslide (Labour 393, Conservatives 213, Liberals 12, others 22): Clement Attlee PM. Allies meet at Potsdam June-July. Atomic bombs dropped on Hiroshima and Nagasaki, Japan

FOCUS ON THE WAR EFFORT

World War II had a huge impact on the lives of ordinary people. Everyone expected extensive bombing raids on British cities. So in the summer of 1939 over 1,500,000 children were evacuated to stay with families in the countryside. In London and Liverpool, many people who remained had to sleep on the underground station platforms during air-raids. Others sought refuge in Anderson shelters in their gardens. Blackout curtains kept all lights hidden, and wardens went round to ensure this. As food was rationed, people were encouraged to "Dig for Victory" and grew their own food in allotments and back gardens and on any available piece of land.

PLANNING FOR A WELFARE STATE

Even when the war was at its height the government began planning for peace. In 1942 the economist Sir William Beveridge brought out a government report on Social Insurance and Allied Services, which laid the foundations for the modern welfare state. Beveridge proposed that free unemployment benefit, health treatment, sickness pay, retirement pensions and family allowances should all be combined in one simple scheme.

In 1944 the Minister of Education, R.A. Butler (known as Rab Butler), sponsored the Butler Act which provided for three stages of free education (primary, secondary and further) and introduced the grammar school and secondary modern school systems. It also planned that the school-leaving age should be raised from 14 to 16.

LABOUR SWEEPS TO POWER

The coalition government which had fought the war did not survive long after the end of fighting in Europe. There had been no election for nearly ten years – twice the normal time allowed and people wanted a change. So Churchill resigned, and a general election was held in 1945.

The result was a sweeping victory for the Labour Party, which was returned with a majority of 146. Its leader, Clement Attlee, who had been deputy to Churchill in the coalition government, became prime minister. Labour won with a policy of social and economic reconstruction which was similar to the Beveridge plan, while the Conservatives bore the blame for much of the hardship and discontent of the 1930s.

Below: Many women joined the armed forces or took up the call to "dig for victory" by joining the Women's Land Army.

AMERICAN AID

Labour's plans for the future were greatly hampered by thehuge debts left by the war. Britain's exports had dropped sharply, while it had to borrow hugely to pay for supplies. It had also had to sell off a quarter of its overseas investments thereby losing the income from them. Worse still, the Lend-Lease scheme, by which the United States provided goods on a more or less free-gift basis, abruptly ended. Britain had also lost millions of tonnes of merchant shipping. A huge loan from the United States, called the Marshall Loan, went only part way towards bridging the financial gap. For several years after the war had ended people in Britain faced clothes and food rationing.

NATIONAL INSURANCE

Despite financial difficulties, the Labour government managed to carry through part of its welfare programme including the introduction of National Insurance against old age and unemployment: every man and woman who worked had to pay some money every week into a national insurance fund – as did the employers. Then, if they became unable to work through illness, having a baby, unemployment or retirement, they could claim financial benefits (support). The National Health Service was launched in 1948, providing free health care. Even funerals were paid for, so for the first time the government helped its citizens "from cradle to grave" as William Beveridge proposed. Legal aid was also established to help poor people meet the cost of court cases.

NATIONALIZATION

The Labour government also believed that the major utilities of the country, such as coal, electricity and the railways, should not be owned by private companies run for shareholders' profits but should be owned and run by the government in the interests of the British public.

With this in mind, the coal mines were nationalized in 1947, the railways, electricity and gas in 1948, and the steel industry and the Bank of England. The government hoped that the profits made from these industries could be spent on the new machinery and equipment needed to run them properly.

CHANGES IN THE HOUSE OF LORDS

The Labour government reduced the power of the House of Lords to delay bills that the Commons had passed. In 1911 this power had been set at two years; a new act in 1949 reduced it to one. Another reform removed the right of businessmen to have a vote for their business premises as well as at home. One person, one vote became the rule. The House of Lords continued to be criticized because all its members, apart from the bishops and the Law Lords, inherited their titles and their right to sit in the Lords.

Below: **In August 1948 the Olympic Games were held in London. These were the first games to be held for twelve years.**

- **1945** Lend-lease ends: financial crisis. United Nations inaugurated. US lends Britain $3.75 billion. Family allowances begin. Labour government elected; Clement Attlee PM. German war trials begin in Nuremberg. George Orwell's *Animal Farm* published

- **1946** Trade Disputes Act (1927) repealed. Bank of England nationalized. New Towns Act passed. Civil Aviation nationalized. Churchill's Iron Curtain speech at Fulton, Missouri. BBC resumes TV (suspended since 1939), with 12,000 viewers. Bread rationed (world shortage). BBC Third Programme begins (forerunner of Radio 3). National Health Act

- **1947** Coal mines nationalized. Fuel crisis: shortage of coal. Road transport nationalized. India partitioned to form independent India and Pakistan. First atomic pile installed at Harwell. Princess Elizabeth marries Philip Mountbatten, Duke of Edinburgh. School-leaving age raised to 15

- **1948** Railways, power and gas industries are nationalized. British control in Palestine comes to an end. Act declares that all Commonwealth citizens are automatically British. Bread rationing ends. Corporal punishment is abolished. National Health Service is established. Olympic Games are held in London. Nottingham University is founded

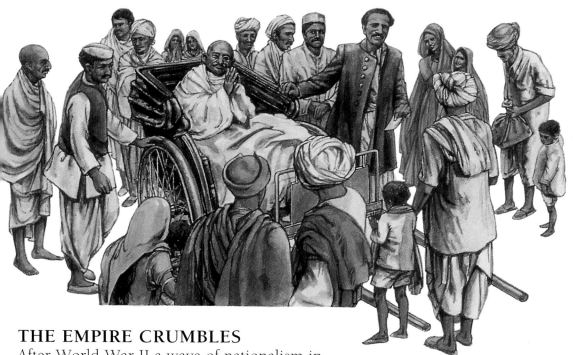

Left: **Mahatma Gandhi led India to independence from the British in 1947. He did this by organizing passive (non-violent) resistance to British rule on a mass scale and was imprisoned several times. Gandhi was assassinated in 1948 by a Hindu fanatic.**

THE EMPIRE CRUMBLES

After World War II a wave of nationalism in Britain's colonies was accompanied by a growing belief among the British that having an empire was morally unjustified and uneconomic. As a result, the dominions (former British empire colonies) were swiftly given independence. In 1947 the Indian empire was split into two countries, India and Pakistan. This led to mass emigration and hideous massacres across India as it did not go far enough towards solving religious conflicts. Burma (now Myanmar) and Ceylon (now Sri Lanka) both became independent in 1948. Burma opted to leave the Commonwealth, as did Ireland, which declared itself an independent republic in 1949.

CHANGE OF GOVERNMENT

After five difficult years the Labour Party went into the general election of 1950 considerably divided, and although it won, its overall majority was cut to only six. After struggling on for 20 months, it called another election with a manifesto which made little mention of any further nationalization – once the main plank of the Labour platform.

The Conservatives were returned with a majority of 16. Winston Churchill, now 76, became prime minister again. Hardly had the dust of the election settled than George VI, who had survived an operation for lung cancer, died suddenly in his sleep. He was succeeded by his 25-year-old daughter, Elizabeth II, who had been prepared for her future role as queen since childhood.

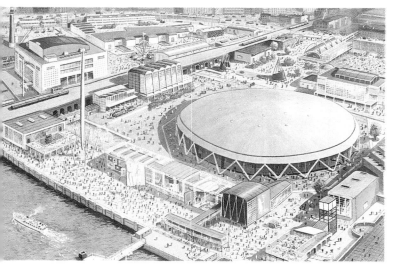

Left: **The Festival of Britain took place in 1951 on London's South Bank. It was a centenary celebration of the Great Exhibition of 1851 and also promoted British-made products, design and architecture. The Festival Hall and Dome of** Discovery can be seen here. British people, homes and gardens, schools, sport, television and cinema were all celebrated, and household names like Ovaltine, Creda, Heinz, Hoover, Morris, EMI and Lloyds Bank were featured.

THE COLD WAR

Despite having been joined by Russia as an ally during World War II, Britain and the United States became increasingly worried about Russia's plans in Eastern Europe (and the world) after the war. British intelligence services were convinced that Russia wanted to dominate the world with its Communist system.

Under the Soviet leader, Joseph Stalin, Russian military might was formidable, but the West had atomic weapons to counter this. However, when Russia developed its own atomic bomb in 1949, and a more powerful hydrogen bomb in 1953, worsening east-west relations reached a stalemate: a Cold War developed, based on fear and calculations about who could defeat whom in a nuclear war. This stalemate dominated foreign policy until Mikhail Gorbachev announced cuts in Soviet forces in central Europe in 1988 and Soviet Communism collapsed.

THE KOREAN WAR

The fear of the spread of Communism also brought Britain into the Korean War of 1950-1953, often called the Forgotten War. Communist North Korea, backed by China, invaded South Korea across the 38th Parallel – a Cold War dividing line drawn up by the increasingly hostile allies after World War II. The West suspected that Stalin had a hand in stirring up and supporting this conflict, and sent troops in to support South Korea.
Some 750 British troops lost their lives in this three-year war.

The Korean War put a great strain on Britain's economy, at a time when it needed to keep pace with Germany and other countries in the post-war recovery period.

THE SUEZ CRISIS

After World War II Britain retained a garrison in Egypt to guard the Suez Canal – a vital link between Britain and the Far East. But Egypt's new ruler, Colonel Nasser, demanded that the British withdraw, and in June 1956 the last troops left the Canal Zone.

Meanwhile Nasser was trying to obtain a loan from Britain and other countries to finance the Aswan High Dam across the River Nile. Anti-British broadcasts on the radio by Egypt, plus doubts about the country's ability to repay any loans, led to the withdrawal of all offers of help. At this Nasser nationalized the Canal, a move which threatened access for other countries.

The newly-formed state of Israel, always at loggerheads with its Arab neighbours, proposed a plan whereby Israel would attack Egypt, giving Britain and France, the chief shareholders in the Suez Canal, an excuse to intervene and restore order. This plan was welcomed by the prime minister, Anthony Eden, who had succeeded Churchill in 1955. Eden had been a skilful foreign secretary, but his skill now deserted him.

Israel attacked Egypt as planned: Britain and France demanded a withdrawal of troops on both sides, and proposed an Anglo-French garrison for the Canal. Egypt refused and this was a signal for Anglo-French troops to invade. Pressure from the United Nations, led by the United States, and from Russia forced an immediate withdrawal of the British and French forces. A few months later Anthony Eden resigned as prime minister, due to ill health, and retired from political life.

Left: **On May 29, 1953, Sir Edmund Hillary of New Zealand and Tenzig Norgay, a Nepalese Sherpa tribesman, ascended the summit of Everest. They became the first to scale the highest mountain in the world, just as Elizabeth II ascended to the throne. These two newsworthy events were reported at the same time on the BBC World Service.**

Elizabeth II

IN 1,000 YEARS OF ENGLISH HISTORY only four monarchs have enjoyed a longer reign than Elizabeth II. They are Edward III, Henry III, George III and Queen Victoria. Like her Tudor namesake, Elizabeth came to the throne aged 25 but Elizabeth II celebrated her 70th birthday in 1996, whereas Elizabeth I did not reach hers. Elizabeth II was the eldest daughter of George VI and Lady Elizabeth Bowes-Lyon. She had married Philip Mountbatten in 1947. Her coronation ceremony, in 1953, was a spectacular event.

Above: Queen Elizabeth at her coronation, in 1953. Her reign has become the longest this century and one of the longest in British history.

Below: Elizabeth II's Coronation Crown, now in the Tower of London. It was made in 1660, of gold with over 400 precious and semi-precious stones.

Left: Elizabeth II (1952-) was the eldest daughter of George VI and Lady Elizabeth Bowes-Lyon. She was only 25 when she became queen.

● **1949** Clothes rationing ends. Republic of Ireland is proclaimed. Britain reaffirms position of Northern Ireland in the United Kingdom. Power of the House of Lords is reduced. Apartheid in South Africa begun

● **1950** Scottish Nationalists take Stone of Scone from Westminster (found 1952). General election: Labour majority cut to six. National Service extended to two years (from 18 months). Korean War (to 1953)

● **1951** Festival of Britain. Charges for teeth and spectacles introduced: Labour split. Comet, first jet airliner, developed. General election: Conservatives win majority of 16: Churchill PM

● **1952** George VI dies; succeeded by daughter, Elizabeth II. Identity cards abolished: numbers remain on NH medical cards. Britain makes its first atom bomb. Oil dispute with Iran. Mau Mau disturbances in Kenya. Last London tram runs

● **1953** Queen Elizabeth II's coronation. Disastrous floods on east coast. Myxomatosis reduces rabbit numbers. Commonwealth team climbs Everest. Road transport denationalized. Egypt becomes a republic

● **1954** Tenants gain security of tenure. Hull University founded. "Flying Bedstead" – first vertical takeoff aircraft – developed. Roger Bannister first to run mile in under 4 minutes (3 min 59.4 sec). Food rationing ends. Persian oil dispute settled

● **1955** Winston Churchill retires: Anthony Eden succeeds as PM. General election: Conservatives increase majority to 67. Ruth Ellis is last woman executed for murder. Clement Attlee retires as Labour leader: succeeded by Hugh Gaitskell. Exeter University founded. Duke of Edinburgh's Award Scheme starts. ITV and VHF broadcasts begin

RACE RELATIONS

Until the late 1950s Britain was an almost exclusively white community. But Britain was short of labour after the war and so encouraged immigration from the West Indies, India and Pakistan. Until 1962 anyone from the empire or Commonwealth could come to Britain to live. In 1962 Macmillan's government tried to limit immigration by stating that they must have a job to come to.

The presence of coloured immigrants in large numbers soon resulted in serious racial tensions which the country had not previously experienced. In 1968 many Asians poured in from Kenya and immigration restrictions tightened.

By 1970 the numbers of immigrants had risen to more than one million. To protect these people against racial prejudice in areas such as employment and housing, Parliament passed laws to inflict penalties on people found showing open discrimination, and set up a Race Relations Board to hear complaints and act on them.

● **1956** Premium bonds introduced. First Aldermaston march against nuclear weapons. Suez Canal crisis: Anglo-French intervention fails to stop canal's nationalization by Egypt. Suez Canal is blocked

● **1957 Anthony** Eden ill, retires: succeeded by Harold Macmillan as PM. Jodrell Bank radio telescope tracks Sputnik 1 (first satellite). Treaty of Rome signed: Britain does not join EEC. Vietnam War begins (to 1975)

● **1958** Life peerages introduced. Race riots in London and Nottingham. Elizabeth's eldest son, Charles, created Prince of Wales. Last debutantes presented at Court. Fishing dispute with Iceland. British party under Vivian Fuchs makes first trans-antarctic crossing

● **1959** Christopher Cockerell's Hovercraft first Channel crossing. First part of M1 motorway open. General election: Conservatives increase majority to 100. Hawaii becomes 50th US state

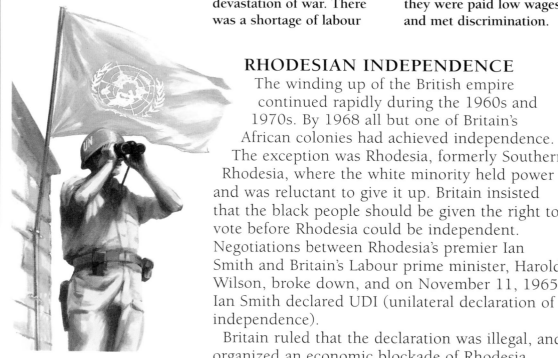

Above: **After World War II the United Nations was created to maintain peace and security in the world.**

Above: **A boatload of immigrants arrives in the 1950s – a time of growth in manufacturing and building after the devastation of war. There was a shortage of labour** and Britain looked to her ex-colonies, particularly India and the West Indies. Thousands emigrated here, hoping for a good life, but they were paid low wages and met discrimination.

RHODESIAN INDEPENDENCE

The winding up of the British empire continued rapidly during the 1960s and 1970s. By 1968 all but one of Britain's African colonies had achieved independence. The exception was Rhodesia, formerly Southern Rhodesia, where the white minority held power and was reluctant to give it up. Britain insisted that the black people should be given the right to vote before Rhodesia could be independent. Negotiations between Rhodesia's premier Ian Smith and Britain's Labour prime minister, Harold Wilson, broke down, and on November 11, 1965, Ian Smith declared UDI (unilateral declaration of independence).

Britain ruled that the declaration was illegal, and organized an economic blockade of Rhodesia. Britain was supported by the United Nations. In 1980 the British government was finally able to negotiate a settlement allowing open elections which led to the establishment of a black majority government, at which point what had been Rhodesia was renamed Zimbabwe.

TROUBLE IN NORTHERN IRELAND

Discrimination was a major factor at the root of the troubles in Northern Ireland which broke out in 1969. The partition of Ireland in 1921, which split the six Protestant and Loyalist counties from the rest of the predominantly Catholic south, left a large number of Catholics north of the border. This Catholic minority faced discrimination in terms of housing, job opportunities and influence in local affairs, and began a civil rights movement to press for better conditions.

Civil rights demonstrations were met by counter-demonstrations from the Protestants, who feared any movement which might bring them into association with Eire rather than with Great Britain. Demonstrations quickly turned into mob violence, with deaths and destruction of property on a scale so serious that later in 1969 British troops were sent in to keep order.

Above: **A British soldier patrols a Belfast street. British troops were sent to protect local communities.**

Left: **The 1960s saw the growth of a social, cultural and artistic revolution highlighted by the Beatles, a pop group from Liverpool. Their records sold in millions and their popularity, which was known as Beatlemania, spread all over the world.**

Below: **Pre-decimal coins were based on multiples of twelve instead of the metric multiples of ten we use now.**

DECIMALIZATION

Decimalization involved countries issuing currency in units that are multiples of ten, for example the French franc is made up of 100 centimes. France was the first European country to decimalize its currency during the French Revolution. By the 1870s most other major powers had adopted a decimal system. Britain and its dependencies were the last to change. On February 15, 1971 Britain adopted a decimal system.

- **1960** Seventeen colonies in Africa, and Cyprus, become independent. Pacemaker for hearts developed

- **1961** Volcanic eruption on island of Tristan da Cunha in the South Atlantic: population evacuated to Britain. Farthings cease to be legal tender. Francis Crick and James Watson solve the structure of DNA. South Africa leaves Commonwealth. New universities: Essex and Sussex. Sierra Leone, Tanganyika independent. Yuri Gagarin is first man in space

- **1962** New Coventry cathedral opened. Thalidomide tragedy: babies born with deformities. Independent: Jamaica, Trinidad and Tobago, Uganda. New Act controls immigration from West Indies and Pakistan. London smog: 750 die. First British satellite (Ariel) launched from US space centre at Cape Canaveral

- **1963** Common Market rejects Britain. Beeching Report begins rail closures. Beatles pop group win international fame. Nuclear power station opens at Bradwell. Dartford Tunnel is opened. Peerage Act gives peers right to disclaim on inheritance. Kenya, Malaysia and Zanzibar gain independence. Haorld Macmillan retires: succeeded as PM by Sir Alec Douglas-Home. New universities: Newcastle, York. French president, General Charles de Gaulle, vetoes Britain's entry to the EEC. Britain signs agreement banning nuclear testing

- **1964** Malawi and Zambia independent. New universities: East Anglia, Kent, Lancaster, Strathclyde, Warwick. General election: Labour victory; Harold Wilson becomes PM. Rolling Stones gain popularity

- **1965** Oil, gas found in North Sea. Greater London created. White Rhodesians make unilateral declaration of independence. First woman high court judge appointed

THE ENERGY BOOM

The 1960s and 1970s were an exciting time for British energy and transport development. Oil and natural gas were discovered beneath the North Sea in 1965, which greatly boosted Britain's economic and financial standing in the world. But there was no manufacturing growth or investment in industrial development to take advantage of this new-found wealth.

THE HOVERCRAFT

In 1959, British engineer Christopher Cockerell produced his first hovercraft, the *SRN1* – it crossed from the Isle of Wight to mainland England. In 1965 the first passenger service using hovercrafts started between Britain and France. Hovercrafts ride on a cushion of low-pressure air, blown downwards by fans. The air is held in by a skirt, or side wall, around the hovercraft. This system is ideal for crossing water and landing on beaches or flat land. Hovercraft can easily reach speeds of 120 kilometres an hour They can carry dozens of cars and up to 400 passengers.

JETS AND CARS

Ordinary people were more mobile than ever before. A network of motorways was springing up all over the country – the M1 was opened in 1959, and Spaghetti Junction in Birmingham linked a staggering 18 roads. Cars became sportier and faster, and more and more people could now afford them. Electric and diesel trains took over from steam. People were also now flying for the first time on package holidays to Spain. The first jet airliners, such as the De Havilland *Comet,* came into operation in the early 1960s. In 1969 a *Concorde* prototype made its first flight. *Concorde* became the first supersonic airliner to enter service. It carries up to 144 passengers at twice the speed of sound, and can cross the Atlantic in three hours.

TECHNOLOGICAL CHANGES

Many labour-saving devices that are now taken for granted began to appear in the 1970s – for example, dishwashers, microwave ovens, food mixers and launderettes. Inventor Clive Sinclair introduced the affordable pocket calculator, as well as home computers and digital watches.

Above: **One of many floating offshore oil platforms in the North Sea. The five steel legs of the platform are lowered into the sea in order to anchor it to the seabed. The discovery of oil in the North Sea in the mid-1960s gave Britain the opportunity to transform its economy.**

Below: **Cutaway drawing of the luxury ship *Queen Elizabeth II,* launched in 1967. The liner is 294 metres long and 32 metres wide. It carries a crew of 906 and can accomodate 2,025 passengers.**

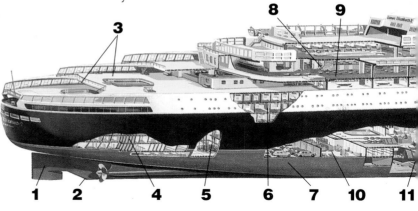

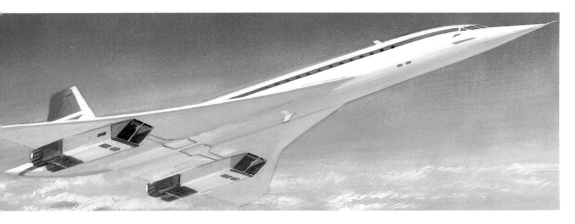

THE COMMON MARKET

The main achievement of Edward Heath's Conservative government was Britain's entry in 1973 into the European Economic Community (EEC), also referred to as the European Community (EC) or the Common Market and more recently as the EU (European Union). Britain declined to join when the EC was formed in 1957, and was turned down when it later changed policy and tried to join in the 1960s. When Labour leader Harold Wilson won the general election of 1974, he negotiated revised terms, and in 1975 invited the public to vote on membership in Britain's first referendum. The vote was a "yes" for staying in the EC. It now comprises 15 Member States: Austria, Belgium, Denmark, Finland, France, Germany, Greece, Ireland, Italy, Luxembourg, The Netherlands, Portugal, Spain, Sweden and the UK. On January 1, 1993, the Single Market came into operation. Its aim is to create a single economic region for people and businesses to travel and trade in freely.

Above: Concorde, the world's only supersonic airliner. Aircraft first broke the sound barrier in the 1940s. Today *Concorde* carries passengers at twice the speed of sound. It was designed and built jointly by Britain and France. The first services were flown in 1976.

Below: **1** Rudder; **2** Screw; **3** Swimming pools; **4** Crew cabins; **5** Car lift; **6** Cabins; **7** Garage; **8** Ballroom; **9** Main lounge; **10** Laundry; **11** Engine room; **12** Stabilizers; **13** Boiler room; **14** Theatre; **15** Reception room; **16** Hospital; **17** Printing shop; **18** Restaurant; **19** Cold stores; **20** Bridge; **21** Bow thrusters; **22** Bow anchor.

● **1966** Barbados, Botswana, Guyana and Lesotho gain independence. Aberfan disaster in Wales: landslip kills 116 children, 28 adults. New universities: Aston, Bath, Bradford, Brunel, City, Heriot Watt, Loughborough, Stirling, Surrey. First Ombudsman appointed. Severn and Tay road bridges open

● **1967** Pirate radios outlawed: BBC launch Radio 1 as pop music station. Breath tests introduced. Homosexuality between consenting adults no longer offence. Liner *QueenElizabeth II* launched. Economic blockade of Rhodesia. Gibraltar votes to stay British. Francis Chichester sails around the world and is knighted. Steel industry renationalized. Sterling devalued by 14.3 percent. New universities: Dundee, Salford

● **1968** Mauritius, Swaziland independent. Welsh nationalists set bombs. Martin Ryle discovers pulsars. Race Relations Act passed. Two-tier postal system introduced

● **1969** Voting age reduced from 21 to 18. School-leaving age up to 16. Rhodesia declares itself a republic. *Concorde* makes its first flight. Robin Knox-Johnston sails round world in first non-stop solo voyage. Wally Herbert leads first trans-arctic expedition. Riots and terrorism in Northern Ireland: troops sent to keep peace. Capital punishment abolished. First men land on the Moon

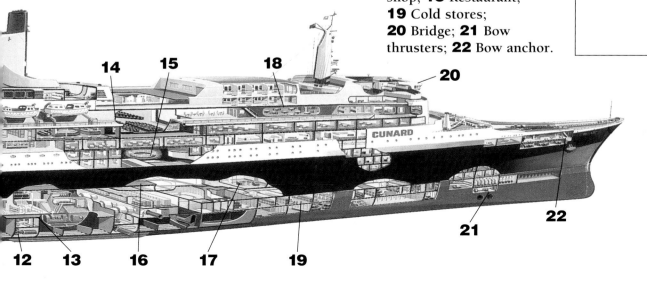

The Maastricht Treaty of 1991 took the Union even further towards a single currency (the ecu, short for European Currency Unit) and a European citizenship that has remained a contentious issue among many members.

THE HEATH AND WILSON YEARS

Economics and labour relations dominated the general elections of the 1970s. In the first, in 1970, most people were confident that the Labour Party would return to power. But in a shock result the Conservatives, under their new leader Edward Heath, won a majority of 31. Britain's heavy international debt was one cause of the defeat.

THE MINERS' STRIKE

In 1974, the miners triggered off the next election. They had been offered a 16 per-cent pay rise but they asked for a pay rise of up to 40 percent, so they threatened to strike. Edward Heath called an election, to get the country's backing for his tough line on wages. The result was a hung Parliament, neither of the two big parties having a majority. Labour took office under Harold Wilson who, after nine months, called a second election which he won with a majority of three.

Left: **Britain and the United States forged a close political alliance under the leadership of Prime Minister Margaret Thatcher (right) and President Ronald Reagan.**

MARGARET THATCHER

Margaret Thatcher came to power as Britain's first ever woman prime minister in 1979, having led the Conservatives to election victory over the Labour Party. She became Britain's longest-serving prime minister last century, and the first to win three general elections in a row for over 150 years.

Margaret Thatcher developed what was called the enterprise culture, which was designed to take people away from dependence on the state (and the welfare state). State-owned industries (such as the telephone, gas, electricity and water services) were transferred into the hands of privately-run companies. The nation's health and school services were made more accountable to public spending.

Thatcher was authoritarian with her ministers – all men – and kept a firm control on the reins of power. But her policies are judged to have encouraged material interests and a decline in moral values.

Internationally Thatcher's tough line earned her the nickname the Iron Lady. Her firm direction during the Falklands War, strong opinions, and the special relationship she developed with US president Reagan, won her widespread renown. At home, however, the introduction of the Community Charge, known as the Poll Tax, was extremely unpopular. Designed to replace the local rates system, this – and her increasingly autocratic style – led to her political downfall. Thatcher resigned on November 22, 1990. She was replaced as leader by John Major, who led Britain for the next seven years.

Left: **On 31 March 1990, 200,000 people descended on central London to demonstrate against the unpopular Poll Tax. Thousands of police were deployed to clear violent protesters from Trafalgar Square.**

THE RISE OF NEW LABOUR

The Labour Party floundered during the Thatcher years, racked with internal divisions. Labour leaders Neil Kinnock and John Smith attempted to modernize and broaden the appeal of the party's policies.

However, it took the election of Tony Blair as party leader in 1994 (after John Smith had died of a heart attack) to make Labour a serious political force. Blair immediately set out a new agenda and revamped the Labour Party's platform, with unprecedented commitments to free enterprise, anti-inflationary policies and to greater integration into the European Union. In May 1997, 'New' Labour won a landslide election victory, with a parliamentary majority of 179. The new government soon put into practice various manifesto commitments, including a minimum wage, devolved parliaments for Scotland and Wales, and a complete reform of the House of Lords. Talks about the future of Northern Ireland – which had begun under John Major – were resumed, and a fragile ceasefire was declared in 1998. In 1999, a new Northern Ireland parliament was formed with substantial powers.

Above: **The 135-metre London Eye stands near the River Thames, offering superb views of the capital. It was one of the main attractions in Britain's Millennium celebrations.**

Below: **Prime Minister Tony Blair enjoys a moment with his new son, Leo, born in the year 2000.**

- **1970** Equal pay for men and women decreed by law. General election: Conservatives win with a majority of 31: Edward Heath becomes PM. First use of rubber bullets in Northern Ireland. First *Concorde* landing at Heathrow

- **1971** Open University starts teaching. Decimal currency introduced. Trade union reform introduced. Margaret Thatcher, education minister, abolishes free school milk

- **1972** "Bloody Sunday": 13 killed in Londonderry riots. Northern Ireland comes under direct rule from Whitehall. Asians expelled from Uganda flee to UK. Industrial Relations Court set up. "Bloody Friday" in Belfast: bombs kill 11, wound 120. Miners' strike. Artefacts from Tutankhamun's tomb on display in British Museum: seen by over one million people. Duke of Windsor (formerly Edward VIII) buried at Windsor

- **1973** Britain joins Common Market. IRA car bomb in London kills 1, injures 216, damages Old Bailey. Counties abolished in Northern Ireland. Power cuts lead to three-day week. Bahamas gain independence. Northern Ireland votes to stay in UK. Israel at war with Arabs: Arabs restrict oil, starting world economic crisis

- **1974** Miners vote to strike: Heath calls general election, and loses. Harold Wilson heads minority Labour government. Miners get 35 percent pay rise. English and Welsh counties reorganized. Second general election: Labour majority three

- **1975** Scottish counties abolished. Cod War with Iceland (to 1976). Britain's first referendum: 60 percent vote to stay in EEC

- **1976** Harold Wilson retires: James Callaghan becomes PM. Betty Williams and Mairead Corrigan form Ulster peace movement and win Nobel peace prize (1977)

Left: **The Falklands operation would have been impossible without Britain's aircraft carriers. The long flat deck acts as a take-off and landing field. To land, aircraft are guided by radar and radio and by signals from the deck. They are stored below the deck.**

Above: **Some of the 10,000 British troops sent with the task force gathered together in April 1982, to recapture the Falkland Islands from the Argentine invaders. This took 73 days.**

Below: **The British Aerospace Sea Harrier FRS Mk 1 achieved great success in the Falklands conflict of 1982. They destroyed 23 enemy Argentine aircraft without suffering a single loss in air combat.**

THE FALKLANDS WAR

For many years Argentina had claimed the Falkland Islands, which they called the Malvinas, but these had been ruled by Britain since 1833. Argentina's sudden invasion of the islands in the South Atlantic on April 2, 1982, took the world by surprise. Lord Carrington, the foreign secretary, and two of his ministers resigned, feeling that they had seriously misjudged the situation. Theirs was not the only misjudgment: Argentina's rulers did not expect such a swift retaliation by Britain.

With a speed which astonished everyone, Britain sent a task force on its way by sea within three days of the invasion, landing the main force on the Falklands on May 21. In a determined and bloody series of battles, British troops recaptured the Falklands 73 days after the invasion. The United Nations condemned Britain's action, and many felt that the aggressive government response had a political motive with a general election not far away. The Argentines finally surrendered at Port Stanley on June 14. The lives lost were 254 British and 750 Argentinian.

At the end of the war, the problem of the Falkland Islands remained unsolved. Britain refused to negotiate with Argentina on the sovereignty question, insisting that the islanders' wish to remain British be respected. The war also led to a major review of Britain's defence strategy, since several of the warships sent to the Falklands had been on the brink of being scrapped or sold.

Left: **Pope John Paul II, from Poland, the first non-Italian pope since the 16th century. He visited Ireland in 1979 and England in 1982. He took part in a joint service with Robert Runcie, Archbishop of Canterbury, thereby healing a rift between England and Rome that had been opened by Henry VIII in 1534.**

STORMS AND DROUGHTS

It is an old joke that the main subject of conversation in Britain is the weather. But from 1987 onwards weather became a very serious topic. The great hurricane of October 16, 1987 was Britain's worst storm for 250 years. It swept across southern England from Cornwall to East Anglia, killing 18 people, leaving a £300,000,000 trail of damage and felling about 9,000,000 trees. In 1989 Britain had its warmest year since records began in 1659, which brought severe droughts. Then early in 1990 a storm on January 25, killed 45 people. 1995 continued to break records with the hottest summer yet recorded and more droughts which seriously affected people's water supplies.

Above: **Remembering Liverpool football fans who died in the Brussels riots in 1985. Liverpool fans fought a running battle with Juventus supporters from Italy during the European Cup Final at the Heysel Stadium in Brussels. A wall collapsed in the chaos and 38 people were killed. As a result, English teams were banned from European Cup Competitions.**

Left: **Damage caused by the 1987 hurricane.**

● **1984** IRA bomb at Brighton's Grand Hotel, aimed at Conservative leaders during the Party Conference, kills 6 people, injures 31. Britain and China agree over Hong Kong's future. Thames Barrier opened. First Cable TV channels open

● **1985** IRA mortar attack kills 9 policemen in Newry, Ulster. Coal strike ends. Bradford soccer ground blaze kills more than 40 fans. Liverpool fans riot in Belgium: 38 people die. Plane fire at Manchester Airport kills 54. Anglo-Irish agreement is signed. Live Aid concert in London raises £40 million for African famine. High-speed train record – Newcastle to London: 2 hrs 19 mins. Race riots in Brixton, Tottenham, Liverpool

● **1986** Michael Heseltine and Leon Brittan resign from the Cabinet. Channel Tunnel agreement signed. Nuclear reactor explodes, Chernobyl, Soviet Union; fallout reaches Britain. Print-workers strike – violence at Wapping. Queen's visit to China first by British monarch. Halley's Comet

● **1987** Ferry *Herald of Free Enterprise* capsizes: 188 people die. Crazed gunman murders 14 people in Hungerford, Berkshire

THE CHANNEL TUNNEL

Napoleon had once approved plans for a tunnel under the Channel in 1802. In 1880 work was begun and then abandoned by British engineers for fear of an invasion. After more than a century of indecision, Britain and France finally signed an agreement in 1986 to dig the Channel Tunnel to link France and Britain by rail. Work began simultaneously in France and England in 1988. The 56-kilometre-long tunnel was dogged by difficulties. Geological problems caused the project to fall behind schedule, and rising costs led to a financial crisis which was solved early in 1990. Some 15,000 workers helped dig the tunnel, and ten lost their lives. Further problems concerned the rail link from Folkestone to London. The Channel Tunnel finally opened in 1993 and passenger services began in 1994. The journey, taking freight, cars and passengers by electric train, takes 40 minutes.

THE GULF WAR

The forces of Saddam Hussein, the Iraqi leader, overran the neighbouring territory of Kuwait in August 1990, causing the United Nations Security Council to authorize the use of force to remove them if they not withdraw by January 15th. Hussein refused and Allied troops from the United States, Britain, France, Italy, Egypt, Saudi Arabia and other Arab nations went to war on January 17th. Conflict ceased on February 27th, with victory for the Allied forces, in what was called Operation Desert Storm, chiefly due to superior air and fire power. The war witnessed 4,000 bombing missions on the first two days alone. The Iraqis counter-attacked using long-range missiles called Scuds. American Patriot missiles shot many Scuds out of the sky.

The Gulf War caused severe environmental problems because over 600 oil wells had been ignited and oil had been emptied into the sea. Kuwait City had been destroyed and Kuwait ransacked. Over 40,000 people were killed, most of them Iraqi, and Hussein remained an unpredictable force in a still unsettled region.

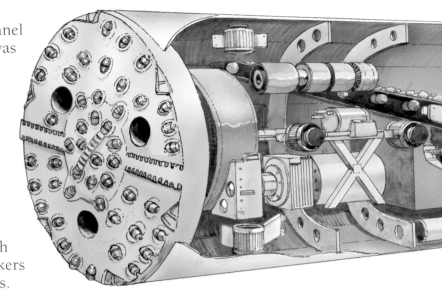

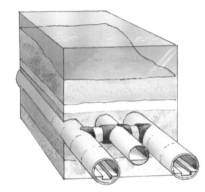

Above: **Cutaway drawing of the Channel Tunnel boring machine.**

Left: **The tunnel is made up of three separate tunnels. Trains run in two of them and the central one is a service shaft.**

Below: **Members of the international coalition who fought in the Gulf War against Iraqi forces.**

In 1991 United Nations troops forced Iraq to withdraw from Kuwait which it had occupied.

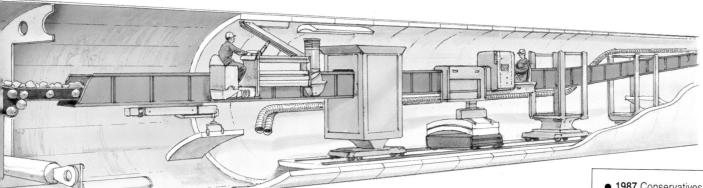

THE HOSTAGE CRISIS

For years Iranian-backed terrorist forces in Beirut had held Western hostages, making a variety of political demands in return for their release. Church of England special envoy Terry Waite made several trips to Beirut to negotiate the release of all the hostages. Waite himself was then captured and held by terrorists for five years.

Long campaigns were conducted by the families and friends of hostages. One of the most notable involved Jill Morrell's poster campaign organized for the release of British journalist John McCarthy. In 1991, after years of negotiations, followed by silence, the hostages were released one by one: journalist John McCarthy on August 8, 1991, after 1,943 days of captivity; September 24, former battle of Britain pilot Jackie Mann kidnapped in May 1989; and on November 18, Terry Waite.

Below: **John McCarthy arrives in England with his father after more than five years in captivity.**

- **1987** Conservatives win third term. Worst storm for 250 years kills 18 people, fells nine million trees. Fire at King's Cross tube station kills 31 people. Terry Waite kidnapped in Beirut. Britain expels 2 Iranian envoys. London stock market collapses. Free dental and eye tests abolished

- **1988** Fire ravages North Sea oil rig *Piper Alpha*: 166 crew die. Triple train crash at Clapham Junction kills 34. Sabotaged airliner crashes on Lockerbie, Dumfriesshire; 270 people die. Australia's bicentenary

- **1989** Airliner crashes on MI: 46 die. President Gorbachev of the USSR visits Britain. John Major succeeds Sir Geoffrey Howe as foreign secretary. House of Commons goes on TV. Chancellor of the Exchequer Nigel Lawson resigns; replaced by John Major. Britain's warmest year since 1659. Hillsborough football stadium disaster kills 94. Guildford Four freed

- **1990** A violent storm lashes southern Britain: 45 people die. Hubble Space Telescope launched. Irish hostage Brian Keenan released after four years captivity in Beirut. Iraq invades Kuwait. Parts for Iraqi supergun seized by Customs. Margaret Thatcher resigns as PM: John Major takes over. Strangeways Prison riot and Poll Tax Riot. British and French tunnel workers meet under the Channel. Britain joins the ERM

- **1991** Gulf War (January 17th-February 27th). Allied victory. Hostages John McCarthy and Terry Waite released from Beirut

AUTHOR DENOUNCED

Salman Rushdie's book *The Satanic Verses* roused a worldwide storm amongst Muslims in 1989. Ayatollah Khomeini, then religious leader of Iran, proclaimed that Rushdie was to be sentenced to death by a *fatwah* (order) for his alleged insult to Islam, and called on Muslims to execute him. In Bradford copies of the book were publicly burned. Rushdie was forced into hiding, although he has managed to make several carefully guarded public and television appearances and to publish new novels.

ENVIRONMENTAL ISSUES

Throughout history, humans have had an immense impact on the Earth, as was terrifyingly demonstrated with the first atomic bomb test in 1945. The atomic bomb made people aware, probably for the first time, that future existence on Earth – a planet which is over 4,500 million years old – depended on looking after the environment.

However, despite having a national Department of the Environment in Britain, appalling pollution continues to cause widespread damage. This ranges from litter on the streets, to industrial chemicals in rivers, seas and oceans, car exhaust fumes choking up the atmosphere, and agricultural pesticides destroying plants and animals.

GREEN PRESSURE GROUPS

The environmental pressure group Greenpeace was founded in 1969. Working in 25 countries, Greenpeace has drawn attention to the problems of whaling, seal hunting, sewage pollution and nuclear testing across the world. When it surveyed Britain's coast in 1986, it found disturbing signs of serious pollution from sewage.

Another pressure group called Friends of the Earth was formed in 1971. This group aims to make people (and their governments) aware of vital world issues such as global warming, pollution, the destruction of tropical rainforests and damage to the ozone layer.

The Environmental Protection Agency was formed in England in 1984, and succeeded in helping to ban the trade in elephant ivory. It continues to campaign against the destruction of whales, dolphins and other wildlife; as do

Left: **View of the Earth from space. In the 1980s and 1990s fears grew about holes in the ozone layer and global warming.**

Below: **When there is an oil spill, environmental groups work hard to clean up the coastline and rescue the animals affected. This otter is being cleaned so that it can be safely returned to the wild.**

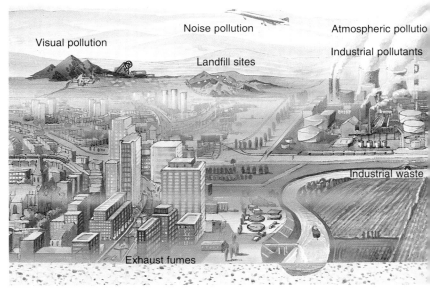

Visual pollution

Noise pollution

Atmospheric pollutio

Landfill sites

Industrial pollutants

Industrial waste

Exhaust fumes

the World Wide Fund for Nature UK, the Royal Society for the Protection of Birds, and the Nature Conservancy Council. Biodiversity – the healthy variety and survival of many species – is considered essential to the survival of the planet. All these groups are concerned with protecting the maximum number of animal and plant species and maintaining the highest numbers within each species.

Conservation and green pressure groups have had considerable influence on the government of the day. However, many environmentalists feel that this influence could be greater, and have formed a political party, called the Green Party, to bring pressure on the government from within Parliament. Their message is to treat the Earth like a living thing, and to treat the environment as a living, breathing organism.

Left: **British zoos play a vital role in public education about wildlife and in preservation programmes which aim to increase populations of rare species such as the giant panda.**

RECYCLING

Since the 1970s the idea of recycling different sorts of household rubbish has caught on. In most British towns today there are recycling centres and bottle banks where glass, for example, can be recycled to save all the fuel needed to make new glass, old newspapers and magazines can be recycled to save trees. Most schools have their own projects and various nationally-organized schemes such the BBC Television programme *Blue Peter's* various initiatives have helped everyone to become involved in protecting their environment.

NUCLEAR PROTEST

Britain's testing of nuclear weapons aroused much public alarm. From 1956, protesters made an annual Easter march from the atomic research station at Aldermaston to Trafalgar Square to urge that tests be stopped. In 1958 the Campaign for Nuclear Disarmament (CND) began a campaign to stop the production of British nuclear weapons.

The collapse of communism and the Soviet Union in 1987 meant the end of the Cold War, in which Russia and the United States had threatened each other with nuclear weapons but never used them. Most nuclear powers eventually signed an agreement to ban the testing of nuclear weapons, but in 1995 France provoked world anger by launching a series of nuclear tests in the Pacific Ocean. Again Greenpeace and Friends of the Earth were active in trying to stop these tests.

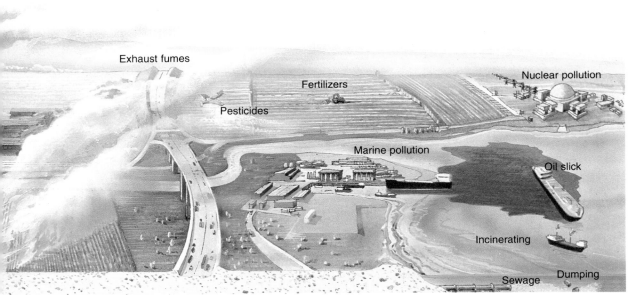

Exhaust fumes

Fertilizers

Pesticides

Nuclear pollution

Marine pollution

Oil slick

Incinerating

Sewage

Dumping

Left: **Some of the causes of pollution: exhaust fumes from road vehicles; smoke from factory chimneys and burning straw; industrial waste, agricultural fertilizers and sewage seeping into rivers and oceans.**

FIRE AND DIVORCE

As Queen Elizabeth II herself stated, 1992 was an "annus horribilis" – a horrible year for the royal family. Princess Anne divorced, the Duke and Duchess of York separated and Windsor Castle was badly damaged by fire.

A growing number of press and television reports speculated about the future of the marriage of Princess Diana and the future king, Prince Charles. Marital difficulties led to their separation in 1992, which was followed by a divorce in 1996.

DEATH OF A PRINCESS

After the divorce, Diana maintained her high public profile, and worked for and supported many charitable causes, especially children's organisations, AIDS awareness, and landmine casualties in war-torn countries. Her unprecedented popularity in Britain and around the world meant that she was dogged by the press, particularly the paparazzi. It was while trying to escape press attention that Diana, her companion Dodi Fayed, and their driver, were killed in a car accident in Paris on 31 August, 1997.

THE FUTURE OF THE MONARCHY

After Diana's death, the Royal Family and their advisors seriously misjudged the mood of the nation, and it was only after pressure from politicians and press that a full state funeral was agreed. Many people saw the Royal Family as cold and uncaring, especially in contrast to the warm and humane image of Princess Diana. Many people began to question why this family should have a special status, and by the end of the 1990s, the future of the British monarchy hung in the balance.

Below: **Princess Diana (1961–1997). In her lifetime, she became far more popular than the Royal Family. In paying tribute to her, Prime Minister Tony Blair described her as the "people's princess".**

Left: **Prince Charles, Prince Harry, Prince William and Diana's brother, Charles (Earl Spencer), watch as Diana's coffin is carried through the streets of London. Princess Diana's death was mourned by people throughout the world, and her funeral watched by many millions on live television.**

- **1992** Conservatives win fourth term. Neil Kinnock resigns as head of Labour Party. Princess Anne divorces and remarries. Church of England Synod votes to allow women priests

- **1993** British and Irish prime ministers sign peace agreement. Shetlands' oil tanker disaster. IRA bombs in Warrington. Grand National race declared void. Britain ratifies Maastricht Treaty

- **1994** Sunday trading allowed by law. John Smith dies of heart attack: Tony Blair elected as leader of Labour Party. Main Irish terrorist groups announce cease-fire. Queen and President François Mitterand of France inaugurate Channel Tunnel. National Lottery introduced

- **1995** John Major fights off challenge for party leadership. Scott Inquiry into government involvement in the illegal sales of arms to Iraq

- **1996** 16 children and 1 teacher gunned down at school gym in Dunblane, Scotland. BSE scare ruins British beef industry. Euro '96: European football championships held in England

- **1997** Labour Party wins General Election with a massive 179 majority. Princess Diana dies in a car crash. IRA declare cease-fire in Northern Ireland

- **1998** Peace agreement successfully introduced in Northern Ireland

- **1999** 750 peers lose their hereditary right to sit in the House of Lords. Elections take place for the new devolved parliaments in Scotland and Wales. Manchester United win an unprecedented FA Cup, Premier League and European Cup treble

- **2000** The old Millennium ends, and a new one begins: official celebrations in London are a moderate success

REFERENCE SECTION

Local History

The history of Britain is not simply the story of its kings and queens, or of momentous events and battles. The history of your town, village, neighbourhood and family can be equally interesting.

You can find out a lot about local history by tracing your own family history (a study called genealogy) or by discovering the history of a local building or street.

WHERE TO LOOK

The best place to start your search is at your local library. Most libraries have a local reference or local studies section. Moreover, your local librarian will be able to give you advice about other sources of information.

Your local church will probably be one of the oldest buildings in the area. Many old churches provide pamphlets about their past that you can buy or make a donation towards. Look at the gravestones too. Their inscriptions might reveal a famous person, or a relative, buried there.

The register of births, marriages and deaths will be in the church safe or local records office. These records will uncover many clues about family history.

Older relatives can recall interesting personal stories from the past, and they may have mementos such as old photographs of their family and possibly of their houses, local towns, streets and countryside.

Your local history museum will have a fascinating array of ancient tools, costumes, maps and pictures of the past. Larger national museums, historic buildings and sites such as castles or cottages run by the National Trust, and other bodies such as local tourist boards, provide all sorts of local history information.

There are other ways to find out about your town's past. For example, do you live near an old coaching inn, canal lock or railway bridge? Is there perhaps an ancient Roman or Anglo-Saxon road nearby? Check with your library if there is any information about their origins. Do you have streets called something like Old London Road, or Turnpike Lane - and if so, do you know why they are called that? If you live in a Chapel Street or Mill Lane, is there a chapel or mill to see? If not, where is it and what happened to it?

BRASS RUBBINGS

In churches you will often see brass plates with engravings of people, often knights, on the walls or floors. They were put up as memorials to important local people who died. You can take rubbings from them provided you get permission first. Some churches have all the equipment ready for hire: paper, tape, and heelball wax. You tape down the paper over the brass then rub the wax over the paper until the complete image appears on the paper.

ROMAN NUMERALS

When exploring famous sights, you will often come across dates engraved on buildings, tombstones or other objects such as milestones:

I = 1	VIII = 8
II = 2	IX = 9
III = 3	X = 10
IV or IIII = 4	L = 50
V = 5	C = 100
VI = 6	D = 500
VII = 7	M = 1,000

So, for example, MDCLXVI=1666, the year of the Great Fire of London.

PLACE NAMES

ROMAN

-caster	} fortified place	Lancaster
-cester		Gloucester
-chester		Chichester

ANGLO-SAXON

-borough	} fortified place	Welingborough
-burgh		Edinburgh
-bury		Canterbury
-combe	valley	Illfracombe
-ham	small village	Chatham
-ing	the clan of	Reading
-ley	meadow	Chorley
-stow	meeting place	Felixstowe
-ton	village	Appleton

DANISH

-by	village	Derby
-thorpe	small village	Scunthorpe
-toft	farmstead	Lowestoft

IRISH

-agh	field	Armagh
Bally-	path	Ballymena
-derry	oak grove	Londonderry
Don-,Down-, Dun-	hill fort	Downpatrick

SCOTTISH

Aber-	mouth of a river	Aberdour
Ach-, Auch-	field	Auchterarder
Ard-	high	Ardrossan
Bal-	house, village	Ballantrae
Car-	rock	Carmoustie
Dum-, Dun-	fort, hill	Dumbarton, Dunfermeline
Loch-	lake	Lochaber
Mon-	moss, moor	Montrose
Mor-	big	Morven
Pit-	croft	Pitlochry
Strath-	valley	Strathclyde

WELSH

aber-	rivermouth	Aberystwyth
betws-	small church	Betws-y-coed
caer-	fortress	Caernarfon
cefn-	ridge	Cefn-y-Bedd
coed-	wood	Betws-y-coed
llan-	enclosure, church	Llandudno
llyn-	lake	Talyllyn
rhos-	moorland	Rhossili
ty-	house	Ty Mawr
y, yr, 'r	the	Betwys-y-Coed
ynys-	island	Ynys Barri

ANCIENT FESTIVALS

DATE	EVENT
January 1st	New Year's Day First Footing, Scotland. Up Helly A', on the last Tuesday: Shetland fire festival, dating back to Viking burials on their blazing ships and marking the end of long winter nights.
February 14th	Blessing the salmon nets in Norham on Tweed, and St Valentine's Day everywhere.
March	Shrove Tuesday pancake race, in Olney, Buckinghamshire.
April 1st	All Fools Day, everywhere.
May 1st	May Day: dancing round the maypole dates back to Celtic celebration of the return of summer. A hobby horse is led through Padstow, Cornwall, and Minehead, Somerset, to represent the old winter.
June	Trooping the Colour, in London. Mid-summer bonfires, especially in Cornwall on June 23rd.
July	Swan-upping, on River Thames, London to Henley: marking swans' beaks.
August	Chairing the Baird at the Royal National Eisteddfod, Wales.
September	Horn Dance in Abbots Bromley, Staffordshire, dates back to medieval hunting rights
October 31st	Hallowe'en
November 5th	Guy Fawkes Night: fireworks and bonfires commemorate the Gunpowder Plot of 1605
December 31st	New Year's Eve, everywhere. Burning the Old Year in Biggar, Strathclyde, and Wick, Caithness.

Things to See

The number by each entry is repeated on a map on page 205.

EARLY BRITAIN

1. Avebury Ring, Wiltshire. This is the largest henge (circle of upright stones) in Europe. Built about 5,000 years ago, it has over 100 stones, some as tall as six metres. Avebury Ring is thought to have been used for sacred rituals for over 500 years.

2. Devizes Museum, Devizes, Wiltshire. Among the collections of finds from Neolithic, Bronze Age and Iron Age sites in Wiltshire, the most important is the Stourhead Collection of Bronze Age urns, beakers, grave goods and ornaments.

3. Grime's Graves, Thetford, Norfolk. Local superstition has named this Neolithic flint mine Grime's Graves – the digging place of the devil. It is one of the first industrial sites in Britain. Archaeologists have found evidence of about 700 mine shafts, and picks made from deer antlers.

4. Jarlshof, near Sumburgh, Shetland Islands, Scotland. Uncovered in a storm in 1905, Jarlshof is a microcosm of Scottish history. The site includes the remains of a Late Bronze Age village, an Iron Age roundhouse, a Viking longhouse, a medieval farmhouse, and a laird's house and hall from the 15th and 16th centuries.

5. Maiden Castle, near Dorchester, Dorset. Probably the best known Iron Age hill-fort, built on the site of a Neolithic defence system. Maiden Castle was the scene of one of the fiercest battles of the Roman conquest of Britain, and was captured by the Romans in AD 43. Archaeologists have uncovered skeletons of badly mutilated bodies buried in shallow graves.

6. Navan Fort, Co. Armagh, Northern Ireland. Three kilometres west of the city of Armagh, this royal fortress is Northern Ireland's most important ancient monument. It was the stronghold of the kings of Ulster until c. AD 332 – a visitors' centre tells their story.

7. Skara Brae, Orkney Islands, Scotland. A Neolithic settlement of stone houses was built c. 2000 BC. The one-room stone houses are remarkably well preserved, having been covered by sand until a storm in 1850. As well as stone furniture such as box-beds and wall cupboards and hearths on the floor for fires, archaeologists have found a pair of dice carved from bone.

8. Stonehenge, on Salisbury Plain, Wiltshire. The most famous megalithic monument of all was built in several stages from c. 3200 to 1300 BC. Huge stones (megaliths) are set in two concentric circles (one within the other). Its exact purpose is unknown but it is thought to have been a religious centre for ceremonies linked to the sun's rising and setting. Another mysterious site on Salisbury Plain is Silbury Hill – 40m high, this was the largest construction in prehistoric Europe. Although it may have been a burial mound, no grave has ever been found inside.

ROMANS

9. Antonine Wall, Strathclyde, Scotland. Named after Emperor Antonius Pius and built in AD 143, the wall stretched about 60km from Bridgeness on the Firth of Forth to Old Kilpatrick on the River Clyde, to relieve Hadrian's Wall from attacks by Scottish tribes. The wall was abandoned in AD 200.

10. Caerleon, Gwent, Wales. This Roman fortress was founded c. AD 75 for the 2nd Augustan Legion. Parts of the fortress wall and some internal buildings still stand. The museum has swords, scabbards, mosaics and models, and a large collections of engraved gemstones.

11. Dover Lighthouse, Dover, Kent. The Roman lighthouse dates from the 1st century AD and is the oldest in Britain. It was built to help sailors in the Channel and was originally over 24m high. The lighthouse stands within the wall of Dover Castle, which was built by the Normans – they decided to leave the lighthouse intact. .

12. Fishbourne Villa, Chichester, West Sussex. This well-preserved Roman villa with superb mosaic floors was built c. AD 75, probably for a British tribal king called Cogidubnus, who was protected by Rome.

13. Hadrian's Wall, from Bowness on the Solway Firth to Wallsend near Newcastle-upon-Tyne. The wall was begun c. AD 120 by order of Emperor Hadrian, to secure the Roman empire's northern-most border by keeping out the rebellious northern tribes. The wall stretched for 117km. Housesteads, one of the legionary forts built along the wall, provides a good view of the remains of the wall snaking across the countryside.

15. Porchester Castle, Portsmouth, Hampshire. This castle was built by the Romans at the end of the 3rd century AD. It was one of several forts built along the Saxon Shore of eastern and southern England as protection against barbarian attacks from the Continent.

16. Roman Baths, Bath, Avon. Known as Aquae Sulis, and dedicated to the goddess of healing, Sulis Minerva, these Roman baths flourished from AD 54 to *c.* AD 410. The town became fashionable again in the 1700s as a spa town.

17. St Albans, Hertfordshire. The Romans called the city Verulamium and it was burnt down by Boudicca, queen of the Iceni, when she led her tribe against the Romans in AD 60. The museum in the city has many magnificent Roman artefacts, including mosaics, and the foundations of a Roman theatre are still visible.

ANGLO-SAXONS

18. Alfred Jewel, Ashmolean Museum, Oxford. This is thought to be a miniature portrait of King Alfred set in gold and crystal. It has the Saxon words for "Alfred ordered me to be made" engraved on it. It may have been made as a brooch or as the decorated end of a bookmark.

14. Offa's Dyke, from the Dee estuary near Prestatyn in Clwyd to the Severn estuary near Chepstow in Gwent, Wales. Offa was the Anglo-Saxon king of Mercia from 757 to 796. The dyke was a huge earthern bank that stretched for 270km and marked the boundary between Mercia and Wales.

19. West Stow, Suffolk. An excellent reconstruction of part of a Saxon village.

20. Yorvik Viking Centre, York. An exciting interactive museum about the Viking settlement in York. Visitors are taken through the different reconstructed settings such as a market or a Viking Great Hall — all the noises and smells of everyday life at this time are vividly reproduced.

NORMANS

21. Battle Abbey, Battle, East Sussex. This Benedictine abbey was built by William the Conqueror in thanks for his victory at the battle of Hastings. There is a legend that the high altar marks the spot where King Harold fell and died with an arrow through his eye. Visitors can relive the battle of Hastings in the Gatehouse Exhibition and "1066 Experience".

22. Domesday Book, Winchester, Hampshire. In 1085 William I ordered a national survey to discover the true wealth of his new kingdom. Population statistics and details about who owned what land were recorded by French clerks in the two volumes of the Domesday Book, now kept in the Public Record Office, London. In the Great Hall at Winchester, a Domesday exhibition tells how the book was compiled and what it reveals. (The Hall also has a Tudor reconstruction of King Arthur's Round Table.)

11. Dover Castle, Dover, Kent. After the battle of Hastings, William the Conqueror captured this strategically important city and refortified its castle. The present castle was begun by Henry II and completed by his son, King John.

23. Durham Cathedral, Durham. Work began on the cathedral in 1093 as a shrine for St Cuthbert, the most famous saint of the north. It is one of England's greatest masterpieces of Norman architecture. The north door has a bronze knocker shaped as a frightening face which, in the Middle Ages, people in trouble could hold on to and claim sanctuary (safety from the law).

24. Leeds Castle, the village of Leeds, Kent. This beautiful medieval castle was built in 1120. Later it was the home of Catherine of Aragon, Henry VIII's first wife, and Elizabeth I was held a prisoner here before she became queen. The castle is surrounded by a wide moat and by grounds that include a maze, aviary, walled garden and vineyard.

25. The Tower of London, London. This is one of the most famous and most popular tourist attractions in London. The oldest part of the building is the White Tower, built of stone brought from Normandy by William the Conqueror. It got its name in 1241 when it was whitewashed. The Tower boasts a long and gruesome history and has been by turns a fortress, a palace for the monarchy, a prison and place of execution, a former home to the Royal Mint and the Royal Armoury (now in Leeds), and home still to the Crown Jewels, the Yeomen of the Guard (in the scarlet Beefeater uniforms worn since Tudor times) and the royal ravens.

26. Wells Cathedral, Wells, Somerset. Begun in 1185, this is a hymn to the stonemason's art, with 400 statues of angels, bishops and kings on the West Front and scenes of medieval life carved on the capitals of the soaring pillars and arches inside – find the cobbler mending a shoe, or the farmer catching two thieves in his orchard. Around the cathedral are the Bishop's Palace, moat and Vicar's Close, which is the only complete medieval street in Britain.

22. Winchester Cathedral, Winchester, Hampshire. The city was Alfred the Great's capital and it shared this role with London for nearly 200 years after the Norman Conquest. Its first castle was built in 1070, and work on the great cathedral began in 1079. The building is 170m long and is one of the longest cathedrals in Europe. The cathedral library contains a 10th century copy of Bede's *Ecclesiastical History*, which was translated by King Alfred, and the 12th century Winchester Bible. The early 19th century novelist Jane Austen is buried in the cathedral.

27. Windsor Castle, Windsor, Berkshire. Home to the monarchy for over 900 years, Windsor was first established by William the Conqueror, then enlarged by Edward III, and restored by George III, George IV and Queen Victoria. It is the largest castle in England. Damaged by fire in 1992, it has been restored to all of its former glory.

20. York Minster, York. The building took 250 years to complete, from 1220 to 1470. Inside there are magnificent stained glass windows – one set of 15 depicts the Last Fifteen Days of the World and was designed to be a warning of what was to come. In the summer, performances of medieval mystery plays are held in the cathedral grounds.

MIDDLE AGES

28. Bannockburn, Stirling, Scotland. The battle of Bannockburn of 1314 between the Scots led by Robert the Bruce and the English forces of Edward II took place within sight of Stirling Castle. The English army was defeated and the result was complete independence for Scotland with Bruce as king. A monument marks the spot where the battle took place, and there is a statue to Robert the Bruce.

29. Beaumaris Castle, Gwynedd, Wales. This was the last castle founded in Wales by Edward I, and was built between 1295 and 1298 to guard the Menai Strait. The castle's outer wall has 12 towers and surrounds a higher inner wall protecting the main part of the stronghold. Small boats could once dock in the saltwater moat. The name comes from the Norman *beau marais*, meaning beautiful marsh.

30. Bradford upon Avon Granary, Bradford upon Avon, Wiltshire. This is a 14th century tithe barn, built by the wealthy Abbess of Shaftesbury to store grain from tenants on her land. It is over 51m long and 9m wide.

31. Caernarfon Castle, Caernarfon, north Wales. Foundations of the castle were laid by Edward I in 1283, during his conquest of Wales, and work was completed in the 1330s. The Eagle Tower was one of the largest towers built in the Middle Ages, and has walls of different coloured stone. The castle was neglected in the 16th century, narrowly escaped demolition after the Civil War in the 17th century, and was repaired in the 19th century. In 1969 Prince Charles, like previous Princes of Wales, was invested here.

32. Cambridge University, Cambridge. The first true college, Peterhouse, was founded in 1284 by the Bishop of Ely. Visitors can go into the college courtyards, chapels, dining halls and gardens out of term time. King's College has a magnificent chapel, which houses a Rubens painting, *The Adoration of the Magi*. Punts and river boats take visitors from Magdalene Bridge for a trip past the Backs – the lawns that slope down to the River Cam.

33. Canterbury Cathedral, Canterbury, Kent. Canterbury has long been an important centre for English Christianity. In 1170 Thomas à Becket, Archbishop of Canterbury, was murdered on the altar steps, and for hundreds of years pilgrims gathered at the site.

The cathedral is also the burial place of Henry IV and Edward the Black Prince, one of the greatest soldiers of the Hundred Years War, and has a magnificent collection of medieval stained glass.

34. Edinburgh Castle, Edinburgh, Scotland. Perched high on Castle Rock, which may have been the site of an Iron Age fort, the castle dominates the city. The oldest part of the castle is St Margaret's Chapel, which dates from c.1100. In 1566 Mary, Queen of Scots, gave birth to her son, the future King James VI of Scotland and James I of England, in the castle. The Scottish Crown Jewels, which are older than the English, are housed here. The famous Edinburgh Military Tattoo takes place within the castle walls each year. (At the other end of the Royal Mile is the Tudor palace of Holyroodhouse.)

35. Fountains Abbey, Ripon, Yorkshire. This beautiful abbey was founded by Cistercian monks from York in the 12th century. By the 16th century it had become very wealthy as a result of the monks' skills in trading in wool. Henry VIII chose Fountains as one of the first religious houses to be sold off in 1540. It is one of the best-preserved medieval ruins and has become a World Heritage Site and a National Trust Property. To the east near Helmsley are the remains of another Cistercian abbey, Rievaulx.

36. Lincoln Cathedral, Lincoln. The present building was built between the 12th and 14th centuries, after an eathquake had ruined the original church in 1185. Its honey-coloured stone seems to change colour as the light varies. It has a magnificent rose window of stained glass, and houses one of the four copies of the Magna Carta.

Magna Carta. In 1215 the powerful barons and leading churchmen of England forced King John to sign the Magna Carta (Great Charter) in Runnymede, Berkshire. This document imposed limitations on the monarchy and was the basis of important liberties for the people. Copies can be seen in the British Museum in London (**25**), and in the cathedrals of Lincoln (**36**) and Salisbury (**37**).

38. Royal Armoury, Leeds, Yorkshire. Opened in 1996, when the famous collection of weapons and suits of armour was relocated from the Tower of London.

37. Salisbury Cathedral, Salisbury, Wiltshire. The cathedral was finished c.1280, but the spire, 123m high and the tallest in England, was not added until 1334. The cathedral has beautifully carved ceilings and some impressive tombs and monuments, as well as Europe's oldest working clock. The cathedral library has a copy of the Magna Carta.

28. Stirling Castle, Stirling, Scotland. Built high on a rock overlooking the Forth Valley, Stirling Castle dates from the 15th century, on the same site as earlier fortifications. It was captured by Robert the Bruce after the battle of Bannockburn in 1314, and remained a Scottish royal palace until James VI of Scotland became James I of England in 1603.

39. Warwick Castle, Warwick. The original castle dates from the 14th century. Although it was converted into a house in the 17th century, it has magnificent towers, turrets and ramparts and is well preserved. The Kingmaker exhibition tells the story of Richard Neville, Earl of Warwick, with life-like figures, sounds and smells.

40. Weald and Down Open Air Museum, Singleton, Chichester, West Sussex. This popular outdoor museum has over 30 rescued historical buildings – there are artisans' workshops, a working water mill, a village school, shepherds' huts and a medieval farm.

25. Westminster Abbey, London. This beautiful building was founded in 1065 by Edward the Confessor. All English kings and queens have been crowned there since 1066, and most are buried there too. Poet's Corner is packed with memorials to some of the greatest British writers, while the tomb of the Unknown Soldier commemorates wartime casualties.

22. Winchester College, Winchester, Hampshire. Britain's oldest public school was founded in 1382, and many of Britain's famous statesmen have been educated here.

TUDORS AND STUARTS

41. Chatsworth House, Bakewell, Derbyshire. This stately home was built in the mid-16th century and contains wonderful collections of paintings, sculpture, manuscripts and furniture. It also has magnificent gardens and a working farm.

42. Cromwell Museum, Huntingdon, Cambridge. In about 1610, Oliver Cromwell went to the old grammar school in Huntingdon, where Samuel Pepys was also a pupil. It opened as a museum in 1962 and contains many of Cromwell's personal belongings, such as the hat he wore when he dissolved the Rump Parliament in 1653.

43. Culloden, near Inverness, Scotland. A cairn (stone monument) marks the spot of the battle of Culloden in 1746, when Charles Edward Stuart (the Young Pretender, also called Bonnie Prince Charlie) and his army were savagely defeated by English forces led by the Duke of Cumberland.

44. Deal Castle, Deal, Kent. This castle was built after Henry VIII's break with Rome in 1531, when fears grew of a possible invasion by the Roman Catholic powers of Europe. It is the strongest and best preserved of five castles built along the south coast.

45. Edgehill, Warwickshire. This was the site of the first battle of the English Civil War in 1642; a stone tower marks the Royalist position.

25. Globe Theatre, London. A faithful reconstruction of the Tudor theatre built in Southwark in 1598 as a permanent base for the Lord Chamberlain's Men, later called the King's Men, the company of actors to which Shakespeare belonged.

25. Hampton Court, Kingston upon Thames, Surrey. Cardinal Wolsey was an advisor to Henry VIII and he wanted to show off his wealth and power by building a splendid home in 1514. Among the many features are a Real Tennis court, the Tiltyard where mock jousting tournaments are held, beautiful gardens and a maze. Wolsey gave his palace to Henry VIII in 1525 in the hope of keeping the king's favour – he failed. Four of Henry VIII's wives lived here, and the ghosts of Jane Seymour and Catherine Howard are said to haunt the long gallery.

46. Hardwick Hall, Mansfield, Derbyshire. This massive house was begun in 1591 – its owner, Bess of Hardwick, Countess of Shrewsbury, was one of the richest and most powerful women in Elizabethan England. At a time when glass was an expensive luxury, Hardwick Hall was fitted with so many windows that it seems to have more glass than stone in its walls.

47. Hever Castle, Kent. In 1462 the castle was bought by the Boleyn family, who carried out an extensive rebuilding programme, and was the setting for Henry VIII's courtship of Anne Boleyn. The castle has a drawbridge, three portcullises and two iron-studded doorways. May Day Morris dancing, archery and jousting take place in the beautiful grounds, where there is also a maze.

34. Holyrood House, Edinburgh, Scotland. Built in the 16th century, at the other end of the Royal Mile to Edinburgh Castle, this handsome palace was home to Mary, Queen of Scots, and later to Bonnie Prince Charlie's court. Charles II extended the palace in the French Classical style popular in the 17th century.

25. Kensington Palace, London. Acquired by William of Orange in 1689, the house was enlarged by Sir Christopher Wren and was home of the reigning monarch until the death of George II in 1760. It now has a dazzling collection of royal costume.

48. Loch Leven Castle, Fife, Scotland. On an island in the middle of the loch (lake) are the romantic ruins of the 15th century Loch Leven Castle. Mary, Queen of Scots, was imprisoned here in 1567, but escaped in 1568.

49. Longleat House, Wiltshire. Work on this superb Elizabethan mansion began in 1568, for Sir John Thynne, an ancestor of the Marquis of Bath who owns it today. It is called a lantern house because it has so many bay windows and glass panes. It is also famous for its collection of lions in the surrounding wildlife park.

25. The Monument, London. Designed by Sir Christopher Wren to commemorate the Great Fire of London of 1666, this column is built on the spot where the fire was thought to have started. It has 311 steps and is topped by a golden ball of flame. (Rudimentary fire-fighting equipment used in 1666 is on display in the Museum of London.)

50. Montacute House, Yeovil, Somerset. This Tudor mansion was built between 1588 and 1601 and is a fine example of Renaissance architecture. It contains a valuable collection of furniture, china, portraits and tapestries, and has beautiful gardens with yew hedges and cedar trees.

25. St Paul's Cathedral, London. The medieval church of St Paul's was destroyed in the Great Fire of London in 1666. In 1675 work began on the stupendous new church designed by Sir Christopher Wren. Standing in the Whispering Gallery, visitors can hear one another's whispers from the other side of the huge dome. The crypt contains the massive tombs of Lord Nelson and the Duke of Wellington. Amazingly, St Paul's survived a second great fire during the Blitz in World War II, when most of the surrounding buildings were completely destroyed by bombing.

51. Stratford upon Avon, Warwickshire. This old market town is the birthplace of William Shakespeare. Many of its buildings have been restored to their original Tudor appearance – half-timbered with black beams that criss-cross whitewashed walls. Visitors can see the house where Shakespeare was born, his school (the King's New Grammar School) and the cottage owned by his wife, Anne Hathaway. The Royal Shakespeare Company performs here.

37. Wilton House, Salisbury, Wiltshire. Wilton House is the home of the Earls of Pembroke and stands on the site of an abbey founded by Alfred the Great. Much of the house was destroyed by fire in 1647 but it was rebuilt by the architect Inigo Jones. Among its many treasures are a fine collection of paintings and 7,000 19th century model soldiers.

HANOVERIANS

25. Apsley House, London. The home of the Duke of Wellington, hero of Waterloo, has an impressive address: Number 1, London. Recently restored, it is full of battle memorabilia, paintings and other treasures collected by the Iron Duke.

52. Blenheim Palace, Woodstock, Oxfordshire. This magnificent palace was built for John Churchill, Duke of Marlborough as a gift from the nation after his famous victory in the battle of Blenheim in 1704. It was designed by Sir John Vanbrugh, the famous architect. Work began immediately after Marlborough's victory but was not completed until 1722, the year the Duke died. The house is set in a magnificent park landscaped by Capability Brown.

25. Buckingham Palace, London. Originally built for the Duke of Buckingham in 1703, George III bought the palace for Queen Charlotte in 1762. It was remodelled by John Nash for George IV in 1826. Huge crowds gathered here at the end of World War II to cheer the royal family. The palace is open to the public during the summer.

53. Burns's Cottage, Alloway, Strathclyde, Scotland. Robert Burns, Scotland's national poet, was born in 1759. His family lived in a two-roomed clay and thatch cottage, now a museum dedicated to him.

54. Captain Cook's House, Whitby, Yorkshire. Captain Cook spent his early life in the fishing port of Whitby, and his famous ship, *Endeavour*, was built here. Cook's House is in Grape Lane and is marked by a plaque.

55. Castle Howard, Malton, Yorkshire. This spectacular debut by the architect Sir John Vanbrugh was built for the 3rd Earl of Carlisle, a member of the Howard family, between 1699 and 1726. Apart from the opulence of the main house, there are collections of historical costumes and carriages in the stables, and fountains, statues, temples, follies and obelisks in the magnificent grounds laid out by Capability Brown.

56. Chawton, Hampshire. Jane Austen and her family lived in Chawton from 1809 to 1817 – their home is now a museum. It contains many of her personal possessions such as letters, jewellery and a patchwork quilt that she and her mother made. It was here that she wrote many of her best-loved novels, including *Emma, Mansfield Park* and *Persuasion*.

57. Darlington Railway Museum, Co. Durham. The railway age began in Darlington, in 1825, when George Stephenson rode his locomotive *Active* (later called *Locomotion No. 1*) along the 40km track to Stockton. *Locomotion* is just one of the trains now on show.

58. Ellesmere Port, South Wirral, Merseyside. The boat museum here has Britain's largest collection of traditional canal boats.

59. Exeter, Devon. Britain's first canal was built here, in 1594. This historic port now has a huge collection of boats from all over the world (and a fine cathedral).

60. Ironbridge Gorge Museum, Coalbrookdale, Shropshire. The first bridge in the world to be built entirely of iron was opened here in 1780, over the River Severn. It's a fitting site for a museum of Britain's industrial past.

2. Kennet and Avon Canal Centre, Devizes, Wiltshire. The recently restored canal was built by John Rennie to run between the River Thames at Reading and the River Avon at Hanham Lock. By the edge of the canal in Devizes, close to a impressive series of 29 locks, displays show how the canal was planned, built and used.

61. Levant Mine, St Just, Cornwall. There have been tin mines in Cornwall for centuries. The mine at St Just is open to visitors and has, among other things, the powerful beam engines that were introduced in this period.

63. Maritime Museum, Liverpool. The museum is at the Royal Albert Dock and includes an exhibition on the transatlantic slave trade of the 18th century. In the 19th century, so-called coffin ships took thousands of Irish and other emigrants across the Atlantic to North America.

25. National Maritime Museum, Greenwich, London. The Royal Hospital at Greenwich was built for naval veterans in the 18th century and later became a Royal Naval College. It is now home to a marvellous display on Britain's seafaring past: docked here are *Cutty Sark*, a 19th century clipper which carried tea from China and wool from Australia, and *Gypsy Moth IV*, in which Francis Chichester sailed round the world between August 1966 and May 1967 – on his return, Elizabeth II knighted him with the same sword that Elizabeth I used to knight Sir Francis Drake.

64. Portsmouth, Hampshire. At the entrance to the Royal Dockyard is Nelson's great ship HMS *Victory*. Also on view is the *Mary Rose*, Henry VIII's warship, which was raised from the seabed in 1982. Exhibitions vividly recreate sail and rope making, ship building and life in the Royal Navy.

16. Pump Room, Assembly Rooms and Royal Crescent, Bath, Avon. In the 18th century, the Pump Room became the centre of gossip in the thriving spa – they are directly over the Roman reservoir where health-giving waters spring up. The Assembly Rooms were opened in 1771 for twice-weekly balls organized by Richard "Beau" Nash, the uncrowned king of Bath. The Royal Crescent was built by John Wood the Younger from 1767 to 1775. Their Georgian architecture was influenced by the classical styles of ancient Greece and Rome.

65. Royal Pavilion, Brighton, East Sussex. This exotic building with its onion domes and minarets is a mixture of Chinese and Indian styles. It was built for the Prince Regent, later George IV in 1820. The interiors revel in their extravagance, and have to be seen to be believed.

25. Trafalgar Square, London. The city's most famous square was designed to commemorate Nelson's great naval victory in 1805. Dominating the square is Nelson's Column, which has a statue of Nelson on top and is almost 56m high. At its base are four bronze lions designed by Sir Edwin Landseer. The National Gallery overlooks the square on the north side and to the northeast is the church of St Martin in the Fields.

VICTORIANS

25. Albert Hall and Albert Memorial, London. The Albert Hall in Kensington was opened in 1871 to commemorate the life and work of Queen Victoria's husband, Prince Albert. The Albert Memorial was erected in 1861 after his death. It stands opposite the Albert Hall on the site of the Great Exhibition which Prince Albert had promoted. (Two other Victorian treasures, the Victoria and Albert Museum and the Natural History Museum, are within walking distance.)

66. Beaulieu Motor Museum, Hampshire. This museum was founded by Lord Montagu in 1952. It contains about 250 vintage and veteran cars as well as cycles and motor cycles. Malcolm Campbell's record-breaking *Bluebird* is here – he became the first to reach 150mph (241km/h) in 1925, and by 1935 had broken the 300mph (482km/h) barrier. At a slightly slower pace, there are rides and drives such as a monorail, a 1912 veteran bus and the Vauxhall Driving Experience.

67. Beamish Open Air Museum, Stanley, Co. Durham. This museum recreates 19th century life in the northeast. Replicas of a mine, a worker's cottage, a confectioner's shop, a dentist's practice, a farm, a schoolroom and a fairground all help to bring this period to life.

68. Chiltern Open Air Museum, Chalfont St Giles, Buckinghamshire. Replicas of buildings from a wide range of historical periods include an Iron Age house a Victorian working farm, an Edwardian Public Convenience and a 1940s Prefab.

69. The Charles Dickens Centre, Rochester, Kent. An award-winning museum in Eastgate House depicts the life and times of this famous Victorian author. Some of the characters from his novels appear in "Dickens's Dream", an exciting audio-visual attraction which brings his world to life.

25. Houses of Parliament, London. The first Parliament was called at Westminster in 1265. The old palace was almost completely destroyed by fire in 1834, though Westminster Hall survived. The present buildings were designed by Augustus Pugin and Charles Barry in the Gothic style, and were built between 1840 and 1860. The clock tower by the House of Commons is famous for its bell, Big Ben.

70. Lacock Abbey, Lacock, Wiltshire. The abbey was the last religious house in England to be sold off by Henry VIII after the Reformation. In the 1830s it became the home of William Henry Fox Talbot, a pioneer of photography. There is a museum of his early cameras and work in the grounds of the abbey.

62. Maritime Heritage Museum, Bristol. In 1497, John Cabot set sail from Bristol and headed across the Atlantic to discover Newfoundland. Bristol became Britain's second wealthiest port after London, and the centre of the slave trade. Isambard Kingdom Brunel's SS (steamship) *Great Britain* is docked here – 98m long, it was the largest ship afloat and the world's first all-metal ship.

As well as the maritime museum there is an industrial museum, and outside the city Brunel's Clifton Suspension Bridge spans the River Avon. Brunel built all the tunnels, bridges and viaducts on the Great Western Railway, which opened in 1840 and ran between London and Bristol. Paddington and Bristol Temple Meads are two fine examples of railway station architecture.

71 Osborne House, near Cowes, Isle of Wight. This was Queen Victoria's home at the time of her death in 1901. It was partly designed by her husband, Prince Albert, to resemble an Italian villa. Visitors can see the private and state apartments as they were in the queen's time. A Swiss cottage was built in the grounds as a playhouse for the royal children.

72. Port Sunlight Village, Wirral, Merseyside. Towards the end of the 19th century, William Lever expanded his soap manufacturing business and built an attractive village for his workforce. The village is now a museum with a heritage centre.

25. Royal Botanical Gardens, Kew, Richmond upon Thames, Surrey. There have been gardens at Kew since the mid-17th century. In 1730 the estate was taken over by the royal family, and George III's mother, Princess Augusta, started a botanic garden and study centre. The Temperate House and Palm House at Kew were designed by Decimus Burton in the 19th century – the Victorians loved tropical plants and glasshouses. Today, Kew has the world's largest collection of living and preserved plants.

73. Ulster Folk and Transport Museum, Cultra, Co. Down. In the Irish Railway Collection, the fascinating story of Irish railways is told through exhibits such as the gigantic *Maedhbh* (*Maeve*) steam engine, carriages and wagons. Other forms of transport in display are aircraft, a merchant schooner, bicycles and donkey creels. Visitors can also watch horse ploughing and roof thatching, and walk among 19th century farmhouses, mills, churches, schools and a forge.

MODERN

74. Fleet Air Arm Museum, Yeovilton, Somerset. During a display of aircraft from the pioneering days to the present, visitors can see the original model of *Concorde* and sit in the cockpit and passenger seats.

25. HMS *Belfast*, London. This World War II cruiser took part in the Normandy landings on D-Day in 1945. It is now a floating museum moored by Tower Bridge.

25. Imperial War Museum, London. Every aspect of Britain at war since World War I is on display here, including the effect on people's lives – for example, photographs show children being evacuated in World War II.

25. Museum of the Moving Image (MOMI), London. An interactive museum traces the history of photography and film by showing cameras, photographs and film clips. Actors invite visitors to take part in excerpts from cinema classics. There are also fascinating examples of great moments in history that have been captured on film.

GENERAL

18. Ashmolean Museum, Oxford. In the same city as Britain's oldest university is the oldest public museum. Among the British treasures are the Alfred Jewel and the lantern held by Guy Fawkes in the Gunpowder Plot.

25. British Museum, London. This world-famous museum has a vast collection of treasures including the Elgin Marbles from Greece, Roman glass, and the famous Viking burial ship from Sutton Hoo.

32. Fitzwilliam Museum, Cambridge. Founded in 1816, this museum has a large collection of Roman artefacts, illuminated manuscripts, English pottery and porcelain, and paintings from the Middle Ages to the present.

25. London Dungeon, London. Reconstructions show the most gruesome people and events, including medieval torturers at work, witch hunting and bloody murders. These are viewed in very damp, dark conditions, with the appropriate sound effects – not for the squeamish ...

25. Madame Tussaud's, London. Probably the most famous waxworks museum in the world. It has models of famous people from around the world and from every walk of life. A Chamber of Horrors includes scenes of famous murders.

25. Museum of London, London. Everything about the history of London from the earliest times to the present day, and finds from the latest archaeological digs. Look for the shirt worn by Charles I at his execution, or a firehelmet and bucket used in the Great Fire.

25. National Portrait Gallery, London. A fantastic number of portraits and minatures of famous men and women from British history is on display here, together with exhibitions of new photographs and paintings of people.

25. Science Museum, London. Amazing interactive exhibits cover such subjects as the history of British transport and communications, science and medicine, exploration and industry – Caxton's printing press, a model of the Pilgrim Fathers' *Mayflower* and Stephenson's record-breaking *Rocket* are just some of the treasures here.

25. Victoria and Albert Museum, London. This is a museum of arts and treasures from around the world. It has superb displays of historic costume, tapestries and furniture, stained glass and sculpture, silver and porcelain, exquisite miniature portraits of Elizabethen courtiers, musical instruments – everything

GETTING IN TOUCH:

Ancient Monument Society, St Ann's Vestry Hall, 2 Church Entry London EC4V 5HB (Study and conservation of historic buildings)

English Heritage, 23 Saville Row, London W1X 1AB (Responsible for looking after over 400 historic properties)

Ermine Street Guard, Oakland Farm, Dog Lane, Witcombe, Gloucester GL3 4UG (Charity dedicated to study of Roman army and Roman military equipment)

Heraldry Society, 44–45 Museum Street, London WC1A ILY (Encourages interest of heraldry, armoury, chivalry and genealogy)

National Trust, 36 Queen Anne's Gate, London SW1H 9AS (Conserves and opens to the public places of historic interest and natural beauty, including stretches of coastline and over 200 country houses)

Sealed Knot, PO Box 2000, Nottingham NG2 5LS (Recreate battles of English Civil War and promotes public interest in the history of this period)

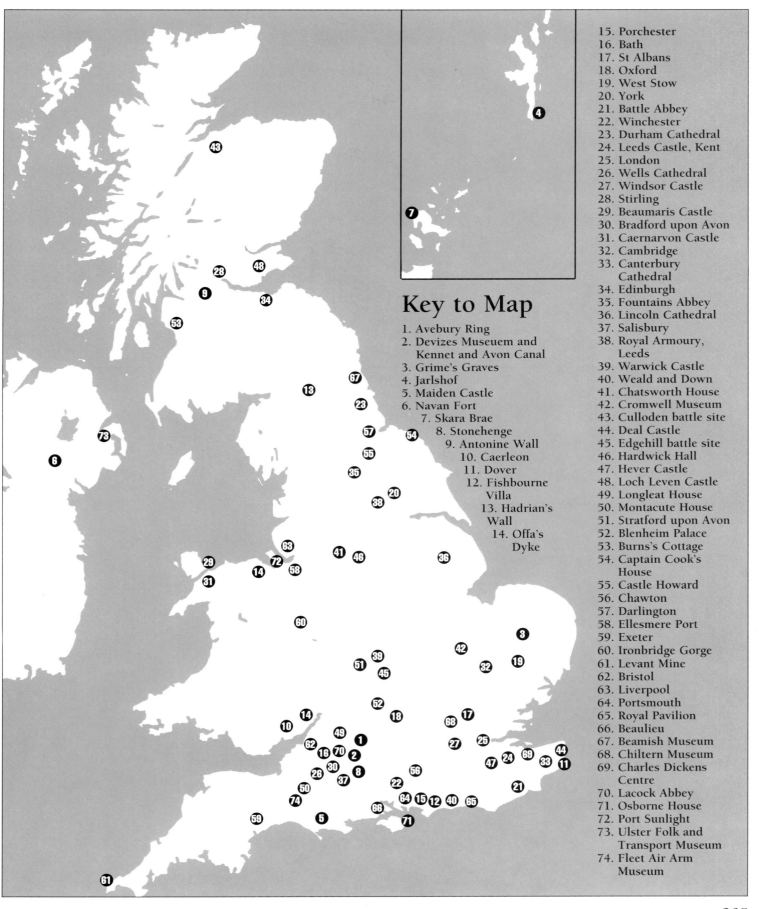

Key to Map

1. Avebury Ring
2. Devizes Museuem and Kennet and Avon Canal
3. Grime's Graves
4. Jarlshof
5. Maiden Castle
6. Navan Fort
7. Skara Brae
8. Stonehenge
9. Antonine Wall
10. Caerleon
11. Dover
12. Fishbourne Villa
13. Hadrian's Wall
14. Offa's Dyke
15. Porchester
16. Bath
17. St Albans
18. Oxford
19. West Stow
20. York
21. Battle Abbey
22. Winchester
23. Durham Cathedral
24. Leeds Castle, Kent
25. London
26. Wells Cathedral
27. Windsor Castle
28. Stirling
29. Beaumaris Castle
30. Bradford upon Avon
31. Caernarvon Castle
32. Cambridge
33. Canterbury Cathedral
34. Edinburgh
35. Fountains Abbey
36. Lincoln Cathedral
37. Salisbury
38. Royal Armoury, Leeds
39. Warwick Castle
40. Weald and Down
41. Chatsworth House
42. Cromwell Museum
43. Culloden battle site
44. Deal Castle
45. Edgehill battle site
46. Hardwick Hall
47. Hever Castle
48. Loch Leven Castle
49. Longleat House
50. Montacute House
51. Stratford upon Avon
52. Blenheim Palace
53. Burns's Cottage
54. Captain Cook's House
55. Castle Howard
56. Chawton
57. Darlington
58. Ellesmere Port
59. Exeter
60. Ironbridge Gorge
61. Levant Mine
62. Bristol
63. Liverpool
64. Portsmouth
65. Royal Pavilion
66. Beaulieu
67. Beamish Museum
68. Chiltern Museum
69. Charles Dickens Centre
70. Lacock Abbey
71. Osborne House
72. Port Sunlight
73. Ulster Folk and Transport Museum
74. Fleet Air Arm Museum

Rulers of Britain

HOUSE	NAME	REIGN	MARRIED	CHILDREN
WESSEX	Egbert First King of all the English	802 – 839	Raedburh	Ethelwulf
	Ethelwulf	839 – 856	1. Osburh. 2. Judith	Ethelbald, Ethelbert, Ethelred I, and Elfred (Alfred the Great)
	Ethelbald	856 – 860	Judith (his stepmother)	
	Ethelbert	860 – 865		
	Ethelred I	865 – 871		
	Alfred the Great	871 – 899	Ealhswith	Edward the Elder, Ethelfleda
	Edward the Elder	899 – 924	1. Egwina	Ethelstan (Athelstan)
			2. Elfleda	
			3.Edgifu	Edmund I, Edred
	Athelstan	924 – 939		
	Edmund I	939 – 946	Aelfgifu	Edwy, Edgar the Peaceable
	Edred	946 – 955		
	Edwy	955 – 959		
	Edgar the Peaceable	959 – 975	1. Ethelfled	Edward the Martyr
			2. Elfreda	Ethelred II the Unready
	Edward the Martyr	975 – 978		
	Ethelred II, the Unready	978 – 1013	1. Aelfgifu	Edmund II Ironside
		1014 – 1016	2. Emma of Normandy (also married Canute)	Edward the Confessor
DANES	Sweyn	1013 –1014	Gunhilda	Canute
	Edmund II, Ironside	1016	Ealdgyth	Edward
	Canute	1016 – 1035	1. Aelfgifu	Harold I Harefoot,
			2. Emma of Normandy	Harthacanute
	Harold I	1035 – 1040		
	Harthacanute	1040 – 1042		
SAXONS	Edward the Confessor	1042 – 1066	Edith (sister of Harold II)	
	Harold II, Godwinsson (died at the Battle of Hastings)	1066		
NORMANS	William I	1066 – 1087	Matilda of Flanders	Robert, William II, Henry I, Adela (married Count of Blois)
	William II, Rufus	1087 – 1100		
	Henry I	1100 – 1135	1. Edith (Matilda)	William and Adela (drowned on *White Ship*), and Matilda (married Geoffrey of Anjou)
			2. Adela of Louvain	
	Stephen of Blois	1135 – 1154	Matilda of Boulogne	Baldwin, Matilda, Eustace

HOUSE	NAME	REIGN	MARRIED	CHILDREN
PLANTAGENET	Henry II	1154 – 1189	Eleanor of Aquitaine	Henry the Young King, Richard I, Geoffrey, John
	Richard I the Lionheart	1189 – 1199	Berengaria of Navarre	
	John	1199 –1216	1. Hadwisa of Gloucester	
			2. Isabella of Angoulême	Henry III, Eleanor (married Simon de Montfort)
	Henry III	1216 – 1272	Eleanor of Provence	Edward I, Margaret (married Alexander III of Scotland), Edmund Crouchback
	Edward I the Lawgiver	1272 – 1307	1. Eleanor of Castile	Edward II
			2. Margaret of France	
	Edward II	1307 – 1327	Isabella of France	Edward III
	Edward III	1327 – 1377	Philippa of Hainault	Edward the Black Prince, Lionel, John of Gaunt, Edmund Duke of York
	Richard II (son of the Black Prince)	1377 – 1399	1. Anne of Bohemia	
			2. Isabella of France	
LANCASTER	Henry IV (son of John of Gaunt)	1399 – 1413	1. Mary de Bohun	Henry V, John Duke of Bedford, Humphrey Duke of Gloucester
			2. Joan of Navarre	
	Henry V	1413 – 1422	Catherine of Valois	Henry VI
	Henry VI	1422 – 1461	Margaret of Anjou	Edward
YORK	Edward IV (descended from Lionel)	1461 – 1483	Elizabeth Woodville	Edward V and Richard (Princes in the Tower), Elizabeth (married Henry VII)
	Edward V	1483		
	Richard III	1483 – 1485	Anne Neville	
TUDOR	Henry VII	1485 – 1509	Elizabeth of York	Arthur, Henry VIII, Margaret, Mary
	Henry VIII	1509 – 1547	1. Catherine of Aragon	Mary I
			2. Anne Boleyn	Elizabeth I
			3. Jane Seymour	Edward VI
			4. Anne of Cleves	
			5. Catherine Howard	
			6. Catherine Parr	
	Edward VI	1547 – 1553		
	Mary	1553 – 1558	Philip II of Spain	
	Elizabeth I	1558 – 1603		
STUART	James I	1603 – 1625	Anne of Denmark	Henry, Charles I, Elizabeth
	Charles I	1625 – 1649	Henrietta Maria of France	Charles II, James II, Mary
	Commonwealth	1649 – 1653		
	Protectorate	1653 – 1660		
	Charles II	1660 – 1685	Catherine of Braganza	
	James II	1685 – 1689	1. Anne Hyde	Mary (marries William of Orange), Anne
			2. Mary of Modena	James Francis Edward (Old Pretender)
	William and Mary	1689 – 1702		
	Anne	1702 – 1714	Prince George of Denmark	

HOUSE	NAME	REIGN	MARRIED	CHILDREN
HANOVER	George I	1714 – 1727	Sophia of Brunswick	George II
	George II	1727 – 1760	Caroline of Anspach	Frederick Prince of Wales, William Duke of Cumberland
	George III (son of Frederick)	1760 – 1820	Charlotte-Sophia of Mecklenberg-Strelitz	Edward Duke of Kent, George IV, William IV
	George IV	1820 – 1830	Caroline of Brunswick	
	William IV	1830 – 1837	Adelaide of Saxe-Meiningen	
SAXE-COBURG	Victoria	1837 – 1901	Albert of Saxe-Coburg	Victoria, Edward VII, Alice, Alfred, Helena, Louise, Arthur, Leopold, Beatrice
	Edward VII	1901 – 1910	Alexandra of Denmark	Albert, George V, Louise, Victoria, Maud
	George V	1910 – 1936	Victoria Mary of Teck	Edward VIII, George VI, Mary, Henry, George, John
	The House of Saxe-Coburg became the House of Windsor from 1917			
WINDSOR	Edward VIII (Abdicated)	1936		
	George VI	1936 – 1952	Elizabeth Bowes-Lyon	Elizabeth II, Margaret
	Elizabeth II	1952 –	Philip Mountbatten, Duke of Edinburgh	Charles, Anne, Andrew, Edward
	The House of Windsor became the House of Windsor Mountbatten from 1995			

The Commonwealth of Nations

This is a voluntary association of independent states. The head of the Commonwealth is Her Majesty Queen Elizabeth II. Present members of the Commonwealth (with date of joining) are:

Antigua & Barbuda (1981)
Australia (1931)
The Bahamas (1973)
Bangladesh (1972)
Barbados (1966)
Belize (1981)
Botswana (1966)
Brunei (1984)
Cameroon (1995)

Canada (1931)
Cyprus (1961)
Dominica (1978)
Fiji (1997)
The Gambia (1965)
Ghana (1957)
Great Britain (1931)
Grenada (1974)
Guyana (1966)
India (1947)
Jamaica (1962)
Kenya (1963)
Kiribati (1979)
Lesotho (1966)
Malawi (1964)
Malaysia (1957)
Maldives (1982)
Malta (1964)

Mauritius (1968)
Mozambique (1995)
Namibia (1990)
Nauru (1968)
New Zealand (1931)
Nigeria (1960)
* Pakistan (1947)
Papua New Guinea (1975)
St Kitts and Nevis (1983)
St Lucia (1979)
St Vincent and The
    Grenadines (1979)
Samoa (1970)
Seychelles (1976)
Sierra Leone (1961)
Singapore (1965)
Solomon Islands (1978)
** South Africa (1994)

Sri Lanka (1948)
Swaziland (1968)
Tanzania (1961)
Tonga (1970)
Trinidad and Tobago (1962)
Tuvalu (1978)
Uganda (1962)
Vanuatu (1980)
Zambia (1964)
Zimbabwe (1980)

* Pakistan suspended following a military coup in 1999.
** Union of South Africa expelled in 1961 but reinstated in 1994 following the end of apartheid.

British Prime Ministers

NAME	PARTY	OFFICE	NAME	PARTY	OFFICE
Sir Robert Walpole	Whig	1721-1742	Benjamin Disraeli	Conservative	1874-1880
Earl of Wilmington	Whig	1742-1743	William Gladstone	Liberal	1880-1885
Henry Pelham	Whig	1743-1754	Marquess of Salisbury	Conservative	1885-1886
Duke of Newcastle	Whig	1754-1756	William Gladstone	Liberal	1886
Duke of Devonshire	Whig	1756-1757	Marquess of Salisbury	Conservative	1886-1892
Duke of Newcastle	Whig	1757-1762	William Gladstone	Liberal	1892-1894
Earl of Bute	Tory	1762-1763	Earl of Rosebery	Liberal	1894-1895
George Grenville	Whig	1763-1765	Marquess of Salisbury	Conservative	1895-1902
Marquess of Rockingham	Whig	1765-1766	Arthur Balfour	Conservative	1902-1905
William Pitt the Elder, Earl of Chatham	Whig	1766-1767	Sir Henry Campbell-Bannerman	Liberal	1905-1908
Duke of Grafton	Whig	1767-1770	Herbert Asquith	Liberal	1908-1915
Lord North	Tory	1770-1782	Herbert Asquith	Coalition	1915-1916
Marquess of Rockingham	Whig	1782	David Lloyd-George	Coalition	1916-1922
Earl of Shelburne	Whig	1782-1783	Andrew Bonar Law	Conservative	1922-1923
Duke of Portland	Coalition	1783	Stanley Baldwin	Conservative	1923-1924
William Pitt the Younger	Tory	1783-1801	James Ramsay MacDonald	Labour	1924
Henry Addington	Tory	1801-1804	Stanley Baldwin	Conservative	1924-1929
William Pitt the Younger	Tory	1804-1806	James Ramsay MacDonald	Labour	1929-1931
Lord Grenville	Whig	1806-1807	James Ramsay MacDonald	Coalition	1931-1935
Duke of Portland	Tory	1807-1809	Stanley Baldwin	Coalition	1935-1937
Spencer Perceval	Tory	1809-1812	Neville Chamberlain	Coalition	1937-1940
Earl of Liverpool	Tory	1812-1827	Winston Churchill	Coalition	1940-1945
George Canning	Tory	1827	Winston Churchill	Conservative	1945
Viscount Goderich	Tory	1827-1828	Clement Attlee	Labour	1945-1951
Duke of Wellington	Tory	1828-1830	Sir Winston Churchill	Conservative	1951-1955
Earl Grey	Whig	1830-1834	Sir Anthony Eden	Conservative	1955-1957
Viscount Melbourne	Whig	1834	Harold Macmillan	Conservative	1957-1963
Sir Robert Peel	Tory	1834-1835	Sir Alec Douglas-Home	Conservative	1963-1964
Viscount Melbourne	Whig	1835-1841	Harold Wilson	Labour	1964-1970
Sir Robert Peel	Tory	1841-1846	Edward Heath	Conservative	1970-1974
Lord John Russell	Whig	1846-1852	Harold Wilson	Labour	1974-1976
Earl of Derby	Tory	1852	James Callaghan	Labour	1976-1979
Earl of Aberdeen	Peelite	1852-1855	Margaret Thatcher	Conservative	1979-1990
Viscount Palmerston	Liberal	1855-1858	John Major	Conservative	1990-1997
Earl of Derby	Conservative	1858-1859	Tony Blair	Labour	1997-
Viscount Palmerston	Liberal	1859-1865			
Earl Russell	Liberal	1865-1866			
Earl of Derby	Conservative	1866-1868			
Benjamin Disraeli	Conservative	1868			
William Gladstone	Liberal	1868-1874			

Government of Britain

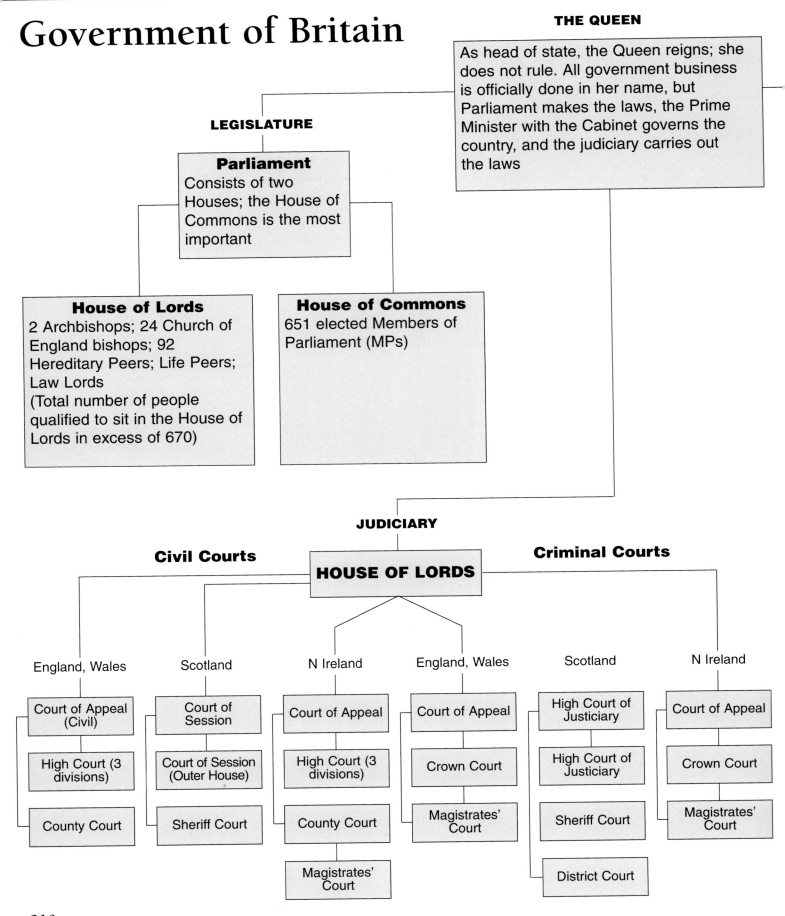

THE QUEEN

As head of state, the Queen reigns; she does not rule. All government business is officially done in her name, but Parliament makes the laws, the Prime Minister with the Cabinet governs the country, and the judiciary carries out the laws

LEGISLATURE

Parliament
Consists of two Houses; the House of Commons is the most important

House of Lords
2 Archbishops; 24 Church of England bishops; 92 Hereditary Peers; Life Peers; Law Lords
(Total number of people qualified to sit in the House of Lords in excess of 670)

House of Commons
651 elected Members of Parliament (MPs)

JUDICIARY

Civil Courts

HOUSE OF LORDS

Criminal Courts

England, Wales

Court of Appeal (Civil)

High Court (3 divisions)

County Court

Scotland

Court of Session

Court of Session (Outer House)

Sheriff Court

N Ireland

Court of Appeal

High Court (3 divisions)

County Court

Magistrates' Court

England, Wales

Court of Appeal

Crown Court

Magistrates' Court

Scotland

High Court of Justiciary

High Court of Justiciary

Sheriff Court

District Court

N Ireland

Court of Appeal

Crown Court

Magistrates' Court

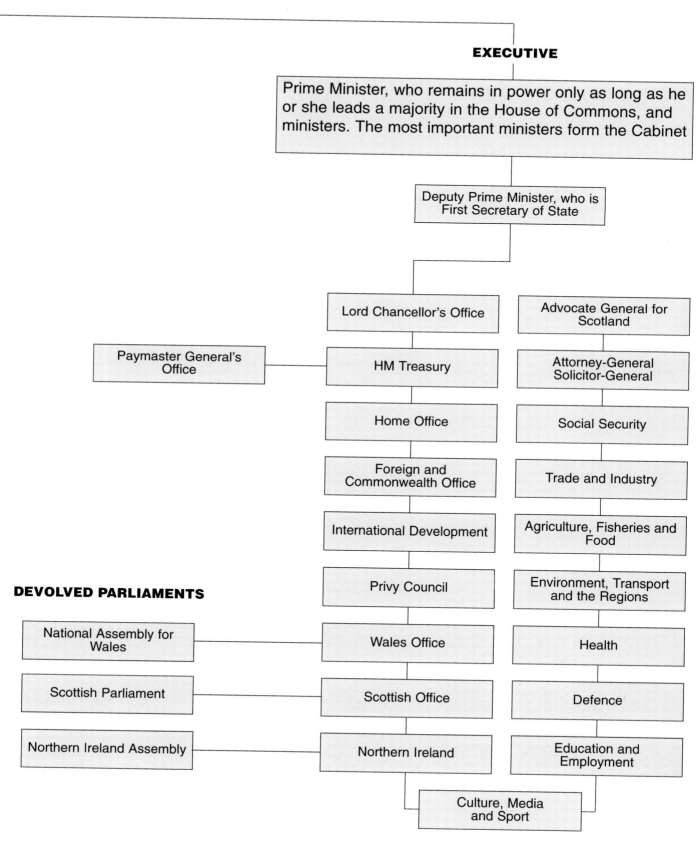

EXECUTIVE

Prime Minister, who remains in power only as long as he or she leads a majority in the House of Commons, and ministers. The most important ministers form the Cabinet

Deputy Prime Minister, who is First Secretary of State

Lord Chancellor's Office

Advocate General for Scotland

Paymaster General's Office

HM Treasury

Attorney-General Solicitor-General

Home Office

Social Security

Foreign and Commonwealth Office

Trade and Industry

International Development

Agriculture, Fisheries and Food

DEVOLVED PARLIAMENTS

Privy Council

Environment, Transport and the Regions

National Assembly for Wales

Wales Office

Health

Scottish Parliament

Scottish Office

Defence

Northern Ireland Assembly

Northern Ireland

Education and Employment

Culture, Media and Sport

Great Britons

Anderson, Elizabeth Garrett (1836–1917) First woman doctor to be allowed to practise in England, at the East London Hospital. It was later renamed the Elizabeth Garrett Anderson Hospital For Women, in her honour. She successfully campaigned for the acceptance of women as doctors and she was also the first woman mayor in England.

Austen, Jane (1775–1817) Novelist who described the manners and behaviour of everyday life in her perceptive and entertaining stories. Her six great novels are *Sense and Sensibility*, *Northanger Abbey*, *Emma*, *Persausion*, *Mansfield Park* and *Pride and Prejudice*.

Ashton, Sir Frederick (1904–1988) Founder and director of The Royal Ballet. He is famous not only as a dancer but also as a great choreographer. He created works such as *La Fille mal gardée*, for which he brought together Margot Fonteyn and Rudolf Nureyev, *Cinderella* and *Tales of Beatrix Potter*.

Astor, Nancy (1897–1964) American-born British politician. She was the first woman to take a seat in the House of Commons, on the death of her husband William Waldorf Astor, the Conservative MP, in 1919. She was a supporter of the temperance movement and of women's rights.

Baird, John Logie (1888–1946) Scottish electrical engineer and television pioneer. He began research into the possibilities of television in 1922, and in 1926 gave the first demonstration of a television image. His system was adopted by the BBC in 1929, and he continued to research and develop television technology until his death.

Bannister, Sir Roger (1929–) First person to break the four-minute mile, running it in 3 minutes 59.4 seconds in 1954. He was a finalist in the 1500 metres in the 1952 Olympic Games in Helsinki. He also had a distinguished medical career as a neurologist.

The Beatles The most successful group in the history of pop music. John Lennon, Paul McCartney, George Harrison and Ringo Starr began performing in Liverpool in 1960, and started recording two years later. Their songs and tours made them world famous. John Lennon was shot dead in the street in New York City in 1980.

Becket, Thomas à (118–1170) Archbishop of Canterbury who defended the Church from the Crown and had a series of bitter quarrels with Henry II. He was murdered by four of the king's men on the steps of the altar in Canterbury Cathedral. His tomb there became a place of pilgrimage, and he was made a saint in 1173.

Boudicca, or Boadicea (died AD 60) Wife of the king of the Iceni, a Norfolk tribe. Humiliated by the Romans on her husband's death, she raised a rebellion, burned towns and Roman army camps, and massacred 70,000 soldiers. When finally defeated, she took her own life.

Burke, Edmund (1729–1797) Irish-born statesman, orator, writer. He vigorously opposed George III's policy of arbitrary rule, and accused the Tory government of suppressing public opinion. He advocated liberal treatment of the American colonies, championed Catholic emancipation and supported abolition of the slave trade.

Burns, Robert (1759–1796) National poet of Scotland, born in Alloway near Ayr to a poor farming family. His first poems were published in 1786, when he was facing poverty, and were a great success. Among his famous works are the song *Auld Lang Syne* and the poems *Tam o' Shanter* and *The Address to a Mouse*.

Britten, Benjamin (1913–1976) A composer of classical music who began his career by writing scores for plays and documentary films. His most well-known works are *A Young Person's Guide to the Orchestra*, the operas *Peter Grimes* and *Billy Budd*, and the *War Requiem* set to poetry by Wilfred Owen.

Brontë sisters The three sisters and their brother, Branwell, lived in isolation near the moors in Yorkshire, where they spent their childhood making up stories. As adults they made a remarkable contribution to English literature. Their best-known novels are *The Tenant of Wildfell Hall* by Anne (1820–1849), *Jane Eyre* by Charlotte (1816–1855), and *Wuthering Heights* by Emily (1818–1848).

Brunel, Isambard Kingdom (1806–1859) Engineer famous for the design of the Clifton Suspension Bridge in Bristol, completed in 1864. He designed the SS *Great Britain*, the first all-metal ship, and the SS *Great Western*, the first steamship to cross the Atlantic. He was also responsible for the design and construction of the Great Western Railway from London to Bristol.

Carroll, Lewis (1832–1898) Novelist and mathematician, whose real name was Charles Lutwidge Dodgson. He was a lecturer of mathematics at Christ College, Oxford, but is famous as the author of *Alice's Adventures in Wonderland* (1865) and the sequel *Through the Looking Glass* (1872). He was also a master at writing nonsense verse, such as *The Hunting of the Snark*.

Caxton, William (c.1422–1491)
Born in Kent, he lived in Bruges in Belgium where he set up a printing press and produced the first book in English, *Recuyell of the Historyes of Troye*, in 1475. The following year he set up the first English press in Westminster, London.

Chaplin, Sir Charles Spencer
(1889–1977) Film actor and director in the heyday of silent movies at Hollywood. Charlie Chaplin was the son of a poor music-hall performer in London. He became famous for his comic but touching role as a skinny tramp with a cane, bowler hat and moustache. Among his many films are *The Gold Rush*, *Modern Times* and *The Great Dictator*.

Charlton brothers, Bobby (1935–) **and Jack** (1937–) Two of England's greatest football heroes. Bobby was a fast and deadly striker who played for Manchester United (1954–1973), scoring 245 goals and winning many medals. Jack played in defence for Leeds United (1965-1975) before going on to manage Middlesborough (1973), Sheffield Wednesday (1977,; Newcastle United (1984), and the Republic of Ireland (1986–1995). Both played for England and were in the team that won the World Cup in 1966.

Chaucer, Geoffrey (c.1345–1400)
One of England's earliest and greatest poets, famous for his *Canterbury Tales* (1386), a collection of stories told by pilgrims on their way to the tomb of Thomas à Becket at Canterbury. Chaucer's works were

the first to be written and printed in English. He is buried in Poet's Corner in Westminster Abbey.

Christie, Agatha (1890–1976)
Writer of many detective novels. Her two most well-known characters are the Belgian detective, Hercule Poirot, and the spinster, Miss Marple. She is also the author of *The Mousetrap*, the longest running play in London.

Linford Christie (1960–)
Europe's fastest and oldest Olympic 100-metre champion. He has won more gold medals (11) at major championships and more medals (23) than any other British athlete. At one point he held all six top international 100-metre titles. He is also a successful 200-metre runner and a member of the British 4 x 100 metres relay squad.

Churchill, Sir Winston Spencer Leonard (1874–1965) Soldier, statesman and author. He served in the Boer War, entered Parliament (1900) and held office as President of the Board of Trade, Home Secretary and First Lord of the Admiralty. As Conservative prime minister during World War II, he led the country to victory – his wartime speeches are probably the most quoted of any British politician. He was awarded the Nobel prize for literature in 1953.

Clive, Robert (1725–1774)
Soldier and colonialist who first went to India as a clerk in the East India Company. He then entered the army and was sent back to India to avenge the atrocity of the Black Hole of Calcutta. As governor of Bengal, he won sovereignty of the East India Company over the whole province, founding the empire of British India. Criticized in Parliament for the methods he used to acquire his wealth, he committed suicide.

Constable, John (1776–1836)
A prolific artist, known especially for landscape paintings. He studied at the Royal Academy in London, and had his first success with his famous landscape *The Haywain* in 1821, which won a gold medal in Paris – his work greatly influenced French artists of the time. Many of his paintings take Flatford in Suffolk or Salisbury Cathedral in Wiltshire as their subject.

Cook, James (1728–1779)
Known as Captain Cook, this navigator and explorer sailed twice round the world and discovered Australia and Antarctica. On his ship the *Endeavour*, he charted the coasts of Australia, New Zealand and New Guinea, and discovered other island groups in the Pacific. He also discovered how to prevent scurvy. He was killed by natives in Hawaii on his third voyage.

Crick, Francis Harry Compton (1916–) Molecular biologist educated at universities of London and Cambridge. Together with American scientist James D Watson he explained the structure of DNA, one of the greatest advances in modern science, which lead to far-reaching discoveries about genetics. They were awarded the Nobel Prize for Medicine in 1962.

Cromwell, Oliver (1599–1658)
Soldier and statesman who opposed Charles I in Parliament. With the Puritans, he led the parliamentary armies during the Civil War and defeated the Royalists at the battle of Naseby. After the execution of the king, Cromwell became Protector of the Commonwealth. It was the only period of republican government in English history.

Darling, Grace (1815–1842)
The daughter of a lighthouse keeper on one of the Farne Islands off the

coast of Northumberland, remembered for her bravery. She and her father rescued many survivors from the shipwreck of the *Forfarshire* in heavy seas on September 7th, 1838.

Darwin, Charles (1803–1884) Naturalist who formulated the theory of evolution by natural selection, causing a storm of controversy when he applied it to humans. Darwin's theory suggested that man was not created by God on the sixth day but was descended from the ape. His most famous works are *On the Origin of Species* and *The Descent of Man*.

Disraeli, Benjamin (1804–1881) Tory politician, writer and prime minister from 1874 to 1880. Witty and flamboyant, he was a favourite of Queen Victoria and an adversary of William Gladstone. Disraeli had the queen assume the title Empress of India, promoted the empire's expansion in Africa, and bought shares in the Suez Canal. He also wrote two political novels, *Coningsby* and *Sybil*.

Dickens, Charles (1812–1870) Famous for novels which dealt with many social problems of the Victorian period, such as poverty and child labour. His novels were first published under the name of Boz in weekly episodes in a magazine. Among his many famous works are *A Christmas Carol*, *Oliver Twist*, *David Copperfield* and *Great Expectations*. He is buried in Westminster Abbey.

Drake, Sir Francis (*c.*1540–1596) Seaman and explorer, he was the first Englishman to sail round the world, on the *Golden Hind*. He is most famous for his part in the defeat of the Spanish Armada in 1588. He died of fever in the West Indies.

Faraday, Michael (1791–1867) Scientist famous for his research into the relationship between electricity and magnetism, which led to the invention of electric motors and generators. The farad, a unit to measure electrical capacity, is named after him.

Fonteyn, Margot (1919–1991) One of the greatest ballerinas of all time, she made her debut in *The Nutcracker* in 1934. She is best known for her roles in *The Sleeping Beauty*, *Giselle* and *Swan Lake*, and for her partnership with the Russian dancer, Rudolf Nureyev.

Fleming, Alexander (1881–1955) Scottish scientist who discovered penicillin, a drug which kills infections. Its manufacture and use has been one of the most important developments of modern medicine.

Fry, Elizabeth (1780–1845) Quaker prison reformer who, during a visit to Newgate in 1813, was appalled at conditions. In 1817 she formed an organization for the reform of prisons. She also founded hostels for the homeless.

Gibbon, Edward (1737–1794) Historian whose great work, *The Rise and Fall of the Roman Empire*, published in six volumes between 1776 and 1788, is still considered a masterpiece.

Gilbert, Sir William Schwenck (1836–1911), and **Sullivan, Arthur** (1842–1900) Between them, Gilbert and Sullivan created many popular light operas such as *HMS Pinafore* (1878) and *The Mikado* (1885). Gilbert wrote the words, Sullivan composed the music.

Gladstone, William Ewart (1809–1898) Liberal politician, four times prime minister. He introduced important reforms, including an Education Act which established the first national school system in Britain, and a Great Reform Act which gave many more men the vote.

Gordon, Charles George (1833–1885). Known as Gordon of Khartoum, this soldier, surveyor and engineer was also known for his good works in helping the poor and the sick. In 1884 he defended the city of Khartoum in the Sudan from an Arab rebellion and was killed after a five-month siege.

Grace, William Gilbert (W G) (1848–1915) One of cricket's greatest players. He trained as a doctor and had a practice in Bristol, but devoted most of his time to cricket. He toured Canada and the US and twice captained the English team against Australia. An all-rounder, during his long career from 1864 to 1908 he made 126 centuries, scored 54,896 runs and took 2,864 wickets.

Halley, Edmond (1656–1742) Astronomer who sighted a comet and predicted its return in 1758 – it did reappear, and was named after him. In 1721 he became the Astronomer Royal. Halley also studied wind, weather patterns and tides, and invented the diving bell.

Hitchcock, Sir Alfred (1899–1980) Film maker famous for thrillers such as *The Thirty-Nine Steps* (1935) and *The Lady Vanishes* (1938). He moved to Hollywood in 1940. His later successes include *Psycho* (1960) and *The Birds* (1963).

Johnson, Amy (1903–1941) Aviator who set new records for long-distance flights. In 1930 she was the first woman to fly from London to Australia, in a record-breaking 191 days. She flew from London to Japan via Moscow and back in 1931, and made a record solo flight to Cape Town and back in 1936. She disappeared when baling out over the Thames estuary.

Johnson, Samuel (1709–1784)
Poet, critic and writer, Dr Johnson compiled one of the first English dictionaries over a period of eight years. He was great friends with James Boswell, who wrote his biography, *Life of Samuel Johnson*. He founded the Literary Club in 1764.

Keats, John (1795–1821)
One of England's best-known poets. In 1820 he published a volume of works entitled *Lamia and Other Poems* which included *Ode on a Grecian Urn*, *Ode To A Nightingale* and *The Eve of St Agnes*.

Keynes, John Maynard (1883–1946) Economist whose theories have been adopted by many governments since World War II, especially in dealing with economic depression and unemployment. He suggested that government spend money on public works such as roads and bridges, to provide people with jobs and wages and so create demand for other products and boost the economy.

Lane, Sir Allen (1902–1970)
Publisher and founder of Penguin and Puffin Books, low-priced paperbacks that made good writing affordable for more people. The first Penguins issued in 1936 cost only a few pence.

Lawrence, Thomas Edward, Lawrence of Arabia (1888–1935)
Scholar and soldier who became famous after his exploits in the north African desert. He helped to organize the Arab Revolt against the Turks, but felt the Arabs had been betrayed by the post-war settlement. He changed his name and joined the Royal Air Force.

Lear, Edward (1812–1888)
Artist and writer of humorous verse, known for his nonsense rhymes or limericks which he illustrated himself with cartoons. He also travelled extensively in Italy and Greece making landscape sketches and oil paintings.

Livingstone, David (1813–1873)
Scottish missionary and explorer of Africa who discovered the Victoria Falls. He disappeared for several years on an unsuccessful search for the source of the Nile. He was found by the American journalist and explorer, Henry Morton Stanley, who greeted him with the now famous words, "Doctor Livingstone, I presume".

Macdonald, Flora (1722–1790)
Scottish Jacobite heroine. After the battle of Culloden in 1746 she protected the would-be king, Charles Edward Stewart (also known as Bonnie Prince Charlie and the Young Pretender), by disguising him as her maid and helping him escape to France.

Moore, Henry (1898–1986)
One of the most original of modern sculptors, specializing in huge abstract forms of single figures or groups. His sculptures can be seen at St Matthew's Church in Northampton, the Time-Life Building in London, the UNESCO building in Paris, and The Lincoln Center in New York. He was England's official war artist from 1940 to 1942.

Nelson, Horatio (1785–1805)
Admiral and celebrated hero, whose most famous victory was during the battle of Trafalgar when he defeated Napoleon's invasion fleet. He lost an eye in battle in 1794, and his arm three years later. In 1798 he destroyed nearly all of Napoleon's fleet off the coast of Egypt. He was

received as a hero in Naples where he met the beautiful wife of the British ambassador, Lady Emma Hamilton. He was killed at the moment of victory at Trafalgar.

Newton, Sir Isaac (1642–1727)
One of the greatest scientists of all time. From an early age Newton spent his time inventing sundials and water-powered clocks. In the autumn of 1665 or 1666, he is said to have been sitting in an orchard when an apple fell from a tree. This set him thinking about gravity and at the age of 23, he developed the laws of gravity and of the movements of planets and tides. He also discovered that light is made up of different colours, built the first reflecting telescope, and made important discoveries in mathematics.

Nightingale, Florence, the Lady with the Lamp (1820–1910)
Nurse who reformed military hospitals and founded the modern nursing profession. At her own initiative, she went with 38 other nurses to Scutari, to care for the wounded of the Crimean War. Despite the opposition of military commanders she introduced new rules of cleanliness and hygiene, and the number of deaths in the hospital fell drastically. On her return to England she raised money and founded a school of nursing at St Thomas's Hospital.

Olivier, Laurence (1907–1989)
Actor, producer and director. His first appearance on stage was in 1924. He went on to play all the major Shakespearean roles and appeared in and directed successful films such as *Hamlet* and *Henry V*. In 1962 he became director of the newly established Chichester Theatre Festival and was director of the National Theatre until 1973.

Orwell, George (1903–1950)
Author, whose real name was Eric Arthur Blair. He was born in India and served with the Burma police before leaving to travel around Europe. He changed his name and became a writer, best known for his political novels, *Animal Farm* (1945) and *Nineteen Eighty-Four* (1949).

Owen, Wilfred (1893–1918)
Poet famous for his insights on the horror of war, including *Dulce et Decorum Est* and *Anthem for Doomed Youth*. He enlisted in World War I in 1915 and in 1917 suffered concussion and trench fever in the Somme. He was killed in action one week before the end of the war.

Pankhurst, Emmeline (1858–1928)
Campaigner for women's rights who led the movement to gain the vote for women. She began the Women's Social and Political Union, which used increasingly violent methods to further its cause. She was imprisoned several times and was force fed when she went on hunger strike. She and other members of the movement, including her daughters Christabel (1880–1958) and Sylvia (1882– 1960), became known as suffragettes.

Peel, Sir Robert (1788–1850)
Tory prime minister from 1841 to 1846, who encouraged free trade and eliminated taxes on corn imports to make food cheaper. He founded the Metropolitan Police, who became known as Bobbies from Peel's first name, Robert.

Potter, Beatrix (1866–1943)
Author and illustrator of children's books which have become world-famous classics, such as *The Tale of Peter Rabbit* and *The Tailor of Gloucester*. Although she was born in the city, she loved the country and left her farm in the Lake District to the newly formed National Trust.

Quant, Mary (1934–)
World famous fashion designer and hair-stylist of the Swinging Sixties, a time when the young were challenging convention. In 1964, Mary Quant introduced the mini-skirt and revolutionized fashion.

Raleigh, Sir Walter (1552–1618)
Navigator and adventurer. He established the colony of Virginia, in North America, named in honour of Elizabeth I, the Virgin Queen, and introduced potatoes and tobacco to England. He organized an expedition to the West Indies looking for gold on behalf of the new king, James I, but found none. James was suspicious and imprisoned him on a charge of treason – Raleigh was later executed.

Red Rum (died 1995)
Arguably the most famous horse in the world and certainly the most famous winner of the Grand National steeplechase. Red Rum was stabled and trained at Aintree, Liverpool, where he won the race three times – in 1973, 1974 and 1977. A bronze statue of him now stands at the racecourse.

Robin Hood (*c.*12th century)
Legendary outlaw, said to have lived in Sherwood Forest with his Merry Men, in the reign of Richard I. According to folk tales and ballads popular in the 15th century, he and his men robbed wealthy nobles to give to the poor and needy.

Rolls, Charles Stewart (1877–1910) Pioneer aviator and maker of automobiles. With Frederick Royce, he formed the Rolls-Royce firm in 1906. He was the first to fly non-stop across the English Channel and back, but died in a plane crash one month later.

Russell, Bertrand (1872–1970)
Welsh philosopher and mathematician. He wrote many philosophical works but the most well known is the best-selling *History of Western Philosophy* (1945). From 1949 onwards he campaigned for nuclear disarmament.

Scott, Robert Falcon (1868–1912)
Explorer, known as Scott of the Antarctic because of his expeditions to the South Pole. His first visit was between 1901 and 1904. In 1911 he and his team embarked on a second expedition and reached the South Pole on January 12th, 1912, only to find that the Norwegian explorer Roald Amundsen had reached the Pole a month earlier. They began the return journey in treacherous weather – all members of the team died and their bodies and diaries were found eight months later.

Shakespeare, William (1564–1616) The most famous playwright of all time, born in Stratford upon Avon. He wrote comedies such as *A Midsummer Night's Dream* and histories such as *Henry V*, but the best-known works are tragedies such as *Romeo and Juliet*, *Hamlet* and *Macbeth*. He also acted and was joint manager of an acting company, The King's Men, which performed at the Globe Theatre in London.

Sidney, Sir Philip (1554–1586)
Poet, courtier and soldier, "the jewel of Elizabeth's court". He was regarded, both in England and on the Continent, as the ideal gentleman of his age and the finest prose writer of his generation. His long poem *The Faerie Queen* was left unfinished when he died.

Stephenson, George (1781–1848)
Engineer and founder of English railways. Born near Newcastle, he began working in a coal mine aged only seven. His first railway engine was capable of a steady 6mph (10km/h). In 1825 he built the

world's first public railway, between Stockton and Darlington, although horses were used to pull the carriages. But four years later, his design for a steam powered locomotive, the *Rocket*, won £500 in a competition. It was capable of 30mph (48km/h).

Thatcher, Margaret (1925–)
First woman prime minister in Britain. In 1988 she celebrated ten continuous years in office, having won three consecutive elections for the Conservative Party. She was replaced as Leader of the Conservative Party in 1990, in part because of her antagonism to the European Community.

Thompson, Daley (1958–)
Superb athlete, specializing in the decathlon. He won a gold medal at the Olympic Games in 1980 and 1984.

Turner, Joseph Mallord William (1775–1851) One of the great masters of watercolour painting, who specialized in sea scenes and landscapes. Turner started exhibiting in the Royal Academy at the age of 15. He was interested in capturing the effects of light. His revolutionary technique paved the way for Impressionism. Outstanding paintings include *The Fighting Téméraire* and *Rain, Steam and Speed*. A magnificent collection of his work is on show in the Clore Gallery at the Tate in London

Valois, Dame Ninette de (1898–)
Irish-born ballerina who first appeared on stage in 1914. She toured with the Russian choreographer Diaghilev's Ballets Russes as a young girl. She was a founding member of the Vic-Wells Ballet which became the Sadler's Wells Ballet and The Royal Ballet.

Wellington, Arthur Wellesley (1769–1852) The first Duke of Wellington, who succeeded in defeating Napoleon at the battle of Waterloo in 1815. He had already had a distinguished military career in the Peninsular War, and his ability to inspire his troops to hold a position against overwhelming odds earned him the nickname of the Iron Duke. After Waterloo, Wellington entered politics and was Tory prime minister from 1828 to 1830.

Wilberforce, William (1759–1833) Politician who campaigned for the abolition of slavery. He became a priest in the Church of England and in 1780 was elected as member of parliament for Hull. In 1784 he started his campaign to end the slave trade. In 1807 a law was finally passed making it illegal for slaves to be bought or sold anywhere in the British empire.

Wren, Sir Christopher (1632–1723) Prolific architect of St Paul's Cathedral and over 50 churches to replace those destroyed by the Great Fire of London in 1666. He was already a distinguished mathematician and astronomer and had helped found the Royal Society. He is buried in St Paul's, where his monument reads *Si monumentum requiris, circumspice* (if you seek a monument, look around you).

Timeline of British History

DATE	EVENT
8000 BC	Ice cap begins to retreat
6000 BC	Rising sea-level forms English Channel, cutting Britain off from the Continent
3200 BC	First known houses in Britain, in Skara Brae, Orkneys
3000 BC	Stonehenge is begun
AD 43	Roman invasion of Britain
61–62	Boudicca's revolt
122–126	Hadrian's Wall is built
363	Saxon raids
406	Last Roman legion leaves Britain
597	Pope Gregory I sends Augustine to bring Christianity to Britain
624–625	Raidwald, king of East Anglia, buried at Sutton Hoo
664	Synod of Whitby accepts Church of Rome
698	Lindisfarne Gospels are written and illuminated
731	Bede completes his *Ecclesiastical History of the English People*
787	Viking raids
871	Alfred the Great becomes king
1066	Norman invasion. Battle of Hastings. William the Conqueror becomes king
1071	Canterbury Cathedral is founded, the oldest in Britain
1086	Domesday Book is compiled
1096–1099	First Crusade
1154	Henry of Anjou arrives from France and becomes first Plantagenet king. Nicholas Breakspear becomes Hadrian IV, the only English Pope
1166	Constitutions of Clarendon: clergy to be punished by secular courts
1169	Strongbow invades Ireland
1170	Thomas a Becket murdered at Canterbury
1189–1192	Third Crusade: Richard the Lionheart held hostage in 1192, ransomed in 1194
1204	Loss of Normandy to France
1215	Magna Carta signed
1258	Provisions of Oxford: barons impose constitutional limitations on monarchy
1265	First House of Commons: representatives from every shire and town summoned
1277–1284	Conquest of Wales
1290	Jews expelled from England
1314	Battle of Bannockburn: Scots defeat English
1337	Start of Hundred Years War: Edward III claims French Crown
1344	Most Noble Order of the Garter founded
1345–1400	Chaucer, author of *Canterbury Tales*
1346	Battle of Crécy: French defeated
1348	Black Death
1381	Peasants' Revolt: 100,000 rebel against poll tax
1399	Henry IV becomes first Lancastrian king
1415	Invasion of France: Henry V wins battle of Agincourt
1455	Wars of the Roses begin: houses of Lancaster and York fight for the throne
1485	Battle of Bosworth: Yorkist Richard III killed by Henry Tudor, who becomes king
1497	John Cabot sights land off Nova Scotia, and claims North America for England
1534	Papal authority abolished: Henry VIII is Supreme Head of Church of England
1558	Elizabeth I succeeds Mary Tudor as queen
1564–1616	Shakespeare
1577	Francis Drake sets off round the world in his *Golden Hind*. Returns in 1580

1584	Sir Walter Raleigh sends expedition to America to claim lands for Elizabeth I
1587	Mary Queen of Scots executed
1588	Defeat of the Spanish Armada
1605	Gunpowder Plot: Catholics try to blow up Houses of Parliament. Guy Fawkes executed in 1606
1620	Pilgrim Fathers sail from Plymouth in the *Mayflower* to colonize America
1628	Petition of Right: condemns king's actions
1642–1646	Civil War
1649	Exection of Charles I. Oliver Cromwell declares a Commonwealth
1660	The Restoration: Parliament recalls Charles II as king
1665	Great plague reaches London: kills 68,596
1666	Great Fire of London
1675–1710	St Paul's Cathedral is built
1679	Act of *Habeas Corpus* forbids imprisonment without trial
1688	The Glorious Revolution: Protestants call in Dutch William of Orange to be king
1690	Battle of the Boyne: William of Orange defeats James II in Ireland
1692	Glencoe Massacre: 37 members of Clan MacDonald slain by Clan Campbell
1694	Bank of England established
1701–1713	War of the Spanish Succession: Gibraltar taken
1707	Union of England and Scotland as Great Britain
1715	Jacobite rebellion in support of the Old Pretender, James Edward Stuart
1731	Downing Street becomes prime minister's official residence
1745	Jacobite rebellion in support of the Young Pretender, Charles Edward Stuart
1756	Seven Years' War begins against France: fight for colonies in America and India. Black Hole of Calcutta: 123 Britons die
1757	Clive wins battle of Plassey and controls Bengal: start of the empire
1759	Battle of Quebec: British conquer Canada
1768	Captain Cook sets sail in the *Endeavour*, bound for Tahiti
1773	Boston Tea Party: American protest at British taxes on tea
1775	American War of Independence begins
1776	American Declaration of Independence
1783	Treaty of Versailles: American Independence formally recognized
1788	*The Times* first published
1801	Union of Great Britain and Ireland
1802	Factory Acts regulate employment in factories
1805	Battle of Trafalgar: Nelson defeats Napoleon's invasion forces
1808	Peninsular War begins: Duke of Wellington helps Spain expel Napoleon's forces
1815	Battle of Waterloo: Napoleon defeated
1819	Peterloo Massacre: 11 die after meeting to call for parliamentary reform
1825	World's first railway: Stockton–Darlington
1829	Roman Catholic Relief Act: frees Catholics from discrimination
1832	First Reform Act extends the right to vote
1834	Tolpuddle Martyrs transported for organizing a trade union
1846	Repeal of the Corn Laws: allows import of cheap corn to fight Irish famine; but one million die
1850	Stone Age Skara Brae uncovered in storm
1851	The Great Exhibition
1853-1856	Crimean War against Russia: Florence Nightingale pioneers modern nursing
1854	David Livingstone discovers Victoria Falls
1857-1858	Indian Mutiny. British take over control of India from East India Company

1863	World's first underground railway: Metropolitan line, London
1867	Second Reform Act: gives one million more men the vote
1867	Canada becomes first Dominion
1877	Queen Victoria proclaimed Empress of India
1884	Third Reform Act: electorate increased to five million.Includes agricultural labourers
1897	Victoria's Diamond Jubilee: 60 years on throne
1901	Australia becomes a Dominion
1910	Union of South Africa becomes a Dominion
1911	Parliament Act: curbs the power of the House of Lords; ensures sovereignty of House of Commons
1912	Scott of the Antarctic reaches South Pole. *Titanic* hits iceberg and sinks: 1,513 die
1914-18	World War I: Britain, France and Russia fight aggressors Germany, Austria, Italy
1916	Easter Rising, Dublin
1919	Nancy Astor becomes first woman MP. First Atlantic flight, by Alcock and Brown (in 16 hours, 28 minutes)
1921	Irish Free State: 26 southern counties become a Dominion, separated from Ulster
1928	Women get the vote at 21
1929-1935	Great Depression: economic slump worldwide
1931	Statute of Westminster formally recognizes the independence of the Dominions
1936	Abdication of Edward VIII in order to marry American divorcee, Wallis Simpson. First television broadcast
1937	*Dandy* comic first published. *Beano* first published in 1938
1939-45	World War II: Britain, France (until 1940), USSR and USA (from 1941) fight Germany, Italy and Japan, the aggressors
1944	D-Day: allied landing in Normandy, June 6th
1945	First atomic bomb on Hiroshima, August 9th. Japan surrenders
1947	End of the British empire: India and Pakistan independent; all remaining colonies follow by 1980
1948	Republic of Ireland leaves Commonwealth. Northern Ireland votes to remain in UK. Olympic Games held in London
1949	Council of Europe established
1953	Coronation of Elizabeth II. Edmund Hillary and Tenzig Norgay first to reach summit of Mt Everest
1958	European Economic Community (EEC) set up: Britain stays out. CND founded
1961	Amnesty International founded
1964	Dorothy Crowfoot Hodgkin first Brtish woman to win Nobel Prize (for Chemistry)
1965	Capital punishment abolished
1966	Aberfan mining landslip kills 144 (mostly children), South Wales
1967	Oil tanker *Torrey Canyon* spills 120,000 tonnes of oil, off Scilly Isles
1972	Bloody Sunday: 13 killed in civil rights protest, Northern Ireland
1973	Britain joins the EEC
1976	First passenger service on *Concorde*, world's first supersonic plane
1979	Margaret Thatcher becomes Britain's first woman prime minister
1982	Falklands War: Argentina seizes British Falkland Islands, recaptured in 10 weeks. *Mary Rose* raised from seabed
1985	*Live Aid* concert raises £40m for African famine relief
1991	Gulf War: Iraq seizes Kuwait; US and European (mainly British) forces liberate it in a few days, with an unprecedented display of military power
1997	Labour win General Elcetion

Glossary

abdication giving up a claim and renouncing any right to a duty or office, especially the Crown (as with Edward VIII)

abolition ending of the slave trade

Act a law formally recorded in writing, resulting from a decision taken by Parliament

AD *anno Domini* (Latin for In the year of Our Lord). Opposite to BC (before Christ). This dating system ties in with the Christian calendar, with the year AD 1 being the year Jesus Christ was said to have been born.

Agricultural Revolution changes in the 1700s in farm machinery and sowing, planting and harvesting methods

allegiance loyalty to a person or cause

Allies the powers in World War II, including Britain, France, the United States and Russia, which opposed Hitler and the Axis powers

Anglican belonging to the Church of England, with its doctrine and rituals

appeasement the policy of seeking peaceful solutions to aggressive acts; used to describe Britain's policy to Hitler's expansion before 1939

aqueduct a bridge which carries canal boats on water, or the water supply

archbishop chief bishop, in charge of all other bishops, clergy and churches in a particular area. The Archbishop of Canterbury is head of the Church of England

armada a fleet of warships. Generally refers to the Spanish Armada against England in 1588

armisitice agreement to end conflict temporarily in order to discuss peace terms. Armistice Day on November 11th commemorates the end of World War I

Axis the powers of Germany, Italy and Japan which fought the Allies in World War II

bailiff lord of the manor's chief officer

barbarians a term used by the Romans to describe the nomadic invaders of their empire

Baroque a style of music, art, architecture and sculpture that developed in western Europe from the late 16th century to the early 18th century. It aimed to produce spectacular and ornate effects

baron lowest rank of the nobility. In feudal times, granted estates (manors), and the workers on them, in return for paying taxes and providing knights to the Crown

BC before Christ. *see* AD

besiege to surround a town or castle, cutting off supply lines and attacking with the aim of capturing

bill a proposal to change or introduce a new law in Parliament that is debated and voted for or against (if passed, it becomes an Act)

blockade closing up of a place or country, by military or naval forces, generally to starve it into obedience or surrender

Boer Dutch South African, or descendant of

cabinet originally a small group of close advisers to the monarch; slowly this became a group who formed the policy of government

canonize to formally declare a person a saint. Used by the Roman Catholic Church

Catholics supporters and followers of the Church of Rome and the Pope

cede to give up land to another person or country

Celts Iron Age tribes from Europe

chancellor chief minister to the Crown. For example, Becket was Henry II's chancellor. Still a high-ranking title today: the Chancellor of the Exchequer is the chief minister of finance, while the Lord Chancellor is head of the judiciary and Speaker of the House of Lords

chivalry from the Middle Ages, a religious, social and moral code practised by knights

civilization a society where people have developed skills and a way of living together in communities and towns

civil war war between different groups of people within the same country. In particular, the English Civil War of 1642–1646

clan a group of families having a common ancestor and surname, under the same leader, especially in Scotland and Ireland

colony settlement in a new territory, still subject to its country of origin

Cold War state of hostility between nations, without actual warfare; especially between East and West after World War II

Commonwealth association of independent nations, especially those who are or have been ruled by Britain. Also the period between 1649 and 1653 when there was no monarchy and power rested solely with Parliament

communism a revolutionary brand of Socialism based in theory on workers owning what they produce. In practice it led to the rise of states where power was in the sole hands of the state leader, such as in Russia and China

conscription a system in which citizens are legally bound to serve with the armed forces. In Britain it was introduced from 1916 to 1941

Conservative Party in British politics the party that evolved from the old Tory Party of the 19th century. Opposed to socialism

constitution body of political principles on which a state is governed, written or unwritten, and embodying the rights of the people. Britain has no written constitution

Covenanters Scottish Presbyterians who resisted Charles I's and Charles II's attempts to introduce bishops and Anglican church rituals

crusades series of wars fought by Christians against Muslims for control of the Holy Land (part of the Middle East). The First Crusade was in 1096, the last in 1291

dauphin title of the direct heir to the French throne

democracy from the Greek *demos* (the people), meaning rule by the people. A system of government by elected representatives of the entire adult population of the state

Depression term for an economic slump in the 1930s in Europe (that started in the US in 1929)

Dissenters religious groups that disagree with established ways of worship. Includes groups outside the Church of England such as Catholics, Methodists and Puritans

dissolution breaking up the monasteries; also dismissal of Parliament with a view to summoning a new one as and when the monarch required it

divine right of kings the belief that monarchs received their authority directly from God and so were not answerable to Parliament

dole term used to describe those unemployed collecting national insurance benefits

dominion colonies of the British Empire that achieved self-governing status

dowry money and other assets a rich woman was expected to bring with her when marrying

East India Company trading company given monopoly of eastern trade by Elizabeth I in 1600. Later in conflict with Dutch East India Company Controlled India before British government took over direct authority in 1858

excommunicate to expel from the Church

federation states united under a central government for defence, but independent in internal affairs

Fenians supporters of the Irish Republican Brotherhood, a nationalist organization founded in 1857 in New York and committed to violence as a means to achieving Home Rule for Ireland

feudal system (till 1400s) a system under which people held land in exchange for services to a noble

galleon large three-masted ship used for war or trade, 15th–18th century

Georgian of the Hanoverian period (from the name shared by George I–IV). Often used of this period's style of architecture

Goths German tribes who raided parts of the Roman empire from the 3rd to 5th century

heresy a religious belief that is against the usual, accepted form of religion

Holy Roman Empire a federation of European states and princes that lasted from 800 to 1803

homage a public acknowledgement of respect or honour to a lord or superior

home rule government of a country by its citizens; especially associated with Ireland's demands for self-rule

home secretary government minister responsible for law and order, and immigration

hypocaust Roman underfloor central heating system

impeach to accuse a public official of a crime against the state, such as treason, and the legal process of removing them from office

Industrial Revolution the changes that happened to industry in the 1700s and 1800s as a result of powered machinery and the coming of factories

Inquisition enquiry by Roman Catholic Church into heresy, sometimes involving the torture and execution of disbelievers

IRA Irish Republican Army, terrorist organization seeking to unite Northern Ireland with the Republic of Ireland through violence

Jacobite supporter and follower of those who claimed the throne for the Stuart line of James II

Justiciar chief officer of state, Lord Chief Justice

keep central tower or stronghold in a Norman castle

knight medieval rank, owing military service each year to his lord, including armour, horses and soldiers, in exchange for grants of land

Labour Party in British politics evolved from the Independent Labour Party formed by Keir Hardie in 1893. Largely supported by trade unions, it adopted Socialist ideas in World War I, but remained committed to democracy

Liberal Party one of two major political parties in Britain until the rise of the Labour Party, it grew from the old Whig party of the 18th and 19th centuries

longbow large, pwerful, hand-drawn bow used by British forces in the Middle Ages, for example at the battle of Agincourt

madrigals unaccompanied song for several voices, with different parts sung together. Popular in the 16th and 17th centuries

mandate command ordering a person, group or state how to act

medieval of the Middle Ages

Methodists followers of preacher John Welsey who believe in a very strict method of study and prayer

milecastle Roman fort on Hadrian's Wall

minstrel travelling singer of the Middle Ages. Legend has it that the minstrel Blondel tirelessly searched for and found Richard II during the crusades

monastery residence of a religious male community, bound together by religious vows and living apart from society

monopoly sole possession or control of trade in any commodity

mosaic a pattern or picture made of coloured tiles

motte and bailey Norman fortification consisting of a mound of earth (motte) surrounded by a ditch (or a moat if filled with water), with a walled outer court. Built originally of wood and later of stone, to protect the keep or castle within

munitions weapons and arms manufactured for a nation's war effort

Muslims followers of Islam; those who worship Allah and follow the teachings of Mohammed

mutiny rebellion or uprising by soldiers or sailors against their superiors

National Insurance government-backed pensions and other payments to its citizens

noble person of high birth directly serving the king

Non-Conformists religious groups (including Catholics) who do not agree with the established Church of England. Also called dissenters

pagan a person who follows any pre-Christian religion, especially one with many gods

Parliament Britain's highest governing body, consisting of the House of Lords, House of Commons and the sovereign, and responsible for making laws

peerage a title such as duke, earl, viscount, passed through a family, allowing that person to sit in the House of Lords. Since 1963 peers have been allowed to disclaim their titles and sit in the House of Commons

Picts term coined by the Romans in the 3rd century to describe their enemies north of the Antonine Wall. From the Latin *picti*, painted people, a reference to their war paint

pilgrimage journey to a sacred shrineto give thanks or do penance

Plantagenet originally the nickname of Geoffrey of Anjou, from the sprig of broom, *planta genista*, which he wore as a badge

Pope head of the Roman Catholic Church. During the Reformation in the 16th century, Henry VIII broke with Rome by declaring that the Crown, not the Pope, was the supreme head of the English Church.

pretender someone laying dubious claim to the throne.

prime minister the most senior member of government and leader of the political party in power

Privy Council a group of people appointed for life by the sovereign to be the Crown's private advisers or councillors

Protectorate the period between 1653 and 1660 when Oliver Cromwell took the title of Lord Protector and ruled the country through the army

Protestantism religion of groups of the western Church separated from the Roman Catholic Church

referendum putting issues of national and international importance directly to the people to vote on, rather than Parliament deciding on behalf of the public

Reformation religious and political movement of the 16th century to reform the Roman Catholic Church, which resulted in Protestantism

Regency normally used to describe the period 1811–1820 when the Prince Regent (later George IV) ruled when his father George III was declared insane. The term is also applied to a lavish style of fashion, architecture and interior design

regent person who rules while monarch is either too young (in their minority), too ill or too far abroad to govern effectively at home

Renaissance revival of interest in art and learning of ancient Greece and Rome, *c.*1400–1600

republic a country governed by a president and parliament-style body, such as France and Ireland. A non-monarchist state

Restoration the return of the monarchy in 1660 when Charles II was invited to be king

rotten boroughs voting areas which sent a member to Parliament despite hardly anyone living there (while new industrial towns had no MPs). Reformed in the 19th century

sanitation the clearing up and cleaning of slums by installing drains, sewers and running water to prevent disease; reforms began to improve living conditions in the 1850s.

serf peasant worker bought and sold with the land on which he or she worked, with no individual rights. – The lowest status in the feudal hierarchy of the Middle Ages

ship money a tax to raise money to build ships, revived illegally by Charles I

shire county; now only found as part of many county names

single market referring to the aim of uniting the EU countries into a single economic and monetary and ultimately political union

slave a person legally owned by another without freedom or rights

slums housing built near factories during the Industrial Revolution with no running water or sewage system and families crammed in one or two rooms

socialism a political theory that favours ownership of all resources – land, industry, property, services, energy etc – by all the people, rather than by private individuals

statute a law or rule made by a body or institution, meant to be permanent and expressed in a formal document; especially, an Act of Parliament

suffragettes supporters of votes for women, given particularly to British women who campaigned in the early 1900s

Tory a member of the 18th–19th century political party opposed to political reform. Forerunner of the present-day Conservative

trade union association of workers formed to protect their rights and maintain their earnings; started in the 1800s with the Industrial Revolution

treaty formal agreement between states or governments, often of peace

usurper one who takes the throne without legal authority

vassal a person or country under the control of another

viceroy governor of a country or a province who rules in the name of his sovereign or government

villein feudal peasant owing allegiance, work and produce to a lord in return for small grant of land

Wars of the Roses conflicts between Yorkists and Lancastrians for the English throne, 1455–1485

Welfare State system in which the government take full responsibility for its citizens' social welfare – their health, schooling, employment, housing, retirement and so on.

Whig a member of the British political party of the 18th century favouring social and political reform. The Whig Party later evolved into the Liberal Party

Witan the Anglo-Saxon council meeting of wise men

Index

ACKNOWLEDGEMENTS

The publisher would like to thank the following for supplying additional photographs for this book:

The Bridgeman Art Library: 39*br*, 64*tr*, 72–73*b*, 75*tl*, 82*t*;
Corbis: 184*t*, 184*bl*, 185*t*, 185*br*, 192*t*, 192*bl*;
e t archive: 32*tr*, 61*tl*, 100*b*;
Hulton Deutsch: 168*t*;
The Mansell Collection: 74*t*, 124*b*;
Mary Evans Picture Library: 134*tr*, 145*b*, 166*b*;
National Museum of Labour History: 141*br*;
Mark Peppé: 19*br*, 23*bl*, 29*b*, 35*b*, 52*tl*, 53*b*, 74*b*, 89*cr*, 91*b*, 98*bl*, 100*tr*, 102*tl*, 106*b*, 175*br*;
Popperfoto: 140*cr*, 189*b*;
The Royal Collection: 65;
Sir John Soane's Museum: 127*b*;
Spectrum: 61*b*.